# Special Collections in the Library of Congress

*First motor-powered flight, December 17, 1903, at Kitty Hawk, North Carolina. Before his ascent, Orville Wright positioned the camera and instructed John T. Daniels of the Kill Devil Life Saving Station to snap the picture at the moment the airplane reached the end of the take-off rail. Wilbur and Orville Wright Collection, Prints and Photographs Division. LC–USZ62–6166–A.*

# Special Collections in the Library of Congress

## A SELECTIVE GUIDE

### compiled by Annette Melville

## Library of Congress

### WASHINGTON 1980

Library of Congress Cataloging in Publication Data

United States. Library of Congress.
Special collections in the Library of Congress.

Includes index.
1. United States. Library of Congress. I. Melville, Annette. II. Title.
Z733.U58U54   1980      027.5753      79-607780
ISBN 0-8444-0297-4

The calligraphy for this book was created by Sheila Waters.

For sale by the Superintendent of Documents, U.S. Government Printing Office
Washington, D.C.   20402

# Table of Contents

# *Foreword*

Special collections matter in the Library of Congress. Despite the volume and number of the Library's holdings (about seventy-five million items), some of its most prized research material may be found in special collections, many of which are comparatively small. Without them, the Library would forfeit its standing as one of the world's great research libraries.

Since the nineteenth century special collections have played an important role in the Library's development. Thomas Jefferson's library, purchased by Congress in 1815 and now housed in the Rare Book and Special Collections Division, made the Library comprehensive in most fields of learning. With the addition of the Peter Force Library in 1867, it became a leading repository of Americana. Other special collections brought special strengths. The G. V. Yudin Collection, acquired in 1906, became the basis for renowned holdings for Slavic studies, as the William W. Rockhill gift did for Asian. The Joseph and Elizabeth Robins Pennell collection of Whistleriana and of their own material provided the Library with two major collections, and the Pennell bequest furnished the means to add systematically to the holdings in the fine arts. The John Boyd Thacher, Otto Vollbehr, and Lessing J. Rosenwald collections turned the Library of Congress into the greatest repository of incunabula in the Western Hemisphere. The collections of the Elizabeth Sprague Coolidge Foundation and the Gertrude Clarke Whittall Foundation enabled the Library to achieve comparable distinction in music manuscripts. Examples could be multiplied, affecting every curatorial division of the Library.

This guide has been compiled to introduce readers to nearly three hundred of the Library's special collections and prepare them for research into their contents. Some are famous, and deservedly so. Others are less well known than they should be. All merit examination as examples of the rich and diversified special holdings of the Library.

JOHN C. BRODERICK
*Assistant Librarian for Research Services*

# Introduction

The special collections selected for inclusion in this guide comprise thematically related groups of material maintained as separate units within the general holdings of the Library of Congress. They were either acquired as a unit or specifically assembled by the Library. Special collections are usually formed around a subject or person (such as gastronomy or Abraham Lincoln), the interests of a private collector (for example, the illustrated books and manuscripts assembled by Lessing J. Rosenwald), or the activities of an organization (such as the photographs produced by the Farm Security Administration).

While separated from the general collections for a number of reasons such as provenance, bibliographic significance, or the wishes of a donor, special collections share the important trait of bringing together individual items that grow in research value by their association with the other material in the collection. Whether they contain dime novels or rare operatic recordings, special collections provide the opportunity for studying items of scholarly interest in context.

While the special collections included here represent some of the Library's chief treasures, they are in some respects among the most challenging resources to use. Most are made available to researchers in specialized facilities which are described in the appendix. Over the years each custodial unit has developed finding aids particularly suited to its holdings. Thus, unlike the Library's general classified book collections, the special collections are not recorded in a single card catalog or machine-readable data base but rather in a variety of bibliographic guides. Generally, catalogs, inventories, registers, indexes, calendars, or other research tools must be tailor-made to describe their contents, since in many cases special collections unite materials that have not been brought together elsewhere. Furthermore, some special collections are so vast—the collection of *Look* magazine photographs contains an estimated five million items—that it is not feasible to provide an item-by-item listing.

As a general rule, collections are separated by format at the time of receipt and assigned to the custodial units within the Library that specialize in their maintenance and service. For example, a researcher wishing to use the *Meet the Press* Collection (no. 158) would find radio and television broadcasts of this public affairs series in the Motion

Picture, Broadcasting, and Recorded Sound Division, the custodial unit with facilities for playing sound recordings, videotapes, and television films; publicity photographs and cartoons pertaining to the program are kept together in the Prints and Photographs Division; and letters from viewers, transcripts, and related papers are available in the Manuscript Division.

## Purpose and Scope

Confronted with the variety and scale of the Library's special collections, the user may experience difficulty in locating the full range of materials they contain. This volume seeks to guide the researcher to resources that might otherwise be overlooked. Organized as a series of brief essays, it describes special collections that have been singled out by the Library's reference staff for their rarity or potential interest to scholars and summarizes information from many sources on the history, content, scope, subject strengths, and organization of these groups of materials. Though limited to 269 of the Library's many special collections, it illustrates an approach that can be applied for the effective use of similar resources within the Library and offers a glimpse at the diverse holdings of its custodial divisions. This is the Library's first attempt to describe such a large number of its collections in one guide.

This volume covers special collections of books and pamphlets as well as drawings, films, manuscripts, maps, music, musical instruments, prints, photographs, sound recordings, videotapes and other nonbook materials. In addition, descriptions are provided for a few collections of great historic or bibliographic interest which no longer exist as distinct units. These dispersed collections have been integrated within the classified collections and figure prominently in the development of the Library's resources in such fields as aeronautics and Russian history. For each of the dispersed collections treated in this volume, inventories or catalogs survive from which its original contents can be determined.

Excluded from this guide are collections composed entirely of microforms and collections of personal papers and nonmusic manuscripts which fall within the scope of the *National Union Catalog of Manuscript Collections (NUCMC)*. However, *NUCMC* material which is integrally linked with special collections in nonmanuscript formats is discussed in context.

Also omitted are "format" collections such as globes, miniature books, and piano rolls which are stored together only because of space considerations or preservation purposes.

# Preparation of the Guide

When I began work on this volume in February 1977 under the direction of the Research Department, it was envisaged as a revised edition of *A Guide to the Special Book Collections in the Library of Congress* (Washington: 1949. 66 p. Z733.U62U65), compiled by Shirley Pearlove. Long out of print—although available on microfilm—the 1949 *Guide* listed information on over 140 special book collections and was prepared chiefly from the Library's accession records and the acquisitions summaries published in the *Annual Report of the Librarian of Congress*. The new edition was to have been expanded to cover major special collections of all nonbook materials except microforms and nonmusic manuscripts. It soon became apparent that other Library publications, most notably the division guides and survey articles cited in the appendix to the present volume, provided a more useful model. Copies of these publications had already been assembled in research files in the early 1970s when the possibility of preparing a revised guide to the special collections was first explored. Drawing from these files as well as from the Librarian's annual reports, articles in the Library's *Quarterly Journal* and *Information Bulletin,* and published special collection catalogs, I prepared working lists of groups of material in each of the Library's custodial units that fit the definition of a special collection discussed above. The staff of the custodial units then reviewed the lists and recommended deletions and additions, giving preference to collections of unusual merit and potential research value.

I then gathered information on the selected collections. While the type of information varied to some degree according to the format of the materials in the collection, I asked certain general questions in each case: What administrative units within the Library have custody of the collection? How and when was the collection acquired or formed? For collections acquired as a unit, what activities or interests of the collector had some bearing on the content of the collection? What types of material does the collection contain? What is its estimated size in number of items or linear feet? What are the collection's scope and areas of particular strength? Does it include items of outstanding interest or rarity? How is the collection organized? What special lists, inventories, registers, indexes, bibliographic guides, or other finding aids have been prepared to provide access to the material? Are there articles, catalogs, or other publications which describe the collection?

In addition to Library publications, I also consulted internal files, unpublished finding aids and access tools, and relevant published accounts. Of course, the single most valuable source of information was the staff of the Library's custodial units. I discussed each collection with the staff members most familiar with its contents and in some cases with the donor or an outside expert who had worked with the material. Except for films, nonmusic manuscripts, sound recordings, and videotapes, I examined the material firsthand.

The final stage was to draft descriptions of the special collections. To ensure accuracy, these descriptions were reviewed by members of the appropriate custodial units, staff in the Office of the Assistant Librarian for Research Services and the Collections Development Office, and other Library specialists. Generally, revisers read a preliminary draft of each essay and, months later, a more polished form that incorporated suggested changes.

The bibliographic style I have used blends elements from the University of Chicago Press's *Manual of Style* and standard Library of Congress usage. I derived the spelling of corporate, geographic, and personal names chiefly from the name authority records created by the Library's Processing Services. When the Library's form differed greatly from standard use, I made *Webster's Biographical Dictionary* the arbiter.

This reference work has been compiled as a research aid and not as a substitute for reading and studying the collections themselves. Undoubtedly, as the first such guide to the Library's special collections, it will have shortcomings. Suggestions from users will be welcome and will serve as a basis for future revisions.

ANNETTE MELVILLE
Collections Development Office
July 1979

# How to Use This Guide

The descriptions of the special collections are arranged alphabetically by the first word of the full collection title; however, collections bearing the name of a person are alphabetized under the surname. Each description is composed of three parts:

*Heading*. The collection name is followed by a brief description of the collection's contents and the custodial unit or units where the researcher must go to use the material. Only custodial units in which the material is maintained as a distinct special collection are listed. The custodial unit holding the greatest quantities of material is listed first.

*Essay*. The essay describes the collection's acquisition, size, scope and contents, subject strengths, items of particular interest, bibliographic control, and finding aids as of September 1978, unless a more recent date is indicated. Generally, for multiformat collections, the material housed in each custodial unit is discussed in separate paragraphs. Also included in the essay are citations to publications of related interest. Full bibliographic citations are not provided for publications referred to as examples.

*References*. The references at the conclusion of each essay cite sources which discuss the collection as a whole. Each list is highly selective and intended as a guide to more detailed published descriptions rather than documentation for the essay. General reference works and published accounts containing less information than the essay provides are not cited.

## Abbreviations of Frequently Cited Works

Full references to works frequently abbreviated or cited by short titles in this volume are given below.

*ARLC*    U.S. *Library of Congress*. Annual report of the Librarian of Congress. 1865/66+ Washington. illus.

Z733.U57A

| | |
|---|---|
| *G&M Div. Guide* | U.S. *Library of Congress. Geography and Map Division.* The Geography and Map Division, a guide to its collections and services. Rev. ed. Washington, Library of Congress, 1975. 42 p. illus.    Z733.U63G46 1975 |
| *Guide,* Vanderbilt | U.S. *Library of Congress. Reference Dept.* Guide to the special collections of prints & photographs in the Library of Congress, compiled by Paul Vanderbilt. Washington, 1955.  200 p.    NE53.W3A52 |
| *Handbook of MSS. in LC* | U.S. *Library of Congress. Manuscript Division.* Handbook of manuscripts in the Library of Congress. Washington, Govt. Print. Off., 1918. xvi, 750 p.    Z6621.U55 |
| *LCIB* | U.S. *Library of Congress.* Information bulletin. v.  1+  Jan.  23,  1942+ Washington.  illus. weekly.    Z733.U57I6 |
| *Law Library* | The Law Library of the Library of Congress, its history, collections, and services, edited and compiled by Kimberly W. Dobbs and Kathryn A. Haun. Washington, Library of Congress, 1978.  47 p.  illus. (part col.)    Z733.U63L224 |
| *Mus. Div. Guide* | U.S. *Library of Congress.* The Music Division, a guide to its collections and services. Washington, 1972. 22 p.  illus.    ML136.U5M9 1972 |
| *NUCMC* | The National union catalog of manuscript collections.  1959/61+  Washington, Library of Congress.    Z6620.U5N3 |

QJLC

U.S. *Library of Congress.* Quarterly journal. v. 1+ July/Sept. 1943+ [Washington] illus. Z881.U49A3

*Rare Bk. Div. Guide*

U.S. *Library of Congress. Rare Book Division.* The Rare Book Division, a guide to its collections and services. Rev. ed. Washington, Reference Dept., Library of Congress, 1965. 51 p. illus. (part col.)
Z733.U63R23 1965

*Viewpoints*

U.S. *Library of Congress. Prints and Photographs Division.* Viewpoints, a selection from the pictorial collections of the Library of Congress; a picture book by Alan Fern, Milton Kaplan, and the staff of the Prints and Photographs Division. Washington, Library of Congress, 1975. 223 p. illus. E178.5.U54 1974

—— —— Reprint. New York, Arno Press [1976] 223 p. illus.
E178.5.U54 1976

# The
## Special Collections
## Described

*An Alphabetical*
*Arrangement*

*Interior of the Imperial Library, Constantinople (now the Beyazit Devlet Kütüphanesi Istanbul). This nineteenth-century photograph is by Abdullah Frères. Abdul-Hamid II Collection, Prints and Photographs Division. LS–USZ62–70193.*

# 1

## Abdul-Hamid II Collection

Photographs of Turkey, late nineteenth century

Prints and Photographs Division

In 1893 Sultan Abdul-Hamid II of Turkey (1842–1918) presented to the Library of Congress a fifty-one-volume photographic survey of his country. These elaborately bound photograph albums were designed to illustrate the achievements of Turkish culture and the activities of the sultan's government. The collection consists almost exclusively of formal views of military installations and personnel, naval vessels, schools, hospitals, historic monuments, fire-fighting and lifesaving equipment, major cities, palaces and stables of the Imperial Court, and other subjects of official interest. Abdullah Frères, a well-known commercial firm in Istanbul, produced many of the 2,250 gold-toned photoprints. The captions are written in French and Ottoman Turkish, and the collection is represented in the catalog of the Prints and Photographs Division.

*Guide,* Vanderbilt, no. 2.

# 2

# Accademia della Crusca Collection

## Italian-language publications, 1500–1887

The Accademia della Crusca Collection, purchased by the Library in 1914, was composed largely of publications cited as examples of good Italian usage in the *Vocabolario,* the authoritative dictionary of the Italian language prepared by the Accademia della Crusca in Florence. The collection embraced works in many fields of the humanities and sciences—literature, history, politics, theology, ancient philosophy, art, and medicine—and the published writings of 350 authors. At least one imprint from each decade between 1500 and 1887 was included. Although the collection was broken up at the time of purchase, many rare volumes are presently located in the general collections of the Rare Book and Special Collections Division. An inventory categorized by author lists the 1,134 titles that originally formed the collection.

*ARLC,* 1914, p. 35.

# 3

# Joseph S. Allen Collection

## Photographs of American architecture

Prints and Photographs Division

In 1977 and 1978 Joseph S. Allen, who retired as editor in the Library's Subject Cataloging Division after thirty-two years of service, presented to the Library his collection of architectural photographs dating chiefly from the period 1915 to 1967. Inspired by the Historic American Buildings Survey (HABS, no. 117), Mr. Allen methodically photographed churches, colleges, government buildings, residential structures, and historic monuments in twenty-seven eastern and midwestern states. One building type that is particularly well documented is the county courthouse. The collection includes photographs of almost nine hundred, including all the courthouses in fourteen states. The photographs of Washington, D.C., constitute the most comprehensive regional survey in the collection and include views of all public monuments and outdoor sculpture, government buildings, churches, high schools, and colleges as well as most grade schools, libraries, fire and police stations, large apartment buildings, chanceries, banks, department stores, hotels, theaters, bridges, large office buildings, and a selection of smaller commercial structures. The collection contains 11,427 black-and-white negatives. The numbered images are reproduced as contact prints, mounted in albums, and listed in a geographic card file in the Prints and Photographs Division. Mr. Allen is currently cataloging his photographs to correspond with the system used for the HABS records.

U.S., Library of Congress, Prints and Photographs Division, "Former Employee Gives Architectural Photographs to LC," *LCIB,* v. 37, October 6, 1978: 607–608.

# 4

# Alternative Press Collection

American "underground" newspapers, mid-1960s to present

Serial and Government Publications Division

Housed in the Serial and Government Publications Division is a collection of alternative press periodicals that have been acquired by the Library through copyright deposit. The collection includes American newspaper-format publications that have been issued outside the publishing mainstream since the mid–1960s. Approximately 350 titles from twenty-six states are represented, including some single issues of short-lived periodicals that are retained in a separate sample file. Few runs are complete. The Newspaper and Current Periodical Room of the Serial and Government Publications Division services the Alternative Press Collection and maintains a record of holdings by title. Subject access is provided by the commercially issued *Alternative Press Index*.

Of related interest is the Underground Newspaper Microfilm Collection, a commercially published set covering publications from 1963 to the present day. Over five hundred titles are reproduced and listed by title and place of publication in an accompanying index. This collection is available in the Microform Reading Room.

# 5

## *Amateur Hour* Collection

Broadcast recordings, films, and applications of the *Amateur Hour*

Motion Picture, Broadcasting, and Recorded Sound Division
Music Division

*Major Bowes' Amateur Hour* became an overnight sensation when introduced on national radio in 1935. During its second year it received an estimated ten thousand applications weekly from amateurs aspiring to compete on evening radio and win a spot in Major Bowes's traveling variety shows. Although it eventually declined in popularity, the series continued until shortly before Edward Bowes's death in 1946. Ted Mack, a former *Amateur Hour* talent scout, revived the program on radio and television in 1948. The *Amateur Hour* remained on television for twenty years, following the tested formula of its predecessor.

The Library of Congress has unusually comprehensive documentation of both the Major Bowes and the Ted Mack series. The Motion Picture, Broadcasting, and Recorded Sound Division maintains original radio recordings (1935–44) that were donated in 1969 by the program's producer, Lewis Graham. In addition to salutes to cities across America, the 2,200 broadcast transcription discs include performances by prominent artists at the beginning of their careers, among them Frank Sinatra of "The Hoboken Four," Beverly Sills, Stubby Kaye, Pat Boone, and Teresa Brewer. In 1970 Ted Mack added over nine hundred disc and five hundred tape recordings of his shows. Also available is television coverage of the Ted Mack series (1948–68). Most of the over 550 16mm kinescopes donated in 1969 by Lloyd Marx are from after the early 1950s.

The performances of specific radio contestants may be located by using notes kept in the division and a file of applications from the period 1935–44. The 7,000 applications and accompanying correspondence and news clippings were deposited at the Library in 1970 by Joseph Brown and are in the custody of the Music Division. These papers are identified in the division as the Major Bowes Collection.

Waters, Edward N., "Notable Music Acquisitions," *QJLC*, v. 28, January 1971: 71.

APPOINTMENT:

MAJOR BOWES'
AMATEUR HOUR

POSSIBILITY FOR:

(Please print plainly in ink)

Name — *Sills* — *Beverly*
 Last Name — First Name

New York Address — *580 Empire Blvd Bklyn*

New York Telephone — *SLb-6457*
 Residence

Home Address — *580 Empire Blvd Bklyn, N.Y.*
 City — State

Street Address —
 Home Telephone Number

How long do you intend to remain in New York? —

Type of Entertainment: *I'm 10 years old I'm studying singing*
Give facts of your vocations, Past and Present
and all Details of Interest: *with Miss Estella Liebling*
*I have 22 arias on my repertoire*
*I have done 2 pictures with*
*Educational Films and have*
*appeared at many entertainments*
*Professional and Amateur.*

List all Previous Radio — *A.C.R. & Y.M.C.A.*
Appearances if any:

FOR AUDITION DEPARTMENT USE ONLY
(DO NOT FILL IN)

M. R. *A--1*                                   D. R.

Date: OCT 25 1939        Auditioned by: *Heller (Reed)*

Selection: *"Caro Nome"*

Alternate:

Application from Beverly Sills, age 10, to appear on Major Bowes' Amateur Hour. *She sang "Caro Nome" from* Rigoletto *on the October 26, 1939, broadcast.* Amateur Hour *Collection, Music Division.* LC–USZ62–67594.

8

# 6

## American Almanac Collection

American almanacs, seventeenth through nineteenth centuries

Rare Book and Special Collections Division

The earliest American almanacs in the Library of Congress have been brought together as a collection in the Rare Book and Special Collections Division. Represented are imprints from at least thirty-five states and the District of Columbia, including the only known copy of *Kikinawadendamoiwemin,* a Chippewa almanac for the year 1834 which is probably the first book printed in the state of Wisconsin. The collection is strongest in eighteenth- and nineteenth-century material and contains all the editions of *Poor Richard's Almanack* issued after 1735 and many examples by Nathaniel Ames, Samuel Clough, Nathaniel Low, John Tulley, and Nathaniel Whittemore. Some almanacs have been annotated. Hugh Alexander Morrison's *Preliminary Check List of American Almanacs, 1639–1800* (Washington: Govt. Print. Off., 1907. 160 p. Z1231.A6M7) is based largely on the collection. The 3,895 volumes are recorded in a card index by date, title, and place of publication and reported in Milton Drake's *Almanacs of the United States* (New York: Scarecrow Press, 1962. 2 v. Z1231.A6D7). Microprint cards of the almanacs listed in Charles Evans's *American Bibliography* (New York: P. Smith, 1941–59. 14 v. Z1215.E923) can be consulted in the Microform Reading Room. A few almanacs containing diary entries are kept in the Manuscript Division.

Title page from Davy Crockett's Almanack (1836), a humorous publication begun by Crockett in 1835. Comic almanacs were immensely popular in the United States during the three decades before the Civil War. American Almanac Collection, Rare Book and Special Collections Division. LC–USZ62–67575.

# 7

# American Colonization Society Collection

## Records and photographs of the American Colonization Society

Manuscript Division
Prints and Photographs Division

The American Colonization Society, organized in 1817 to resettle black Americans in West Africa, presented its records to the Library of Congress in 1913, 1964, and 1965. While spanning the period 1792 to 1964, the majority of the society's correspondence, reports, and financial and business papers date from the years 1823 to 1912. Correspondence covers such subjects as administrative matters, the status of slaves and freedmen in antebellum America, and the society's role in founding and colonizing Liberia and supporting Liberian education. Correspondents include Thomas Buchanan, Ralph R. Gurley, John H. B. Latrobe, J. W. Lugenbeel, William McLain, Anson Greene Phelps, and Joseph Jenkins Roberts. The Manuscript Division has described the 190,000-item collection in a register that will be published. The records have been microfilmed.

Approximately 550 photographs in the Prints and Photographs Division depict founders and promoters of the society, nineteenth-century Liberian officials, government activities, and the life of the indigenous West African peoples. Included are daguerreotype and tintype portraits. The collection is arranged by subject and is recorded in the division catalog.

*Guide,* Vanderbilt, no. 14.

*NUCMC,* 69–2026.

[Register in press.]

# 8

## American Film Institute Collection

American films

Motion Picture, Broadcasting, and Recorded Sound Division

Under a collaborative agreement of 1968, films acquired by the American Film Institute (AFI) are added to the collections of the Library of Congress. The AFI actively collects American features and shorts produced before 1950, especially those made between 1912 and 1942, the period during which the Library did not retain prints of copyrighted films. The collection consists largely of silent pictures produced by independent companies in the 1910s and 1920s before the emergence of the major studios and sound films contributed by RKO, Columbia, Hal Roach Studios, MCA, Inc. (Universal films and silent features produced by Paramount), and other companies. Preserved are such titles as Allan Dwan's *Zaza* (1923) with Gloria Swanson; Cecil B. De Mille's *The Ten Commandments* (1923); the first all-talking, full-length drama, *The Lights of New York* (1928); John Ford's *The Informer* (1935); Frank Capra's *Mr. Smith Goes to Washington* (1939); Howard Hawks's *His Girl Friday* (1940); and Orson Welles's *Citizen Kane* (1941). Smaller bodies of material within the collection include short sound films of operas, minstrel shows, vaudeville acts, and speeches independently produced by Lee De Forest in the early 1920s (De Forest Phonofilms); Yiddish-language films produced in the United States and Poland in the 1930s and 1940s; and features and shorts with all-black casts made for black audiences during the same period. As of September 1978, approximately twelve thousand titles have been received. The Library is converting the 35mm nitrate film stock to safety film. Reference prints of many important acquisitions are available. Films are recorded by title in the shelflist and also listed by distinct collections (such as donor or thematic group) within the AFI Collection.

John Culhane summarizes the history of the AFI-LC preservation film program in his article "Nitrate Won't Wait," in *American Film* (PN1993.A167), v. 2, March 1977, p. 54–59. Selected films in the AFI Collection are discussed in *The American Film Heritage: Impressions from the American Film Institute Archives* (Washington: Acropolis Books [1972] 184 p.  PN1993.U6A86), by Tom Shales, Kevin Brownlow, and others. The published catalog lists films in the collection as of September 1, 1977.

American Film Institute, *Catalog of Holdings, the American Film Institute Collection and the United Artists Collection at the Library of Congress* (Washington: American Film Institute, 1978. 214 p. PN1998.A575 1978).

# 9

## American Forces Radio and Television Service Collection

Broadcast recordings of the AFRTS, 1940s to present

Motion Picture, Broadcasting, and Recorded Sound Division

Since 1942 the American Forces Radio and Television Service (AFRTS), formerly the Armed Forces Radio Service, has supplied educational, music, and dramatic programs for broadcast on military stations overseas and aboard ships. Through special agreement with musicians, unions, and copyright claimants, the AFRTS distributes shows originally aired by domestic radio as well as programs specifically produced for its own use. The Library of Congress holds the largest known collection of AFRTS recordings—approximately 150,000 disc recordings in 1979. While by no means a complete archive of AFRTS programs, the collection contains disc recordings transferred to the Library as early as 1945 as well as selected early wartime broadcasts. Since 1967 the Library has received AFRTS's complete radio program package, a total of approximately three thousand recordings yearly. Of particular interest are the early recordings of *Mail Call* and *Command Performance,* two radio series that are significant in the history of broadcasting for their use of prerecorded music and innovative editing techniques. The collection is organized by series prefix and program number. An index by series title is being prepared. By an agreement between the Library of Congress and the Department of Defense, researchers wishing to order duplicates of AFRTS material must first obtain written authorization from those holding proprietary rights.

Hickerson, Joseph C., and James R. Smart, "All That Is Audible: Recent Recorded Sound Acquisitions in the Music Division," *QJLC,* v. 32, January 1975: 52–53.

# 10

## American Institute of Aeronautics and Astronautics Archives

Research files, papers, and pictorial material pertaining to the history of aeronautics

Manuscript Division
Prints and Photographs Division

Between 1964 and 1966 the American Institute of Aeronautics and Astronautics, an organization formed in 1963 by the merger of the Institute of the Aerospace Sciences and the American Rocket Society, presented to the Library material from its extensive Aeronautical Archives. The archives were formed by the Institute of the Aerospace Sciences between 1939 and 1962 and incorporated primary source material donated by Hart O. Berg, Lester D. Gardner, Bella C. Landauer, Charles Lindbergh, and Thaddeus S. C. Lowe. The collection, most of which is in the Manuscript Division, documents the history of aeronautics from the Montgolfier brothers to Gen. William ("Billy") Mitchell, Gen. Henry H. ("Hap") Arnold, and the development of the modern air force. The biographical files contain clippings, articles, questionnaires, printed matter, and original manuscripts pertaining to individual aeronauts. Of special note are the personal papers (1859–1943) of balloonist Thaddeus S. C. Lowe, "Chief Aeronaut of the Army of the Potomac." The corporate files consist entirely of printed information on aircraft companies. The 30,000-item collection is described in an unpublished finding aid.

The Prints and Photographs Division maintains a collection of pictorial aeronautica assembled by Bella C. Landauer (1874–1960), a fellow of the Institute of Aerospace Sciences, and received by the Library as part of the initial 1964 gift. An expert on the history of commercial printing, Mrs. Landauer collected what she termed "scraps of old paper"—tradecards, bookplates, wine labels, canceled railroad passes —many of which she donated to the New-York Historical Society. The Library's Landauer Collection is a miscellany of aeronautical prints, drawings, posters, photographs, clippings, and printed ephemera dating from the 1780s to 1945. While most of the 1,400 items relate to late nineteenth- and twentieth-century developments, the collection includes portraits of early aeronauts and depictions of balloon ascents. Mrs. Landauer reproduced items from her collection in *Bookplates from the Aeronautica Collection of Bella C. Landauer* (New York: Priv. print. at the Harbor Press, 1930. [38] p. Z993.L25) and *Some Japanese Balloon Prints from the Collection of Bella C. Landauer* ([New York] 1935. 8 leaves. TE537.J3L3). The collection is accompanied by the original card indexes and is being organized.

Books received from the American Institute of Aeronautics and Astronautics have been integrated with the Library's general collections.

# 11

## American Map Collection

### Maps of North America, 1750–90

Geography and Map Division

Some of the rarest printed maps of North America in the Geography and Map Division were acquired by the Library of Congress from an unknown source before the creation of the Hall of Maps and Charts in 1897. Now known as the American Map Collection, these 167 works produced between 1750 and 1790 include copies of "A Map of the Most Inhabited Part of Virginia" by Joshua Fry and Peter Jefferson (1755 and 1775 editions), John Montrésor's "A Map of the Province of New York" (1777), William Gerard De Brahm's "A Map of South Carolina and a Part of Georgia" (1757), and "A Plan of the City of Philadelphia" (1776) by Benjamin Easburn. The collection was formerly bound as a six-volume set and retains its original organization and table of contents. The maps are listed by area, with the collection designation "American maps," in Philip Lee Phillips's *A List of Maps of America in the Library of Congress* (Washington: Govt. Print. Off., 1901. 1137 p. Z881.U5; reprint, Amsterdam: Theatrvm Orbis Terrarvm [1967]) and individually described in the Library's computerized map catalog. They will also be included in the bibliography being compiled by the Library's American Revolution Bicentennial Office.

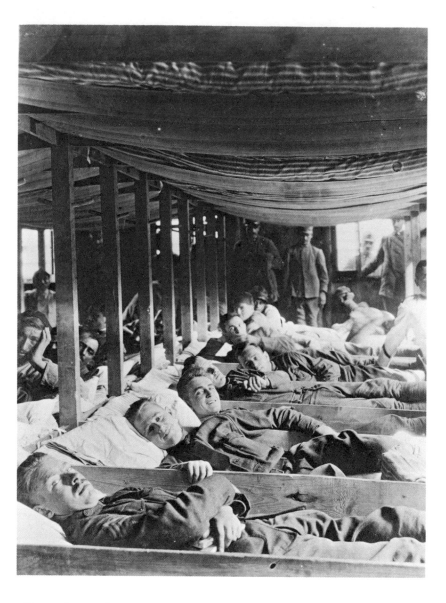

*Troops in transit resting at a Red Cross facility at the central railroad station in Milan, Italy (1918). American National Red Cross Collection, Prints and Photographs Division. LC–USZ62–34120.*

# 12

## American National Red Cross Collection

Photographs of Red Cross relief work and staff members,
early twentieth century

Prints and Photographs Division

In 1944 the American Red Cross transferred to the Library of
Congress 62,000 captioned photoprints and a smaller number of glass
plate negatives documenting the history and relief work of the organization during the early decades of the twentieth century. The collection in the Prints and Photographs Division is composed largely of
photographs taken by Red Cross staff members during and following
World War I. These depict living conditions, medical facilities, refu-
gees, U.S. military personnel, buildings, and topography in over sixteen
European and Asian countries. Paul Ramey and Lewis Hine are among
the World War I photographers represented. Although domestic coverage is less extensive, the collection includes staff portraits and photographs of Red Cross conventions, instructional programs, and disaster
relief operations. A small amount of World War II material was received in 1952. The photoprints are grouped by country and subject
and, in some cases, include the name of the photographer and date.

*Guide,* Vanderbilt, no. 16.

Milhollen, Hirst D., "The American Red Cross Collection of Photographs and
Negatives," *QJLC,* v. 2, February 1945: 32–38; included in *A Century of
Photographs, 1846–1946, Selected from the Collections of the Library of Con-
gress* (Washington: Library of Congress, 1980. TR6.U62.D572), compiled by
Renata V. Shaw.

# 13

## American Records and Briefs and British Appeal Papers Collection

### Published records of the higher courts of appeal in the United States and Great Britain

Law Library

The Law Library has brought together an unsurpassed collection of the records, briefs, and papers of the appellate courts of the United States and Great Britain. The U.S. Supreme Court cases are documented by one of the three complete sets of printed records and briefs in existence, the records beginning in 1832 and the briefs in 1854. The collection contains more than eleven thousand volumes, arranged according to the citation of the case in the *United States Reports;* all current unbound briefs are filed by term and docket number. The Law Library has compiled two finding aids for the briefs and has available a second set of records and briefs and microfilm. The Law Library also collects the records and briefs of the eleven U.S. Courts of Appeals, particularly for the First, Second, Fourth, Fifth, Sixth, Eighth, and District of Columbia Circuits. The records and briefs of the Second Circuit are received on microfiche.

The British courts of appeals are represented by three sets of documents. The series of appeal papers prepared for cases before the House of Lords, the highest court of Great Britain, begins in 1900 and is available on microfilm for the years 1900 to 1976. The records are indexed by case title. Dating back to 1934 are the appeal papers for the Judicial Committee of the Privy Council, the final court for cases of the British colonies and territories, the ecclesiastical courts of the Church of England, medical tribunals, and the Admiralty Court of the Queen's Bench. The Library has microfilmed most of the available material from 1934 to 1974. Both these series of appeal papers are the only known sets outside of the British Commonwealth. The third group of British documents in this collection consists of approximately one hundred appeal papers addressed to the English Privy Council by the colonies of Virginia, Massachusetts, New Hampshire, Rhode Island, Jamaica, Barbados, Antigua, and St. Christopher. Acquired by the

Library in 1938–39, the eighteenth-century records provide a glimpse at colonial cases for which few documents survive. The material was formerly owned and annotated by British lawyer and politician, Sir George Lee (1700–1758).

*Law Library,* p. 16–17.

# 14

## Anarchism Collection

Anarchism publications prepared for U.S. foreign-language communities

Rare Book and Special Collections Division

In 1977 the Library acquired through exchange and purchase nearly fourteen hundred books, pamphlets, serial issues, and ephemeral items relating to the study of anarchy. These publications were printed between the 1850s and the 1970s primarily for the French-, German-, Italian-, Russian-, Spanish-, and Yiddish-speaking communities within the United States. While touching upon many political and social issues, the collection focuses on the history and philosophy of anarchism and the lives and writings of its major proponents. Of particular interest are pamphlets documenting the beliefs and activities of local organizations and short-lived movements. Items are listed by author or title in the card file received with the collection. Additions to the collection are anticipated.

U.S., Library of Congress, Rare Book and Special Collections Division, "New Rare Book Acquisition Noted," *LCIB,* v. 37, February 10, 1978: 97.

# 15

## George Antheil Collection

Music manuscripts, papers, and recordings of composer
George Antheil

Music Division
Motion Picture, Broadcasting, and Recorded Sound Division

George Antheil (1900–1959), self-styled "Bad Boy of Music," was
a leading American avant-garde composer of the twenties and thirties.
An acquaintance of Jean Cocteau, James Joyce, Ezra Pound, and Erik
Satie, Antheil sought a musical equivalent of surrealism. During his
years in Europe he wrote works evocative of the machine age such as
the famous *Ballet mécanique,* a piece originally scored for xylophones,
electric bells, airplane engines, pianos, and player piano. Antheil returned to the United States in 1933 and moved to Hollywood in 1936
to write music for motion pictures.

Since the early sixties Elizabeth Antheil, his widow, has presented
to the Library holographs ranging from Antheil's early orchestral works,
such as *Zingareska* (1921), to chamber music and film scores from the
forties and fifties. The music manuscripts are described in the *Quarterly Journal* and represented in the catalog of the Music Division.
Correspondence was added to the collection by Mrs. Anna T. Hart in
1968 and Mrs. Cary W. Bok in 1975. The latter group consists chiefly
of letters written by Antheil to his patron, Mary Curtis Bok, regarding
his finances and current music projects (1921–40). The 339 items are
listed in an inventory and discussed by Wayne Shirley in his article,
"Another American in Paris: George Antheil's Correspondence with
Mary Curtis Bok," in *QJLC,* v. 34, January 1977, p. 2–22. The remaining letters are addressed to the composer's friend, Stanley Hart,
and are closed to researchers. The collection of music holographs and
correspondence measures four linear feet.

In 1976 Mrs. Antheil donated to the Library recordings of six of
her husband's film scores, among them *Angels over Broadway* (1940)
and *In a Lonely Place* (1950). The eighty-six short "sequences" were
used by Antheil during editing to time his music to specific scenes.
They included passages omitted from the final soundtrack. The discs

have been copied on tape and are represented in the catalog of the Motion Picture, Broadcasting, and Recorded Sound Division.

*NUCMC,* 77–376.

Waters, Edward N., "Music," *QJLC,* v. 20, December 1962: 31.

# 16

## Susan B. Anthony Collection

Library and papers of Susan B. Anthony

Rare Book and Special Collections Division
Manuscript Division

In 1903 Susan B. Anthony (1820–1906), one of the founders of the woman suffrage movement in America, presented her personal library of feminist and antislavery literature to the Library of Congress. The collection contains inscribed volumes presented by admirers, the official reports of the national suffrage conventions, addresses made at congressional hearings after 1869, and files of reform periodicals such as *The Woman's Journal*. In many of the 272 volumes Miss Anthony has written notes about the donor or author. Perhaps the outstanding feature of the library is Miss Anthony's thirty-three scrapbooks of newspaper clippings, programs, handbills, and memorabilia. The scrapbooks were begun at the suggestion of her father in 1855 and document changes in public opinion toward Miss Anthony and the suffrage movement. Publications are listed in author and shelflist files in the Rare Book and Special Collections Division. Microfilms of the scrapbooks are serviced through the Microform Reading Room.

Miss Anthony's papers in the Manuscript Division were donated by her family over a period of years and include scrapbooks assembled by her sister, Mary S. Anthony, correspondence, speeches, and related material. Diaries from the years 1865 to 1906 contain brief comments regarding her lecture tours on behalf of woman suffrage and references to such associates as Amelia Bloomer, Lucretia Mott, and Lucy Stone. An unpublished finding aid has been prepared for the 500-item collection. The papers have been microfilmed.

Beck, Leonard N., "The Library of Susan B. Anthony," *QJLC*, v. 32, October 1975: 324–335.

*NUCMC*, 72–731.

# 17

## Archive of Hispanic Culture

### Photographs of Latin American art and architecture

Prints and Photographs Division

The Archive of Hispanic Culture is a photographic reference collection for the study of Latin American art and architecture. The collection illustrates indigenous art works dating from the colonial period through the twentieth century as well as artistically influential monuments in Spain, Portugal, the Philippines, and the United States. During its most active period, 1940 to 1944, the archive was supported in part by the Rockefeller Foundation and amassed over twelve thousand photoprints, thirty-four hundred transparencies, and forty-nine hundred photographic negatives (these figures include duplicates). Work was continued on a reduced scale until 1947. While most material was acquired by gift, purchase, or exchange with other institutions, the archive commissioned photographic surveys in several regions. The photographs are arranged by medium—architecture, decorative arts, sculpture, painting, and graphic arts—and subdivided by location, type of object, or artist. A card index lists corresponding slides and negatives for many items. The formation of the archive was accompanied by the preparation of *A Guide to the Art of Latin America* (Washington: [Govt. Print. Off.] 1948. 480 p. Z5961.S72S5; reprint, New York: Arno Press, 1971), edited by Robert C. Smith and Elizabeth Wilder.

*Guide,* Vanderbilt, no. 34.

Smith, Robert C., "The Archive of Hispanic Culture," *QJLC,* v. 1, October/ December 1943: 53–57.

# 18

## Archive of Hispanic Literature on Tape

Voice recordings of Hispanic literary figures, 1940s to present

Hispanic Division

The Archive of Hispanic Literature on Tape is a repository of recorded poetry and prose from the Spanish- and Portuguese-speaking world. The collection was begun in 1942 when Emilio Oribe read a poem, dedicated to Archibald MacLeish, in the Library of Congress Recording Laboratory. Largely with the assistance of the Rockefeller Foundation, the archive was expanded to include recordings made abroad expressly for the collection. As of October 1979 the archive contained tapes of 409 writers reading selections from their own works in Spanish, Portuguese, Catalan, French, Quechua, Nahuatl, and Zapotec as well as accompanying interviews and commentaries. Almost all of the outstanding Hispanic literary figures of the last thirty years are represented, including the five writers who have received the Nobel Prize. The archive is also of interest for its documentation of distinctive regional dialects and speech patterns and of social criticism voiced by many writers. Reference tapes for the collection are housed in the Hispanic Society Room of the Hispanic Division and are supplemented by notebooks containing lists and texts of the selections read by each author. The published guide to the archive describes the collection in detail, providing biographic and bibliographic information on each writer. A few recordings have been reproduced as LP records and are available for purchase.

The Motion Picture, Broadcasting, and Recorded Sound Division has custody of the archive's master preservation tapes. Of related interest is the program initiated by the Library in fiscal year 1977 to record major literary figures of foreign countries outside the scope of the Archive of Hispanic Literature on Tape. As of 1978 the Archive of World Literature on Tape comprised approximately twenty recordings.

Dorn, Georgette M., "The Archive of Hispanic Literature on Tape," *The Federal Linguist* (P1.F4), v. 7, 1976: 18–24.

————, "Luso-Hispanic Recordings in the Library of Congress," *Latin American Research Review* (F1401.L345), v. 14, summer 1979: 174–179.

U.S., Library of Congress, Latin American, Portuguese, and Spanish Division, *The Archive of Hispanic Literature on Tape: A Descriptive Guide* (Washington: Library of Congress, 1974. 516 p. Z1609.L7U54 1974), compiled by Francisco Aguilera, edited by Georgette M. Dorn.

# 19

## Archive of Recorded Poetry and Literature

Voice recordings of American literary figures, 1940s to present

Motion Picture, Broadcasting, and Recorded Sound Division

During his tenure as the Library's Consultant in Poetry in English (1944–45), Robert Penn Warren invited thirteen poets and three novelists to record selections from their works for preservation in the Library's collections. Louise Bogan, the succeeding poetry consultant, expanded the program and secured a Bollingen Foundation grant to issue albums of contemporary American poets reading their own poetry. From these efforts in the 1940s has grown the Archive of Recorded Poetry and Literature, a collection of nearly twelve hundred spoken recordings maintained by the Motion Picture, Broadcasting, and Recorded Sound Division. The archive contains discs and tapes of readings made in the Library's Recording Laboratory, literary events held at the Library, readings made outside the Library expressly for the collection, and noncommercial voice recordings received through gift and exchange. Several private collectors, most notably the American poet Lee Anderson (1896–1972), have allowed the Library to copy their collections for the archive. Among the many major literary figures represented by noncommercial recordings are Conrad Aiken, John Berryman, E. E. Cummings, Robert Frost, and Robert Lowell. The Library has issued a checklist for the archive and a series of literary recordings entitled "Twentieth Century Poetry in English." Mary C. Lethbridge discusses the history of the Library's literary programs in "Poets in Washington: The Consultants in Poetry to the Library of Congress" in *Records* of the Columbia Historical Society of Washington, D.C. (F191.C72), v. 69/70, p. 466–488.

U.S., Library of Congress, General Reference and Bibliography Division, *Literary Recordings: A Checklist of the Archive of Recorded Poetry and Literature in the Library of Congress* (Washington: 1966. 190 p. Z663.293.L5).

# 20

## Armed Services Editions Collection

Archival set of paperbacks published for the American Armed Forces, 1943–47

Rare Book and Special Collections Division

The outstanding achievement of the Army Library Service during World War II was the publication and distribution of the Armed Services Editions. Guided by an organization of publishers, booksellers, authors, and librarians known as the Council on Books in Wartime, this publishing effort produced, from 1943 to 1947, over 122 million paperbacks for free distribution to U.S. servicemen. The Armed Services Editions were designed to appeal to a variety of reading tastes and included works ranging from bestsellers to poetry. Only 99 of the 1,324 titles published had previously been reprinted. Between 1943 and 1951 the Library received a complete set of Armed Services Editions, largely as gifts from the Council on Books in Wartime. The paperbacks are shelved in serial order in the Rare Book and Special Collections Division. John Jamieson's bibliography, *Editions for the Armed Services, Inc.: A History, Together with the Complete List of 1324 Books Published for American Armed Forces Overseas* (New York: Editions for the Armed Services [1948] 139 p. Z1039.S6E27), provides access to the paperbacks by serial number and author.

# 21

## *Arthur Godfrey Time* Collection

Broadcast recordings of Arthur Godfrey, 1949–57

Motion Picture, Broadcasting, and Recorded Sound Division

The CBS variety show *Arthur Godfrey Time* was one of the most popular daytime television and radio programs of the 1950s. In addition to its host Arthur Godfrey, the series featured program "regulars" Julius La Rosa, the McGuire Sisters, and Frank Parker; winners from the evening program *Arthur Godfrey Talent Scouts*; and special guests such as Bernard Baruch, Bob Hope, and Robert Kennedy. Some of the winning contestants appearing on the show—Pat Boone, the Chordettes, Vic Damone, and Jonathan Winters—were later to become well-known entertainers In 1970 Charles Horine and Andrew Rooney, two writers for the various Arthur Godfrey series, presented to the Library broadcast transcriptions of *Arthur Godfrey Time* from the years 1949 to 1957 and recordings of several rehearsals and warm-ups. Reference copies of the 3,000 instantaneous disc recordings are being made available to researchers as the material is duplicated on tape.

*Shortstop Honus Wagner (center) of the Pittsburgh Pirates and outfielder Ty Cobb (right) of the Detroit Tigers testing bats at the 1909 World Series. George Grantham Bain Collection, Prints and Photographs Division. LC–USZ62–28936.*

# 22

# George Grantham Bain Collection

## News photographs of New York City, early twentieth century

Prints and Photographs Division

In 1948 the Library of Congress purchased the photographic files of one of America's earliest news picture agencies, the Bain News Service. George Grantham Bain (1865–1944), formerly affiliated with the United Press, founded his New York photo agency in 1898. The news service specialized in New York City news and covered, to a lesser degree, events in the eastern United States. It distributed its own pictures and those purchased from other commercial agencies to about one hundred newspapers. The Bain picture files richly document local sports events, theater, celebrities, crime, disasters, political activities, conventions, and public celebrations. The extensive news coverage provided by the Bain News Service is suggested by the scope of its original card indexes, arranged by subject and personality, which remain an important means of access to the approximately 120,000 glass plate negatives and 240,000 photoprints in the collection. Documentation is virtually complete for the 1910s except for the material destroyed in an early company fire or retained by D. J. Culver of New York at the time of purchase. For the most part, portraits and printed biographical information collected by the news service have been integrated with the division's central portrait file. The remaining photographs are grouped by subject and recorded in the catalog of the Prints and Photographs Division. Because Bain numbered negatives in a chronological sequence, the date of most images can be estimated. Bain's work is discussed in an article by Emma H. Little, "The Father of News Photography, George Grantham Bain," in *Picturescope* (Z692. P5P5), v. 20, autumn 1972, p. 125–132.

*Guide,* Vanderbilt, no. 43.

# 23

# William A. Barnhill Collection

Photographs of North Carolina folklife, 1914–17

Prints and Photographs Division

In 1969 William A. Barnhill presented to the Library of Congress his photo study, "Pioneer Life in Western North Carolina" (1914–17). Barnhill was interested in local technology and handicrafts and recorded local inhabitants performing such daily tasks as milling, weaving, preparing food, and making baskets, shingles, and pottery. The seventy-six gold-toned and seventeen glossy photoprints are accompanied by captions written by the photographer. The collection is represented in the catalog of the Prints and Photographs Division. A number of the photographs were published in Richard M. Ketchum's article, "Appalachia 1914" in *American Heritage* (E171.A43), v. 20, February 1969, p. 26–41, 85.

# 24

## John Davis Batchelder Collection

Books, manuscripts, and other material assembled by John Davis Batchelder

Rare Book and Special Collections Division
Manuscript Division
Music Division
Prints and Photographs Division

During years of foreign study and travel, John Davis Batchelder (1872–1958) collected books, manuscripts, bindings, prints, maps, and coins which he felt illustrated the history of Western culture. His collection, given to the Library in 1936, is housed for the most part in the Rare Book and Special Collections Division. The 1,499 volumes include children's books, early American publications, incunabula, and such significant literary works as the 1599 quarto edition of Shakespeare's *Romeo and Juliet* and the first folio edition of his plays (1623). Many book and nonbook items were acquired because of their connection with famous people, and the division maintains an association file as well as an author/title catalog. Mr. Batchelder's original card index is kept with the collection.

Three other divisions have custody of significant portions of the Batchelder gift. The Manuscript Division maintains a few personal papers and his collection of over fifteen hundred autographs. While spanning the fifteenth through the twentieth centuries, the autographs date chiefly from the 1770s through the 1930s. The specimens are listed by name in an unpublished index.

In the Music Division are autographs, letters, photographs, and ephemera chiefly relating to opera singers and nineteenth-century composers. Among the over eighty items listed in the collection inventory are a leaf containing corrections by Beethoven to the *Piano Sonata no. 32 in C Minor,* op. 111, a letter written by George Sand about Chopin, a salary receipt (1676) signed by Jean Baptiste Lully, and a request for salary made by Francis Hopkinson in 1779.

The Prints and Photographs Division received from the Batchelder gift over eight hundred prints, reproductions, and postcards which pertain chiefly to the French Revolution, Napoleon Bonaparte, and the theater. The items are listed in the division catalog under the collector's name.

*NUCMC,* 61–2074.

U.S., Library of Congress, *Exhibit of Books, Manuscripts, Bindings, Illustrations, and Broadsides Selected from the Collection of John Davis Batchelder* (Washington: [Govt. Print. Off.] 1938. 62 p. Z881.U5).

Waters, Edward N., "Music," *QJLC,* v. 20, December 1962: 31, 46.

# 25

## Harold Bauer Collection

Papers, music manuscripts, and photographs of pianist
Harold Bauer

Music Division

The Anglo-American pianist Harold Bauer (1873–1951) did
much to foster interest in chamber music in America through his
position of leadership in the Beethoven Association of New York and the
Friends of Music in the Library of Congress. Originally trained as a
concert violinist, Bauer turned to the piano in 1892 at the urging of
Paderewski. He became a celebrated soloist and chamber musician,
introducing Debussy's works to English audiences and arranging compositions of Bach, Brahms, Purcell, and Schumann for piano. In 1957,
the papers of Harold Bauer were presented to the Library of Congress
by his widow, Mrs. Harold Bauer. The collection includes over three
hundred letters from friends and professional associates, including
twenty-one from the author and book illustrator Hendrik Willem Van
Loon; 100 photographs; numerous concert programs, awards, press
clippings, and lectures; printed music and holographs of piano arrangements; and the manuscript for his autobiography *Harold Bauer, His
Book* (New York: W. W. Norton [1948] 306 p. ML417.B23A3).
The letters are filed by correspondent and the programs by date. The
collection measures seven linear feet.

Waters, Edward N., "Music," *QJLC*, v. 16, November 1958: 14–15.

# 26

## Alexander Graham Bell Family Collection

Papers and photographs of the Bell family

Manuscript Division
Prints and Photographs Division

The papers of Alexander Graham Bell (1847–1922) and his family were donated to the Library by his heirs in 1975. Soon after his appointment as professor of vocal physiology at Boston University in 1873, Bell began a series of experiments that led to the invention of the telephone. His success enabled him to engage in numerous scientific activities while continuing his career as a teacher of the deaf. Bell's papers in the Manuscript Division include diaries, correspondence, printed matter, financial and legal records, and several hundred volumes of laboratory notebooks which record his daily work from 1865 to 1922. The collection documents patent disputes and early marketing of the telephone as well as Bell's varied scientific research in such fields as aeronautics, eugenics, and physics, his financial support of *Science* magazine, and his participation in the National Geographic Society and the Smithsonian Institution. A family archive, the collection also encompasses materials of Alexander Melville Bell, the inventor's father; Mabel Hubbard Bell, his wife; and Gilbert H. Grosvenor, his son-in-law, as well as correspondence between the Bells and the Hubbards, the Grosvenors, and the Fairchilds, their relatives by marriage. Access to the 140,000-item collection is provided by a container list. Some material has been microfilmed. Nonmanuscript items—musical compositions, maps, and sound recordings—have been transferred to the appropriate custodial divisions. Of related interest are the Grosvenor and Hubbard Family papers, respectively totaling 65,600 and 8,000 items, that were received by the Library in 1977.

Like the Bell Family papers, the Gilbert H. Grosvenor Collection of Alexander Graham Bell Photographs in the Prints and Photographs Division centers on the professional and private life of Alexander Graham Bell. Included are professional portraits of several generations of the Bell family and photographs by family members. At present, annotated family photo albums which are listed in the division catalog are the principal access tool. Subject and portrait files contain a limited number of reference prints.

Brannan, Beverly W., with Patricia T. Thompson, "Alexander Graham Bell: A Photographic Album," *QJLC,* v. 34, April 1977: 73–96; included in *A Century of Photographs, 1846–1946, Selected from the Collections of the Library of Congress* (Washington: Library of Congress, 1980. TR6.U62.D572), compiled by Renata V. Shaw.

*NUCMC,* 78–1688.

U.S., Library of Congress, Manuscript Division, "Frontiers: Recent Acquisitions of the Manuscript Division," *QJLC,* v. 33, October 1976: 360–365.

# 27

## Big Little Book Collection

### Popular children's books, mid-twentieth century

Rare Book and Special Collections Division

The Big Little Book Collection contains a variety of children's books in special formats that were received through copyright deposit in the 1930s and the 1940s. Most numerous are the "Big Little Books" and "Better Little Books" issued by the Whitman Publishing Company, a subsidiary of the Western Printing & Lithographing Company (now Western Publishing Company) of Racine, Wisconsin. Measuring $4\frac{1}{2}$ by 4 by $1\frac{3}{8}$ inches, the Big Little Book presents stories based on comic strips, movies, radio shows, and children's classics and typically matches each page of text with a full-page, black-and-white illustration. Among the 176 Big Little Books and 73 Better Little Books in the collection are volumes featuring Dick Tracy, Flash Gordon, Little Orphan Annie, Mickey Mouse, Tom Mix, and Tailspin Tommie. The collection, totaling 534 items, includes editions from other American series such as the "Big Big Books" and "Chubby Little Books" as well as a few foreign publications. An inventory is being prepared.

# 28

## Katherine Golden Bitting Collection

Publications and manuscripts on gastronomy, fifteenth through twentieth centuries

Rare Book and Special Collections Division

Between 1939 and 1944 Dr. Arvill Wayne Bitting presented to the Library of Congress the 4,346-volume gastronomic collection assembled by his wife, Katherine Golden Bitting (1868–1937), food chemist for the Department of Agriculture and the American Canners Association and author of nearly fifty pamphlets and articles on food preservation and related topics. To facilitate her investigations, as the *Annual Report of the Librarian of Congress* (1940) states, she collected "materials on the sources, preparation, and consumption of foods, their chemistry, bacteriology, preservation, etc., from the earliest times to the present day." The Bitting Collection contains numerous English and American publications on food preparation from the eighteenth and nineteenth centuries and a sampling of notable French, German, and Italian works. American regional cooking is well-documented. The treasure of the collection is a mid-fifteenth century Italian manuscript entitled "Libro de arte coquinaria" of Maestro Martino which was a source for the earliest printed cookbook, Platina's *De Honesta Voluptate* (ca. 1475). Leonard N. Beck discusses the manuscript in his article "Praise Is Due Bartolomeo Platina: A Note on the Librarian-Author of the First Cookbook" in *QJLC,* v. 32, July 1975, p. 238–253. Books in the collection are recorded in the shelflist and author/title file. Items owned by Mrs. Bitting at the time of her death are indicated by an asterisk in her classic work, *Gastronomic Bibliography* (San Francisco: 1939. 718 p. Z5776.G2B6). Of related interest is the cookbook collection of Elizabeth Robins Pennell (no. 183).

*ARLC,* 1940, p. 255–256.

Beck, Leonard N., "Two 'Loaf-givers,' Or a Tour through the Gastronomic Libraries of Katherine Golden Bitting and Elizabeth Robins Pennell," *QJLC,* v. 37, winter 1980: 35–63.

## To dreſs Haddock the Spaniſh Way.

Take two fine haddocks, ſcale, gut, and waſh them well, wipe them with a cloth, and broil them; put a pint of ſweet oil in a ſtew-pan, ſeaſon it with pepper and ſalt, a little cloves, mace, and nutmeg beaten two cloves of garlick chopped, pare half a dozen love apples and quarter them, when in ſeaſon, put them in, and a ſpoonful of vinegar, put in the fiſh, and ſtew them very gently for half an hour over a ſlow fire; put them in a hot diſh, and garniſh with lemon.

Recipe from the first American edition of Richard Briggs's The New Art of Cookery (1792). "Haddock the Spanish Way" is prepared with "love apples," or tomatoes. Katherine Golden Bitting Collection, Rare Book and Special Collections Division. LC–USZ62–67576.

# 29

# William Blackstone Collection

Early editions of the writings of William Blackstone

Law Library

William Blackstone's *Commentaries on the Laws of England,* initially published between 1765 and 1769, was the first systematic treatise on the principles and decisions constituting English common law. Based on the jurist's lectures at All Souls College, Oxford, the four-volume work became the most influential legal textbook in the British Isles and the United States. The Law Library has brought together a special collection of the English jurist's writings and organized the publications following the arrangement of Catherine S. Eller's *The William Blackstone Collection in the Yale Law Library: A Bibliographic Catalogue* ([New Haven] Published for the Yale Law Library by the Yale University Press, 1938. xvii, 113 p. Z8102.-2.Y17). The collection contains English, Irish, and American editions of the *Commentaries,* abridgments and extracts of this work prepared for law students, secondary writings by Blackstone, and books of related interest such as Gilbert à Beckett's parody, *The Comic Blackstone* (1869). Nearly 85 percent of the publications cited in Catherine Eller's bibliography are represented along with several fugitive items such as a third Dublin edition of the *Commentaries,* issued in 1766. American imprints are particularly numerous. Access to the 500 volume collection is through the Law Library's annotated copy of Catherine Eller's catalog and the shelflist. Walter H. Zeydel's article "Sir William Blackstone and His *Commentaries*" in *QJLC,* v. 23, October 1966, p. 302–312, discusses a number of items in the collection.

*Law Library,* p. 13–15.

# 30

## Ernest Bloch Collection

Music manuscripts, papers, and voice recordings of composer
Ernest Bloch

Music Division
Motion Picture, Broadcasting, and Recorded Sound Division

The Swiss-born composer Ernest Bloch (1880–1959) attracted
international attention in 1919 by winning the Elizabeth Sprague Coolidge prize for his *Suite for Viola and Piano*. He became a well-known
conductor and teacher, serving as director of the Cleveland Institute of
Music, director of the San Francisco Conservatory, and, in his later
years, professor of music at the University of California, Berkeley. In
1925, Bloch deposited at the Library a large number of music holographs, correspondence, clippings, scrapbooks, and other personal
papers. The early holographs—his prizewinning piece is now a part of
the Coolidge Foundation Collection (no. 52)—include sketches and
finished scores for symphonic works, chamber music, piano compositions, songs, and the opera *Macbeth*. An inventory of the original
deposit is published in Robert Strassburg's biography. Over the past
decade the composer's children, Ivan and Suzanne Bloch and Lucienne
Bloch Dimitroff, have donated additional items which have been reported in the *Quarterly Journal*. Most letters are closed to researchers
until 1984. The collection occupies nine linear feet and is represented
in the catalog of the Music Division.

The Bloch family has also donated eight recordings of lectures
delivered by the composer at the University of California in 1951
under the title "The Language of Music," recordings of a special
lecture given in 1952, and a broadcast recording of a memorial tribute
aired on Swiss radio in 1959. The collection is represented in the
catalog of the Motion Picture, Broadcasting, and Recorded Sound
Division and is described in an inventory on file.

*ARLC,* 1925, p. 94–95.

Strassburg, Robert, *Ernest Bloch, Voice in the Wilderness: A Biographical Study*
([Los Angeles: Trident Shop, California State University] 1977.   192 p.
ML410.B656S8), p. 101–117.

# 31

## Bollingen Foundation Collection

Records and publications of the Bollingen Foundation

Manuscript Division
Rare Book and Special Collections Division

The Bollingen Foundation was established in 1945 by Paul and Mary Conover Mellon to create a larger audience for Carl G. Jung's theories through the publication of his collected works in English translation. From this initial publishing venture grew the Bollingen Series, a distinguished series of publications on aesthetics, anthropology, literary criticism, philosophy, psychology, and comparative religion. With the transfer of the Bollingen Series to Princeton University Press in 1969, the foundation concluded its activities and presented its records to the Library of Congress four years later.

While some of the material spans the period from 1939 to 1973, most of the correspondence, memoranda, applications, minutes, financial statements, and news clippings forming the Bollingen Foundation records in the Manuscript Division date from the years 1953 to 1968. The extensive administrative files cover the foundation's fellowship program, contributions to special projects, publications, and internal affairs. Among the correspondents are T. S. Eliot, Carl G. Jung, Joseph Wood Krutch, Jacques Maritain, and Allen Tate. The records, which contain approximately seventy-eight thousand items, include an index and are described in an unpublished finding aid. The rejected applications and advisers' reports are closed to investigators until 1993.

An archival set of books published by the Bollingen Foundation or with its financial support is kept in the Rare Book and Special Collections Division. The 607 volumes are recorded in a shelflist file.

Matheson, William, "Recent Acquisitions of the Rare Book Division," *QJLC* v. 31, July 1974: 181.

*NUCMC,* 77–1494.

U.S., Library of Congress, Manuscript Division, "Recent Acquisitions of the Manuscript Division," *QJLC,* v. 31, October 1974: 261–263.

# 32

## Laura Boulton Collection

Field recordings collected by ethnomusicologist Laura Boulton, mid-twentieth century

Archive of Folk Song

Ethnomusicologist Laura Boulton has participated in over twenty expeditions in her efforts to document the music of various world cultures. Recording on five continents, chiefly from the 1930s through the 1960s, she assembled a collection that is particularly rich in the traditional vocal and instrumental music of Canada, Africa, Southeast Asia, American Indians, and Eskimos. In 1973 Columbia University presented Dr. Boulton's original field recordings to the Library of Congress for preservation in the Archive of Folk Song (AFS 15,667–16,972, 17,115–17,194, and 18,102–18,468). In spite of the technical problems she confronted in the field—Laura Boulton describes the primitive conditions under which she worked in her autobiography *The Music Hunter* (Garden City, N.Y.: Doubleday, 1969. 513 p. ML423.B53A3) —the 1,312 discs and 367 tape recordings are of consistently good acoustical quality. The material has been copied on tape and is accompanied by catalogs and commentaries. Instruments, books, prints, slides, and films accumulated by Dr. Boulton are maintained by Columbia University along with tapes of the Library of Congress recordings.

Hickerson, Joseph C., and James R. Smart, "All That Is Audible: Recent Recorded Sound Acquisitions," *QJLC,* v. 32, January 1975: 74–75.

# 33

## Paul Bowles Collection

### Field recordings of Moroccan music, 1959

Archive of Folk Song

In 1959, with the assistance of a Rockefeller Foundation grant, Paul Bowles traveled throughout Morocco recording indigenous vocal, instrumental, and dance music for the Archive of Folk Song. The American author and composer focused his activity on twenty-three settlements along the Mediterranean and Atlantic coasts and in the inland regions of the Grand Atlas, Anti-Atlas, and Middle Atlas mountain ranges. The resulting collection of seventy tape recordings (AFS 11,623–11,687 and 12,016–12,020) reveals a heterogeneity of regional musical styles which Mr. Bowles attributes, in some measure, to the varying degree of Arab influence and the retention of fifteenth-century Andalusian traditions. The performers range from town professionals to rural nomadic musicians and include a player of the *zamar*, a rare double-reed instrument with two mouthpieces and bull's-horn resonators. In addition to Berber and Arab music, Mr. Bowles recorded Sephardic liturgical music and folksongs of the Jewish communities in Essaouira and Meknès. The tapes are accompanied by a small number of photographs, correspondence, and extensive field notes which have been reproduced on microfilm. Selections from the Bowles Collection have been issued by the Library as a two-record set.

Bowles, Paul, comp., *Music of Morocco* (Library of Congress, Recording Laboratory [1972] 4 s. 12 in. 33⅓ rpm. AFS L63–64).

Jabbour, Alan, and Joseph C. Hickerson, "African Recordings in the Archive of Folk Song," *QJLC*, v. 27, July 1970: 284–285.

Leavitt, Donald L., "Folk, Popular, and Art Music of Morocco," *LCIB*, v. 19, October 17, 1960: 589–591.

# 34

## Brady-Handy Collection

Portrait photographs and views of Washington, D.C., from the Brady and Handy studios, nineteenth and early twentieth centuries

Prints and Photographs Division

In 1954 the Library of Congress purchased from Alice H. Cox and Mary H. Evans, the daughters of Levin C. Handy, the photographic files of the L. C. Handy Studio which had been located at 494 Maryland Avenue SW, Washington, D.C. Levin C. Handy (1855?–1932) was apprenticed at the age of twelve to his uncle, famed Civil War photographer Mathew B. Brady (1823?–1896). Handy became an independent photographer in 1871 and upon Brady's death merged the working files of the two studios. Of the 10,000 negatives received by the Library from these combined files, approximately 4,000 are original wet collodion plates and 1,300 duplicates from Brady's studios. Handy and his associates are thought to have produced 1,300 of the original glass plates—largely portraits and local views, including many photographs of the Library building (Handy established the first Library of Congress photoduplication service). The remainder are mostly Brady and Handy copy negatives portraying members of the 50th Congress, Civil War scenes, and material reproduced for customers. Of particular interest are Washington views executed by Brady at the beginning of the Civil War and portraits of congressmen and government leaders (1855–90). Accompanying the negatives is a group of twenty-four Brady daguerreotype portraits of Edwin Booth, Brady, William Cullen Bryant, Jenny Lind, Daniel Webster, and others. Most prints from the Brady-Handy negatives have been organized by subject and recorded in the catalog of the Prints and Photographs Division.

*Guide,* Vanderbilt, no. 80A.

Milhollen, Hirst D., "The Brady-Handy Collection," *QJLC,* v. 13, **May** 1956: 135–142; reprinted in *A Century of Photographs, 1846–1946, Selected from the Collections of the Library of Congress* (Washington: Library of Congress, 1980. TR6.U62.D572), compiled by Renata V. Shaw.

# 35

## British Cartoon Collection

British political prints, seventeenth through mid-nineteenth centuries

Prints and Photographs Division

In 1921 the Library of Congress purchased a large collection of British political cartoons that had been assembled in the nineteenth century by the Windsor Castle Library. This important acquisition forms the core of the British Cartoon Collection in the Prints and Photographs Division, one of the largest collections of British political prints in the United States. The 10,000 caricatures and satires date from the seventeenth through mid-nineteenth centuries and are most numerous for the period from 1780 to 1820. Well represented is the work of Henry Bunbury (1750–1811), George Cruikshank (1792–1878), Isaac Cruikshank (1756?–1811?), Matthew Darly (fl. 1754–1778), James Gillray (1757–1815), and Thomas Rowlandson (1756–1827). The collection is organized following the numeric sequence of *Catalogue of Prints and Drawings in the British Museum: Division I, Political and Personal Satires* ([London]: Printed by order of the Trustees, 1870–1919. 11 v. NE55.L5A3). A copy of the *Catalogue* has been annotated to indicate the division's holdings. The collection also includes approximately twenty-five hundred prints not listed in the *Catalogue.* Arranged by date and title, these prints have been reproduced on microfilm and indexed by title, artist, publisher, and printseller. For some prints there are colored as well as uncolored impressions.

Etching (ca. 1736) satirizing William Wake, archbishop of Canterbury (holding whip), for loading his son-in-law Dr. Lynch (ass) with lucrative ecclesiastical appointments and neglecting the advancement of other clergymen. The legend reads:

In Days of Old the Churchman that could Shine,
If not Apostle, was at least Divine:
A Supple Conscience non, & Front of Brass,
For highest Honours fits the heaviest Ass.

Ten thousand Souls in one Squab Doctor's care,
Give him no Pain, Since Curates are not dear,
Good antient Pastors us'd to feed and keep,
Enought for ours, that they can Shear, their Sheep.

British Cartoon Collection, Prints and Photographs Division. LC–USZ62–67577.

# 36

## Frank C. Brown Collection

Field recordings of North Carolina folk music, late 1910s to early 1940s

Archive of Folk Song

Following his appointment in 1909 as professor of English at Trinity College (now Duke University), Frank C. Brown (1870–1943) organized the North Carolina Folklore Society and began his documentation of the state's oral traditions. He collected folklore of all types—from legends to quilt designs—although his particular area of interest was songs and ballads. Experimenting with the Ediphone as early as 1915, he became one of the first folklorists to use a mechanical recording device for the documentation of Anglo-American folksongs. After Brown's death, the task of publishing his massive folklore collection fell to Newman I. White, who made arrangements for the Library of Congress to duplicate the original wax cylinder and instantaneous disc field recordings. The eighty sixteen-inch disc copies (AFS 8,772–8,851) contain material recorded by Brown primarily in the late 1910s, early 1920s, late 1930s, and the early 1940s. Although a few singing games, tales, instrumental performances, and dance pieces are represented, the collection consists predominantly of ballads and songs and includes much of the vocal music discussed in volumes 2 through 5 of *The Frank C. Brown Collection of North Carolina Folklore* (Durham, N.C.: Duke University Press [1952–64] 7 v. GR110.N8D8). A concordance, list of contributors, and miscellaneous notes and indexes are kept on file in the Archive of Folk Song. The original field recordings are maintained with the Frank C. Brown papers at Duke University.

# 37

## Cabinet of American Illustration

Drawings by American illustrators, late nineteenth and early twentieth centuries

Prints and Photographs Division

Largely through the efforts of William Patten, the art editor of *Harper's Magazine* in the 1880s and 1890s, the Cabinet of American Illustration was established in 1932 to bring together original drawings by American book, magazine, and newspaper illustrators. Donations by artists, publishers, and their families have fostered the growth of the collection. The cabinet contains over four thousand cartoons, cover designs, sketches for posters, and illustrations for magazines, novels, and children's books that were executed chiefly between 1880 and 1910. Among the 200 artists represented are Daniel Carter Beard, Thomas Fogarty, Arthur B. Frost, Charles Dana Gibson, Elizabeth Shippen Green, Oliver Herford, William A. Rogers, William T. Smedley, Frederic Dorr Steele, George H. Wright, and Frederick C. Yohn. The drawings are arranged alphabetically by artist and listed individually in a separate card file in the Prints and Photographs Division. In many cases the place of publication and the original caption are written on the drawing or catalog card.

*ARLC,* 1932, p. 174–175.

*Guide,* Vanderbilt, no. 105.

# 38

## Canon Law Collection

Publications and manuscripts pertaining to canon law

Law Library

While strongest in the works of the seventeenth- and eighteenth-century canonists, the Law Library's Canon Law Collection encompasses manuscripts, early printed sources, contemporary works, and periodicals pertaining mostly to the canon law of the Roman Catholic church. The *Decretum Gratiani,* the twelfth-century work which for centuries was the basic text for the study of canon law, is represented in the collection by copies of the exceedingly rare 1514 Venice edition, the 1560 Lyons edition, the 1584 Venice edition, and the 1613 Lyons edition. The collection also contains decisions of the high tribunal of the Roman Catholic church, the *Rota Romana,* and is rich in decisions published in the seventeenth and eighteenth centuries. Approximately half of the 3,000 volumes are in Latin. Items in the collection are recorded in the Law Library catalog and shelflist.

*Law Library,* p. 29–30.

# 39

## Carnegie Survey of the Architecture of the South

### Photographs of architecture in the southern states

Prints and Photographs Division

The culmination of Frances Benjamin Johnston's work as an architectural photographer is the Carnegie Survey of the Architecture of the South, a systematic record of the early buildings and gardens of nine southern states that was executed between 1933 and 1940 with the financial assistance of the Carnegie Corporation. Miss Johnston (1864–1952) worked chiefly in Maryland, Virginia, the Carolinas, Georgia, Alabama, and Louisiana and to a lesser degree in Florida and Mississippi. She was one of the first to document vernacular building traditions, photographing not only the great mansions of the South, but churches, graveyards, row houses, offices, kitchens, warehouses, mills, shops, farm buildings, and inns. The survey includes records of severely altered and poorly maintained structures and numerous shots of interiors and architectural details. In recognition of the scope and technical excellence of the Carnegie Survey, the American Institute of Architects presented an honorary membership to the photographer in 1945.

Sixty-eight hundred survey negatives that were deposited at the Library by Miss Johnston and then purchased from her estate in 1953 are, for the most part, available as reference prints. Like those from the Historic American Buildings Survey (HABS, no. 117), the photographs are geographically arranged and accessed through a collection card index. Carnegie Survey records are also recorded in the master card catalog for the architectural collections. Material from the survey has been used to illustrate publications by Henry Irving Brock, Frederick D. Nichols, Samuel Gaillard Stoney, and Thomas T. Waterman and has been reproduced for the picture collections of several American museums and universities. Other photographs by Miss Johnston are discussed in entries number 131 and 186.

*Guide,* Vanderbilt, no. 388.

Vanderbilt, Paul, "Frances Benjamin Johnston, 1854–1952," *Journal of the American Institute of Architects* (NA1.A326), v. 18, November 1952: 224–228.

# 40

## Frank and Frances Carpenter Collection

Travel photographs and papers of the Carpenters, early twentieth century

Prints and Photographs Division
Manuscript Division

In 1951, Frances Carpenter (Mrs. W. Chapin) Huntington presented to the Library the extensive photographic files that had been assembled by her father, journalist and traveler Frank G. Carpenter (1855–1924), to illustrate his popular writings on geography. Like *Carpenter's Geographic Readers*, standard school texts for forty years, the photographs deal with human geography and illustrate industry, agriculture, housing, transportation, schools, distinctive customs, and religious practices. Frank Carpenter and his daughter took many of the photographs themselves, particularly those from the period 1910 to 1924, and compiled captioned albums of their travels in Europe, the Near and Far East, Africa, and North and South America. The albums include approximately fifty-six hundred original contact prints, many of which are keyed to the 8,000 negatives in the collection. The Carpenters also collected thousands of commercial photographs which, like the albums, have been grouped by subject and geographic area. Both albums and loose photographs are represented in the division catalog.

Mrs. Huntington, who wrote under her maiden name Frances Carpenter, continued to donate material to the Library until her death in 1972. The collection of 100 items in the Manuscript Division, a gift of 1969, consists of papers relating to the book *Carp's Washington* (1960), which she edited, and a small number of letters.

*Guide,* Vanderbilt, no. 114.

*NUCMC,* 72–1708.

Vanderbilt, Paul, "Carpenter's World Travels," *LCIB,* v. 10, April 23, 1951: 2–3.

*Viewpoints,* no. 43–45.

*Pace eggers in Yorkshire, England (1920s). Following an old English Easter custom, these boys perform a traditional folk play in return for decorated pace eggs and gifts. James Madison Carpenter Collection, Archive of Folk Song. LC–USZ62–67578.*

# 41

## James Madison Carpenter Collection

Field recordings, papers, and pictorial material relating to
British and American folk music, late 1920s–1930s

Archive of Folk Song

James Madison Carpenter began collecting British-American folklore in 1927 as he compiled material for his Harvard doctoral dissertation "Forecastle Songs and Chanties." A Sheldon fellow, he returned
to England and Scotland from 1929 to 1935 and amassed important
collections of sea chanties, ballads, and folk plays before accepting a
teaching position at Duke University. His entire collection of field
notes, transcriptions, recordings, and photographs was purchased by the
Library in 1972. Included are over one thousand ballad texts and 850
tunes of the Francis Child canon, 500 sea chanties, 1,000 other ballads
and songs from Britain and America, 200 children's singing games,
riddles, and nursery rhymes, and 300 British folk plays which Carpenter
pieced together using descriptions provided by spectators and participants. For several mummer and sword dance plays, he recorded
actual performances and obtained drawings of the players. The Library
has taped the 223 discs which Carpenter prepared from his cylinders in
the early 1940s (AFS 14,830–15,052). A concordance is on file in the
Archive of Folk Song. In an interview recorded in 1972, Carpenter
described his collecting activities in England and Scotland (AFS
14,762–14,765). The Carpenter manuscripts measure approximately
four linear feet and, for the most part, have been microfilmed. The
Archive of Folk Song prepared a preliminary inventory for the material.

# 42

## Tom Carter and Blanton Owen Collection

Field recordings of instrumental music of North Carolina and Virginia, 1973–74

Archive of Folk Song

Assisted by a grant from the National Endowment for the Humanities and the loan of blank tape by the Archive of Folk Song, Tom Carter and Blanton Owen conducted a survey of the traditional instrumental music in a five-county area of North Carolina and southwestern Virginia. The two field-workers, both of whom are folklore students and capable musicians, conducted extensive interviews with older musicians on the sources, history, and social functions of their music and recorded them performing on traditional instruments. The 235 field recordings made in 1973 and 1974 have been duplicated for the Library's collections (AFS 18,474–18,706) and are described in a concordance and notes on file in the Archive of Folk Song. While strongest in banjo and fiddle recordings, the collection also includes whistling, songs, and performances on the autoharp, dulcimer, fife, guitar, hammered dulcimer, Hawaiian guitar, Jew's harp, mandolin, and piano. Selections from the field recordings have been commercially released by Rounder Records.

Carter, Tom, and Blanton Owen, comps., *Old Originals: Old-Time Instrumental Music Recently Recorded in North Carolina and Virginia* (Rounder, 1976. 4 s. 12 in. 33⅓ rpm. Rounder 0057–0058).

# 43

## Carrie Chapman Catt Collection

Library and papers of Carrie Chapman Catt, president of the
National American Woman Suffrage Association

Rare Book and Special Collections Division
Manuscript Division

In 1938 Carrie Chapman Catt (1859–1947), the president of the
National American Woman Suffrage Association (NAWSA), donated
her "feminist library" to the Library of Congress on behalf of her organization. Formerly the NAWSA's reference collection, the gift includes
volumes from the libraries of Susan B. Anthony, Alice Stone Blackwell, Julia Ward Howe, Mary A. Livermore, Elizabeth Smith Miller,
Elizabeth Cady Stanton, Lucy Stone, and other reformers. For the
most part, the 912 items retain their original arrangement. Publications
are recorded in the collection shelflist in the Rare Book and Special
Collections Division.

The papers of Carrie Chapman Catt, the Blackwell family papers,
and the records of the NAWSA (three groups of material in the Manuscript Division formerly known as the "Suffrage Archives") were
donated to the Library largely through the efforts of Edna L. Stantial,
archivist of the NAWSA. The Catt papers, presented in 1947 by Alda
Wilson, executrix of Mrs. Catt's estate, and by Mrs. Stantial in 1960,
date chiefly from 1890 to 1920 and pertain to Mrs. Catt's efforts to secure voting rights for women. Material from after 1920 relates primarily
to her world peace movement activities. The 9,500 items include
diaries written during her world suffrage tour (1911–12), speeches,
articles, and correspondence with Alice Stone Blackwell, Ida Husted
Harper, Clara Hyde, Maud Wood Park, and Rosika Schwimmer. The
Catt material has been microfilmed and is described in a published
register.

*NUCMC,* 68–2014.

U.S., Library of Congress, Manuscript Division, *The Blackwell Family, Carrie
Chapman Catt, and the National American Woman Suffrage Association*
(Washington: Library of Congress, 1975. 102 p. Z6621.U58B5 1975).

# 44

## Mrs. E. Crane Chadbourne Collection

Japanese prints of foreigners, nineteenth century

Prints and Photographs Division

The Chadbourne Collection, the gift of Mrs. E. Crane Chadbourne in 1930, consists of 188 late eighteenth- and nineteenth-century Japanese woodcuts of foreign subjects. The collection includes representations of European and American visitors in Japan, fanciful portraits of foreign rulers, scenes from the lives of Western inventors, and imaginary views of foreign cities. A few woodcuts relate directly to Commodore Perry's trade mission in 1853, the event credited with increasing the popularity of this print genre. Although composed largely of prints issued in Edo (Tokyo) in the mid-nineteenth century, the collection includes a few earlier woodcuts published in Nagasaki. The prints are cataloged individually and recorded as a group in the catalog of the Prints and Photographs Division. Of related interest is Renata V. Shaw's article, "Japanese Picture Scrolls of the First Americans in Japan" in *QJLC*, v. 25, April 1968, p. 134–153; reprinted in *Graphic Sampler* (Washington: Library of Congress, 1979. NE400.G7), compiled by Renata V. Shaw.

*Guide,* Vanderbilt, no. 120.

# 45

## Chicago Ethnic Arts Project Collection

Recordings, photographs, and related documentation from the 1977 field study of ethnic arts in Chicago

American Folklife Center

At the request of the Illinois Arts Council, the American Folklife Center undertook a field survey of the ethnic art traditions of Chicago. During the spring and summer of 1977, the project team interviewed community leaders and artists from over twenty ethnic groups. Field-workers assessed the impact of the contemporary urban American setting on traditional art forms as they documented folk music, dancing, and crafts and gathered biographies of individual performers and craftsmen. Information was compiled for the following ethnic groups: Afro-American, Austrian, Chicano, Chinese, Croatian, Cuban, Czech, Danish, Finnish, German, Greek, Irish, Italian, Japanese, Jewish, Korean, Lithuanian, Macedonian, Native American, Norwegian, Polish, Puerto Rican, Serbian, Slovak, Slovenian, Swedish, and Ukrainian. The final project report was submitted to the Illinois Arts Council for use in planning a state sponsored program for ethnic arts.

The American Folklife Center has organized materials related to the project. In addition to field notes and other written documentation, the project collection includes 335 sound recordings, approximately thirty-seven hundred color transparencies, and three hundred rolls of black-and-white film. Contact prints, identification sheets, and logs provide an index to the materials. Plans are underway to transfer materials to the appropriate custodial units.

American Folklife Center, "Chicago Project Highlights," in its *Folklife Center News* (GR105.A63a), v. 1, April 1978: 3, 8.

———, "Chicago's Ethnic Communities and Their Artistic Expression," in its *Folklife Center News* (GR105.A63a), v. 1, January 1978: 6–7.

*Members of local Italian organization carrying their patron saint, St. Rocco di Simbario, through the streets of the Bridgeport neighborhood in Chicago. Chicago Ethnic Arts Project Collection, American Folklife Center. Negative in center.*

# 46

## Children's Book Collection

Children's books, eighteenth century to present

Rare Book and Special Collections Division

The Rare Book and Special Collections Division houses approximately eighteen thousand children's books dating from the early eighteenth century to the present. Particularly strong in American juvenile fiction, the collection contains numerous works by Jacob Abbott (creator of the "Rollo" series), William Taylor Adams ("Oliver Optic"), Louisa May Alcott, Mrs. G. R. Alden ("Pansy"), Horatio Alger, Jr., Rebecca Sophia Clarke, Charles A. Fosdick ("Harry Castlemon"), Samuel Griswold Goodrich, Harriet Mulford Stone Lothrop (the *Five Little Peppers* series), and Susan Warner. Outstanding contemporary children's books, acquired largely through copyright deposit, are selected for the collection each year and preserved with dust jackets and unmarked title pages. Examples illustrating popular reading tastes are also chosen. Among the modern writers represented by first editions are Ludwig Bemelmans, James Daugherty, Meindert DeJong, William Pène Du Bois, Rachel Field, Robert McCloskey, E. B. White, and Laura Ingalls Wilder. Earlier children's books include instructional texts, early nineteenth-century paperbound books, and rare American publications presented to the Library in 1941 by Frank J. Hogan of Washington, D.C.—among them a copy of Goodrich's *The Tales of Peter Parley About America* (Boston: 1827), two late eighteenth-century copies of *Cock Robin's Death and Funeral,* and ten *New England Primers,* six of them printed before 1800.

Children's books held by the Rare Book and Special Collections Division are listed by author and title in the two-volume catalog published in 1975. Subsequent acquisitions are recorded in a card index. Children's books are also found in other special collections in the division such as the Batchelder, Hersholt, and Kipling collections (no. 24, 114, and 134).

Haviland, Virginia, "Serving Those Who Serve Children: A National Reference Library of Children's Books," *QJLC,* v. 22, October 1965: 307–312.

*Trumpeter gadfly from the first edition of William Roscoe's* The Butterfly's Ball *and the* Grasshopper's Feast *(1807), illustrated by William Mulready. The English publication inspired numerous sequels and imitations in the United States. Children's Book Collection, Rare Book and Special Collections Division. LC–USZ62–67579.*

——, and Margaret N. Coughlan, *Yankee Doodle's Literary Sampler of Prose, Poetry, & Pictures: Being an Anthology of Diverse Works Published for the Edification and/or Entertainment of Young Readers in America Before 1900* (New York: Crowell [1974] 466 p. Z1232.H38).

Nolen, Eleanor Weakley, "The National Library Builds a Children's Book Collection," *Horn Book Magazine* (Z1037.A1A15), v. 14, July 1938: 246–248.

U.S., Library of Congress, Children's Book Section, *Americana in Children's Books: Rarities from the 18th and 19th Centuries, An Exhibition Catalog* (Washington: Library of Congress, 1974. 28 p. Z1037.U73 1974).

U.S., Library of Congress, Rare Book Division, *Children's Books in the Rare Book Division of the Library of Congress* (Totowa, N.J.: Rowman and Littlefield, 1975. 2 v. Z1038.U5U54 1975).

# 47

## Civil War Drawing Collection

Eyewitness drawings by Civil War newspapermen

Prints and Photographs Division

In 1919 J. P. Morgan presented to the Library drawings by Alfred R. Waud (1828–1891), William Waud (d. 1878), and Edwin Forbes (1839–1895), three of the leading Civil War artists for *Harper's Weekly, Frank Leslie's Illustrated Newspaper,* and the New York *Illustrated News.* The public clamor for pictorial news of the war created an enormous demand for eyewitness drawings that could be reproduced as wood engravings in illustrated newspapers. Most of the original sketches were discarded after they were copied. The Library's collection of 1,600 drawings is probably the largest group to have survived and provides a priceless record of camp life, marches, and important events of the war. The best represented artist in the collection is Alfred Waud, who primarily followed the Virginia campaigns from 1861 to 1865, producing hundreds of pencil-and-wash drawings for *Harper's* and the *Illustrated News.* His brother William worked largely in Georgia and South Carolina from 1861 to 1865 on intermittent assignments for all three northern papers. Edwin Forbes, special artist for *Leslie's* from 1862 to 1864, created 300 of the field sketches in the collection as well as the award-winning series of etchings entitled *Life Studies of the Great Army* (1876). Reproductions of selected Civil War drawings by all three artists have been arranged in subject and chronological reference files in the Prints and Photographs Division. Many items from the collection are described in the exhibition catalog prepared by the National Gallery of Art, *The Civil War: A Centennial Exhibition of Eyewitness Drawings* (Washington: 1961. 153 p. NC107.A55). A few Alfred Waud letters, also part of J. P. Morgan's gift, are kept in the Manuscript Division.

*Guide,* Vanderbilt, no. 235, 756.

# 48

## Civil War Photograph Collection

Civil War photographs by Mathew Brady's staff and others

Prints and Photographs Division

The best known pictorial records of the American Civil War are the photographs commissioned by Mathew Brady (1823?–1896), a leading portrait photographer of New York and Washington. At the outbreak of the war, Brady sent photographers into the field to record the progress of the conflict in various regions. Although taking few of the photographs himself, Brady employed twenty photographers at the height of his operations. Brady's staff included, at one time or another, Alexander and James Gardner, who left Brady to work for the Army in 1863, James F. Gibson, Timothy O'Sullivan, and Thomas C. Roche. In 1943 the Library of Congress purchased a collection which brings together 10,000 original and copy glass plate negatives attributed to Brady's staff or made by independent field photographers. These images of camp life, artillery, fortifications, railroads, ships, bridges, towns, battlefields, officers, and men in the ranks were published in a series of illustrated works on the Civil War, among them *The Photographic History of the Civil War* (New York: Review of Reviews Co., 1912. 10 v. E468.7.M64 1912), edited by Francis Trevelyan Miller. In addition to the so-called Brady Collection, the Prints and Photographs Division maintains photographs by other Confederate and Union photographers, such as Haas and Peale, whose work is discussed in Milton Kaplan's article, "The Case of the Disappearing Photographers," in *QJLC*, v. 24, January 1967, p. 40–45; reprinted in *A Century of Photographs, 1846–1946, Selected from the Collections of the Library of Congress* (Washington: Library of Congress, 1980. TR6.U62.D572), compiled by Renata V. Shaw.

The photographs are recorded by subject and geographic location in the division catalog. Many reference prints are maintained in the Civil War photograph files in the division reading room. The Library's published catalog of Civil War photographs lists 1,047 copy negatives with accompanying captions; images described in this catalog are available on microfilm through the Photoduplication Service.

*Guide,* Vanderbilt, no. 78–80, 317, 557.

*Ruins of Richmond seen from across the James River (1865). On April 2, with the Union forces within striking distance of the Confederate capital, General Lee telegraphed Pres. Jefferson Davis to begin evacuation. Civil War Photograph Collection, Prints and Photographs Division. LC–B8171–3245.*

Milhollen, Hirst D., "Mathew B. Brady Collection," *QJLC*, v. 1, April/June 1944: 15–19; reprinted in *A Century of Photographs, 1846–1946, Selected from the Collections of the Library of Congress* (Washington: Library of Congress, 1980. TR6.U62.D572), compiled by Renata V. Shaw.

U.S., Library of Congress, Prints and Photographs Division, *Civil War Photographs, 1861–1865: A Catalog of Copy Negatives Made from Originals Selected from the Mathew B. Brady Collection in the Prints and Photographs Division of the Library of Congress* (Washington: 1961. 74 p. E468.7.U57; reprint, Washington: 1977), compiled by Hirst D. Milhollen and Donald H. Mugridge.

*Viewpoints,* no. 75, 77, 79–82, 84–85.

*Superman shielding a wounded GI from Japanese air fire; cover of the July 1943 issue of* Action Comics. *Comic Book Collection, Serial and Government Publications Division. Copyright © 1943, renewed 1971 by DC Comics, Inc. LC–USZ62–67580.*

# 49

## Comic Book Collection

Serial and Government Publications Division

For more than thirty years, the Library of Congress has acquired comic books through copyright deposit. The current collection of 2,300 titles, probably the largest in the United States, contains approximately forty-seven thousand pieces and is growing by about two hundred issues each month. Represented in the collection is the entire range of comic-book subject matter: western, science fiction, detective, adventure, war, romance, horror, and humor. Although scattered issues date from the late 1930s, the holdings are most comprehensive from 1950 to the present. *Action Comics, Archie, Detective Comics, Tarzan,* and *Wonder Woman* are among those with fairly complete runs. A record of the holdings, by title, is maintained in the Newspaper and Current Periodical Room. Because of the rapid deterioration of the paper and the value of older issues, full access to the comic book collection is restricted to readers engaged in serious research. A small sample collection is maintained for the use of general readers and children accompanied by adults.

# 50

## Confederate States of America Collection

Publications issued in the South during the Civil War

Rare Book and Special Collections Division

The Confederate States of America Collection brings together publications selected from the Library's general collections and books received from such sources as the Rebel Archives of the War Department. The 1,812-volume collection is particularly rich in documents issued by the individual state governments and the congress, departments, and offices of the Confederate States of America. A list covering most of these official publications was compiled by Hugh A. Morrison and published in the *Proceedings and Papers* of the Bibliographical Society of America (Z1008.B51P), v. 3, 1908, p. 92–132. The collection also contains Confederate almanacs, textbooks, sermons, and works of history, literature, military science, and politics and provides a comprehensive survey of book production in the South during the Civil War. Books and pamphlets are noted in author/title and shelflist card files and reported in Marjorie Lyle Crandall's *Confederate Imprints: A Check List Based Principally on the Collection of the Boston Athenaeum* ([Boston] Boston Athenaeum, 1955. 2 v. Z1242.5.C7). Over half of the 318 broadsides recorded in Earle L. Rudolph's *Confederate Broadside Verse: A Bibliography and Finding List of Confederate Broadside Ballads and Songs* (New Braunfels, Tex.: Book Farm, 1950. 118 p. Z1242.5.R8) are included in the complementary Confederate Broadside Song Collection. Items are listed in a card file and indicated in the division's annotated copy of the bibliography.

# 51

## Congressional Speech Collection

Pamphlets of speeches delivered by members of Congress, 1825–1940

Rare Book and Special Collections Division

The printed texts of 3,570 speeches delivered by members of Congress between 1825 and 1940 are preserved in the Rare Book and Special Collections Division. The majority of these individually published pamphlets date from the last six decades of the nineteenth century. While many of the post-Civil War speeches were printed in other sources, the full texts of earlier examples survive largely through the pamphlet copies. The speeches are unbound and arranged alphabetically by author. The speaker, date, and length of each item are recorded in a collection inventory. In some Library sources the collection is identified by its general cataloging designation YA5000 J17 Additional copies of some speeches can be found in the Library's general collections.

*Holograph score (page one) of Aaron Copland's* Appalachian Spring *(1944), composed for the Coolidge Foundation. Elizabeth Sprague Coolidge Foundation Collection, Music Division. Courtesy of Aaron Copland. Negative in division.*

# 52

# Elizabeth Sprague Coolidge Foundation Collection

Music manuscripts of chamber music, twentieth century; papers and photographs of Elizabeth Sprague Coolidge

Music Division

In 1935 Elizabeth Sprague Coolidge (1864–1953), one of the great patrons of music, created at the Library of Congress the Elizabeth Sprague Coolidge Foundation for the support of chamber music. Her aim, Mrs. Coolidge wrote in that year's *Annual Report of the Librarian of Congress,* was "to make possible, through the Library of Congress, the composition and performance of music in ways which might otherwise be considered too unique or too expensive to be ordinarily undertaken. Not this alone, of course, nor with a view to extravagance for its own sake; but as an occasional possibility of giving precedence to considerations of quality over those of quantity; to artistic rather than to economic values; and to opportunity rather than to expediency." The scope and quality of the manuscripts in the Coolidge Foundation Collection attest to how fully the foundation has fulfilled Mrs. Coolidge's intentions. Among the over three hundred twentieth-century holographs are those listed below.

| | |
|---|---|
| Samuel Barber | *Hermit Songs* |
| Béla Bartók | *String Quartet no. 5* |
| Ernest Bloch | *Suite for Viola and Piano* |
| Benjamin Britten | *String Quartet no. 1,* op. 25 |
| Carlos Chávez | *Invention no. 2* |
| Aaron Copland | *Appalachian Spring* |
| Luigi Dallapiccola | *Cinque canti* |
| Howard Hanson | *Four Psalms* |
| Roy Harris | *Canticle of the Sun* |
| Paul Hindemith | *Hérodiade* |
| Gian Carlo Menotti | *The Unicorn, the Gorgon, and the Manticore* |

75

| Darius Milhaud | *Jeux de printemps* |
| Francis Poulenc | *Sonata for Flute and Piano* |
| Sergei Prokofiev | *String Quartet no. 1,* op. 50 |
| Maurice Ravel | *Chansons madécasses* |
| Albert Charles Paul Roussel | *Trio for Flute, Viola, and Violoncello,* op. 40 |
| Arnold Schoenberg | *String Quartets no. 3,* op. 30 and *no. 4,* op. 37 |
| Igor Stravinsky | *Apollon Musagète* |
| Virgil Thomson | *The Feast of Love* |
| Anton von Webern | *String Quartet,* op. 28 |

In addition to works commissioned by the foundation over the years, the collection includes Mrs. Coolidge's music compositions and works dedicated to her. Manuscripts acquired since the publication of the 1950 catalog are reported in the *Quarterly Journal.* The holographs are listed by composer in the catalog of the Music Division. Also in the collection are several hundred portrait photographs, many of which are inscribed, and correspondence pertaining largely to the commissioning activities of Mrs. Coolidge and the foundation. Correspondents include Ernest Bloch, Frank Bridge, John Alden Carpenter, Carlos Chávez, Aaron Copland, Martha Graham, Roy Harris, Gian Francesco Malipiero, Darius Milhaud, Lucy Sprague Mitchell, the Pro Arte Quartet, Arnold Schoenberg, Frederick Stock, and Ernst Toch. The letters are arranged by correspondent and measure fifty linear feet.

*ARLC,* 1925, p. 1–6, 93–94, 165–166.

*NUCMC,* 67–642.

U.S., Library of Congress, Music Division, *Autograph Musical Scores in the Coolidge Foundation Collection* (Washington: [Govt. Print. Off.] 1950. 30 p. ML29m.W305).

# 53

## *Coutume* Collection

Books and manuscripts relating to European customary law

Law Library

The *coutumes,* a primary source of modern French law, were developed in central and northern France from regional legal practices and customs. Unofficial compilations of these customary laws appeared as early as the thirteenth century and became so numerous that Charles VII ordered in 1453 that they be set down in a systematic code. During the last forty years the Law Library has built one of the finest collections of French customary legal sources outside of France. The collection contains nearly seven hundred volumes of French *coutumes* and one hundred volumes of the customary laws of Andorra, Belgium, Italy, Luxemburg, the Netherlands, and Switzerland. A treasure of the collection is the fifteenth-century illuminated manuscript containing what is known as "Le grand coutumier de Normandie," a text which contributed directly to the development of English common law. The volumes are shelved alphabetically by jurisdiction and represented in the Law Library catalog and shelflist. The published catalog of the French *coutumes* includes name, author-compiler, and printer-publisher indexes as well as a glossary of geographical terms.

*Law Library,* p. 31–33.

U.S., Library of Congress, European Law Division. *The Coutumes of France in the Library of Congress: An Annotated Bibliography* (Washington: Library of Congress, 1977. 80 p. Z663.5.C68), by Jean Caswell and Ivan Sipkov, edited by Natalie Gawdiak.

*Execution by hanging (detail), folio 44r, third of seven miniatures in the fifteenth-century French manuscript, "Le grande coutumier de Normandie."* Coutume Collection, Law Library. Negative in Law Library.

# 54

## Charles Henry Currier Collection

Photographs of middle class life in Boston, 1890s–1910s

Prints and Photographs Division

The Currier Collection provides a glimpse of middle class life in Boston at the turn of the century. Charles Henry Currier (1851–1930), a successful Boston jeweler, became a professional photographer in 1889. Over a twenty-year period, Currier photographed homes, offices, factories, charitable institutions, and recreational organizations in the Boston area, frequently portraying clients at work or with friends and family. He destroyed all of his glass plate negatives except those acquired by the Library from Ernst Halberstadt in 1950. The negatives have been reproduced as 523 reference prints and are filed by subject. The Currier Collection is recorded in the catalog of the Prints and Photographs Division. Many items from the collection were featured at an exhibition at the Rose Art Museum at Brandeis University and described in the catalog *Charles H. Currier, a Boston Photographer (Active ca. 1887–1910): An Exhibition of the Poses Institute of Fine Arts, Rose Art Museum, March 15–April 12, 1964* ([Waltham, Mass.: 1964] [16] p. TR140.C8B7).

# 55

## Edward S. Curtis Collection

Photographs of North American Indians by Edward S. Curtis, early twentieth century

Prints and Photographs Division

Many of the photographs published by Edward S. Curtis (1868–1952) in *The North American Indian* ([Seattle, Wash.] E. S. Curtis; [Cambridge, U.S.A.: University Press] 1907–30. 20 v. E77.C97) were acquired by the Library of Congress through copyright deposit. Curtis worked over thirty years in remote regions of the United States and Canada to prepare this monumental survey. Through the support of J. P. Morgan, a lavish twenty-volume compilation of Curtis's photographs, in photogravure reproduction, was published in a limited edition of 500 sets. The Curtis images in the Prints and Photographs Division are original photoprints and include examples from each of the regions documented in *The North American Indian*: the plains, the northern Pacific coast, northern and central California, the western desert, and the central plateau. One-third of the more than sixteen hundred photoprints are described in the catalog of the Prints and Photographs Division. The remaining material is numerically arranged. A copy of the original edition of *The North American Indian* can be consulted in the Rare Book and Special Collections Division.

# 56

## Damrosch Family Collection

Papers, music manuscripts, and sound recordings of the Damrosch family

Music Division
Motion Picture, Broadcasting, and Recorded Sound Division

The Damrosch family has figured prominently in American musical life for over a hundred years. The family patriarch, Leopold Damrosch (1832–1885), came to the United States in 1871 to conduct the German male voice choir, the Männergesangeverein Arion. He soon became a leader in New York music circles, organizing the city's first large-scale music festival and introducing German opera at the Metropolitan Opera House. His son Frank (1859–1937) served as chorus master and assistant conductor of the Metropolitan Opera before establishing the People's Choral Union and founding the Institute of Musical Art, now a part of the Juilliard School. Leopold's younger son Walter (1862–1950) directed the New York Symphony Society for over twenty years. He brought classical music to thousands of school children through his special children's concerts and his educational radio program, *The Music Appreciation Hour,* which was broadcast by the National Broadcasting Company (NBC) from 1928 to 1942. The marriage of pianist Clara Damrosch (1869–1948), another of Leopold's children, brought into the family David Mannes (1866–1959), founder of the Mannes School of Music in New York City.

The Damrosch Collection has been formed over the last fifteen years through the gifts of Marya Mannes, Mrs. Robert Littell, Mrs. John Tee-Van, and other family members. The collection is particularly rich in correspondence and contains letters exchanged by Walter and Frank Damrosch with many of the leading musical, literary, and political personalities of the period. Leopold and Walter Damrosch are represented by music manuscripts. The collection also includes biographical writings, concert programs, clippings, photographs, drawings, presentation copies of printed music, and scrapbooks. Most of the collection is listed in inventories on file in the Music Division. The collection measures thirty-eight linear feet.

In 1962 NBC donated to the Library instantaneous disc recordings of *The Music Appreciation Hour* and the accompanying teaching manuals and student workbooks for the years 1929 to 1941. The 254 discs were produced between 1937 and 1941. The recordings have been copied on tape, listed in the catalog of the Motion Picture, Broadcasting, and Recorded Sound Division, and described in notes on file.

*NUCMC,* 72–1785.

Waters, Edward N., "Notable Music Acquisitions," *QJLC,* v. 28, January 1971: 66–67.

——, "Songs to Symphonies: Recent Acquisitions of the Music Division," *QJLC,* v. 25, January 1968: 52–53.

U.S., Library of Congress, Music Division, "Recent Acquisitions of the Music Division," *QJLC,* v. 31, January 1974: 31–32.

# 57

## Arthur Kyle Davis Collection

Field recordings of Virginia folk music, 1930s and 1940s

Archive of Folk Song

Arthur Kyle ("A. K.") Davis, Jr. (1897–1972), a professor of English at the University of Virginia for over forty years, was one of the first scholars to make field recordings of the folk music of Appalachian Virginia. In 1977 the Library of Congress duplicated 180 disc and eight tape recordings (AFS 19,220–19,230) which Professor Davis had made in the 1930s and 1940s and deposited with the Virginia Folklore Society. Davis used his recordings to accompany lectures and as source material for his two important studies *Traditional Ballads of Virginia* (Cambridge, Mass.: Harvard University Press, 1929. xviii, 634 p. ML3551.D2T7; reprint, Charlottesville: University Press of Virginia [1969]), and *More Traditional Ballads of Virginia* (Chapel Hill: University of North Carolina Press [1960] 371 p. M3551.D2M7). In addition to ballads, the collection includes songs, fiddle tunes, and a few radio interviews in which Professor Davis discusses his field work and the history of folklore scholarship in Virginia. Recordings gathered before the late 1940s are listed in his *Folk-Songs of Virginia: A Descriptive Index and Classification of Material Collected Under the Auspices of the Virginia Folklore Society* (Durham, N.C.: Duke University Press, 1949. lxiii, 389 p. ML128.F75D3; reprint, New York: AMS Press [1965]). Titles in the collection are listed in a concordance in the Archive of Folk Song.

*Photograph by F. Holland Day (ca. 1897). Early in his career, Day executed a number of studies showing models in exotic costumes and the play of natural light on folded drapery. F. Holland Day Collection, Prints and Photographs Division. LC–USZ62–52919.*

# 58

## F. Holland Day Collection

Photographs by F. Holland Day

Prints and Photographs Division

In 1934 the Library acquired from an anonymous donor 640 original photoprints by F. Holland Day (1864–1933), a leading American exponent of "pictorial photography." Day experimented with compositions and themes derived from painting and sculpture and executed many portrait and figure studies. The Library's collection, the largest known corpus of the photographer's work, contains images produced between 1895 and 1917. Included are portraits of Kahlil Gibran and his family and the famous series based on the Passion of Christ in which Day himself appears as the principal figure. The photographs are shelved with the master photographs in the Prints and Photographs Division and are recorded in the division catalog. Many images in the collection are described in Ellen Fritz Clattenburg's catalog *The Photographic Work of F. Holland Day: [exhibition] Wellesley College Museum, Wellesley, Massachusetts, February 21–March 24, 1975* (Wellesley, Mass.: The Museum [1975] 64 p. TR647.D38C55).

*Guide,* Vanderbilt, no. 180.

# 59

## Dell Paperback Collection

Archival set of Dell paperbacks

Rare Book and Special Collections Division

In 1976, through the interest of Helen Meyer, chairman of the board of Dell Publishing Company, Inc., a virtually complete set of Dell paperbacks was presented to the Library by Western Publishing Company, the Wisconsin-based firm that has handled production and printing of Dell paperbacks since the first issues of the Dell Books series in 1943. In forming this archival collection, Western Publishing Company tried to document major changes in cover design resulting from marketing strategy, the release of a movie adaptation, and fluctuations in price and in many cases retained successive reissues of a single publication. The four copies of Kurt Vonnegut's *Slaughterhouse-Five* issued under number 8029, for example, exhibit three markedly different covers. Though approximately 90 percent of the books are reprints of titles previously issued in hard cover, the collection includes the Dell First Editions series which was begun in 1953 and features works by George Sumner Albee, George C. Appell, Jack Finney, and Margaret Mead. The 6,501 paperback volumes are grouped by series and arranged in serial order. They are described in an author and title file prepared by Western Publishing Company.

Matheson, William, "Microcosm of the Library: The Rare Book and Special Collections Division," *QJLC,* v. 34, July 1977: 242.

# 60

## Detroit Publishing Company Collection

Photographic views of points of interest in the United States
and foreign countries, early twentieth century

Prints and Photographs Division

The Detroit Photographic Company (renamed the Detroit Publishing Company) was formed in 1898 as a partnership between
William A. Livingstone, owner of the American rights to a process for
lithographically adding color to black-and-white negatives, and wilderness photographer William Henry Jackson (1843–1942). Building
upon Jackson's file of photographic negatives, the Detroit Publishing
Company became one of the largest American publishers of postcards
and souvenir views. Before going out of business in 1924, the company
issued thousands of photographs of excellent quality depicting buildings,
historical sites, natural landmarks, industry, sports activities, and points
of interest throughout the United States and, to a lesser extent,
Europe, Africa, and Asia. The Library's collection of Detroit Publishing
Company views is among the most extensive in the country. It brings
together over twenty-two thousand photoprints obtained largely
through copyright deposit and nearly 18,500 original glass negatives
acquired in 1949 from the State Historical Society of Colorado. The
Library's well-preserved glass plate negatives depict scenes from the
eastern United States and abroad. The photoprints have been grouped
by subject and are described in the division's catalog. Published order
catalogs indicate the scope of the company's original stock files and are
also available for reference in the Prints and Photographs Division.

*Guide,* Vanderbilt, no. 186–189.

# 61

## Dime Novel Collection

Popular paperback fiction, nineteenth century

Rare Book and Special Collections Division

In 1860 Irwin P. Beadle & Company became the first American publisher to issue paperback fiction in a series at the fixed price of ten cents a volume. The first dime novels were largely Indian and pioneer tales that were highly nationalistic in spirit. In the 1870s detective adventures, society romances, and rags-to-riches stories were introduced and soon the term *dime novel* was popularly applied to any sensational, blood-and-thunder novel issued in pamphlet form. Through copyright deposit the Library of Congress has accumulated a dime novel collection of nearly forty thousand titles from 280 different series. The prolific publishing houses of Beadle & Adams, Frank Tousey, and Street & Smith are well represented. The collection also contains serially published songbooks, jokebooks, and handbooks and issues of the popular reprint libraries that specialized in unauthorized editions of foreign novels and stories before the passage of the International Copyright Act in 1891. There is a particularly extensive run of the Seaside Library, the series founded by George Munro in 1877. Issues are recorded in a card file by publishers' series. Seaside Library is indexed separately by author or title. Selected dime novel series have been microfilmed.

# 62

## Luis Dobles Segreda Collection

Publications pertaining to Costa Rica

Collections Management Division

Luis Dobles Segreda relied extensively on his personal library to compile *Indice Bibliográfico de Costa Rica* (San José, Costa Rica: Imprenta Lehman, 1927–36. 9 v. Z1451.D63), a massive bibliography which ceased publication after nine of its projected twelve volumes were issued. The distinguished Costa Rican scholar and diplomat began his collection in 1910 in an attempt to bring together as many writings as possible on his native country. He acquired works published in Costa Rica, material written by Costa Ricans and printed abroad, and pertinent publications by foreigners. When the resulting collection was purchased by the Library of Congress in 1943, it contained over fifty-six hundred books and pamphlets issued between 1831 and the 1930s. The collection is encyclopedic in scope and is of greater interest for the completeness of its coverage than for the rarity of its editions. The items are bound in approximately one thousand volumes. The *Indice* uses the designation L. P. (Letras Patrias) and the bound volume number to indicate many titles in the collection. The contents of the unnumbered volumes are briefly identified in a partial inventory kept with the collection. There is no listing of most publications falling within the subject areas of the projected volumes of the *Indice* —poetry, education, sociology, and demography. While a few items have been separately cataloged, the majority of the collection is kept as a unit and serviced by the Collections Management Division. The Hispanic Division provides reference assistance for researchers wishing to use the material.

Hanke, Lewis, "The Luis Dobles Segreda Collection," *QJLC*, v. 1, January/March 1944: 57–62.

# 63

## Documents of the First Fourteen Congresses

Congressional documents, 1789–1817

Rare Book and Special Collections Division

The extensive collection of early congressional documents held by the Rare Book and Special Collections Division is built upon the War Department collection that was assembled in the late nineteenth century by librarian David FitzGerald and Gen. A. W. Greely and transferred to the Library of Congress in 1904. Containing over 3,680 separate titles, many in multiple copies, these public documents from the first fourteen Congresses (1789–1817) include presidential messages to Congress, legislative journals of both houses, secret proceedings or executive journals of the Senate, reports of congressional committees, communications to Congress by government officials, and petitions, memorials, and miscellaneous publications issued by congressional order. Aside from the legislative journals, the documents are printed in varying sizes, without serial numbering, and sometimes without pagination. Most items are unbound. The documents are arranged following the system used in A. W. Greely's *Public Documents of the First Fourteen Congresses, 1789–1817: Papers Relating to Early Congressional Documents* (Washington: Govt. Print. Off., 1900. 903 p. Z1223.A 1900) and its supplement (Washington: Govt. Print. Off., 1904. 343–406 p. Z1223R 1900 Suppl.; reprint of both works, New York: Johnson Reprint Corp. [1973]). Items are represented in the shelflist and indicated in the division's annotated copy of Greely's work. Of related interest is the division's collection of bills from the seventh through fourteenth Congresses (1801–17). These items are listed in a chronological file.

*ARLC,* 1904, p. 32.

Eaton, Vincent, "Documents of the First Fourteen Congresses," *LCIB,* May 24, 1949: 14–15.

# 64

## Jessica Dragonette Collection

Broadcast recordings of Jessica Dragonette, 1930s

Motion Picture, Broadcasting, and Recorded Sound Division

In 1974 and 1975 Jessica Dragonette, one of radio's most popular singing stars, presented to the Library of Congress recordings of her performances on the *Cities Service Concerts* and *The Palmolive Beauty Box Theatre*. Miss Dragonette joined NBC's *Cities Service Concerts* in 1929 and was soon singing selections from the classical, folk, popular, and operetta repertoire with Frank Parker and the Cavaliers Quartet. She started with *The Palmolive Beauty Box Theatre* in 1937 and performed with partners selected from the Metropolitan Opera. The collection features solos and duets from the *Cities Service Concerts*, a total of 369 disc recordings, and complete transcriptions of thirty-seven *Palmolive* broadcasts, including rare recorded performances of the operettas *Lady in Ermine, The Only Girl, Sari, The Prince of Pilsen, Madame Pompadour,* and *The Blue Paradise.* The broadcast transcriptions have been reproduced on tape and are listed in the catalog of the Motion Picture, Broadcasting, and Recorded Sound Division. Detailed descriptions are kept on file. Scripts of several *Palmolive* broadcasts are maintained in the Music Division and represented in its catalog.

# 65

## Early American Statutory Law Collection

Early editions of the laws of American states and territories

Law Library

Since the early 1900s the Law Library has made a concerted effort to acquire first printings of session laws (the laws enacted by state legislatures during their annual or biennial sessions), state codes and compilations, and special laws of the American states and territories. Probably the collection's greatest strength is the session laws. These are virtually complete for the pre-Civil War years and in some cases include the earliest examples issued in the colonial and territorial periods. A copy of *Check-List of Session Laws* (New York: H. W. Wilson Co., 1936. 266 p. Z6457.A1N34), compiled by Grace E. MacDonald, has been annotated to indicate the Law Library's holdings. While ·not as extensive as the session laws, the state codes and compilations in the collection include a significant number of titles cited in *Check-list of Statutes of States of the United States of America, Including Revisions, Compilations, Digests, Codes, and Indexes* (Providence: Oxford Press, 1937. 147 p. KF2.N38), compiled by Grace E. MacDonald. A copy of this work has also been annotated. Many individual editions in the collection are ·of great bibliographic interest. *A Complete Body of Laws in Maryland,* printed in Annapolis by Thomas Reading in 1700, and *Laws of the Territory of Illinois,* issued by Nathaniel Pope in 1815, are the earliest publications produced in their respective states found in the Library of Congress collections. The 15,000 volumes are arranged by jurisdiction and the majority are recorded in the Law Library catalog.

Microform copies have been obtained for those early state records not in the bound collection. Of related interest are the Law Library's rich holdings of U.S. session laws, session laws of the Provisional and Confederate government of the Confederate States of America, and the tribal laws and constitutions of the Cherokee, Chickasaw, Choctaw, and Creek nations.

*Law Library,* p. 17–19.

# 66

## Early Bulgarian Imprint Collection

Bulgarian-language publications, nineteenth century

Rare Book and Special Collections Division

The Early Bulgarian Imprint Collection, purchased by the Library in 1949 and housed in the Rare Book and Special Collections Division, contains copies of some of the earliest books printed in the modern Bulgarian language. Because printing presses were prohibited within Bulgaria by the Turks before the country achieved national autonomy in 1878, these books were printed chiefly in Constantinople, Vienna, Belgrade, Bucharest, and Budapest. The approximately six hundred "pre-liberation" books in the collection include copies of one hundred fifty religious books, fifty grammars and readers, thirty-five histories, thirty patriotic works, thirty-three translations, and twenty calendars. Approximately 40 percent of the Bulgarian-language publications produced between 1806 and 1877 are represented. Of particular note is the 1806 edition of *Kyriakodromion*, the collection of ninety-six sermons prepared by Bishop Sofronii of Vratsa, which was the first book to be published in modern Bulgarian. Two annotated copies of the standard bibliography *Opis na starite pechatani bŭlgarski knigi* by Valerii Pogorelov (Sofia: Durzh. pechatnitsa, 1923. 795 p. Z2891.P75), one in the division and the other in the European Reading Room, serve as finding aids for the collection. Forty-five titles in the collection that are unrecorded in Pogorelov's bibliography are cited on lists appended to each of the two reference copies. The author-short title index from the bibliography has been annotated and microfilmed. The collection was formerly identified as the Plotchev Collection.

Jelavich, Charles, "Bulgarian 'Incunabula,' " *QJLC*, v. 14, May 1957: 77–94.

# 67

## Early Copyright Records Collection

U.S. copyright registers and accession records, 1790–1870

Rare Book and Special Collections Division

A congressional act signed into law on July 8, 1870, authorized the Librarian of Congress "to perform all acts and duties required by the law touching copyrights" and stipulated that all copyright records and deposits be transferred to the Library of Congress. Before 1870 authors and publishers registered their claims to statutory copyright with the clerks of the U.S. District Court for the jurisdiction in which they resided. The 615 volumes of early records in the Rare Book and Special Collections Division consist largely of the District Court registers from the years 1790 to 1870. Although varying in completeness, the record books often contain indexes by claimant or claimant and title and, particularly after January 1, 1803, include specimens of commercial labels and prints that were submitted for copyright registration. The collection also contains records of the Department of State (1796–1842), the federal body that until the mid-nineteenth century was responsible for deposit copies received as legal evidence. From the Patent Office, which took over the copyright activities of the Department of State in 1859, there are records compiled before August 1870. Other documents include the accession registers of the Library of Congress listing the deposit copies secured for government library use during the mid-nineteenth century. The records are available on microfilm in the Copyright Office. One of the most interesting features of the collection for the bibliographer is the group of 44,032 title pages (1790–1870) which were deposited by authors and publishers as evidence of intention to publish. Some title pages document works that were substantially altered before publication or never printed. The title pages are arranged alphabetically within yearly groupings. In his article entitled "Of Copyright, Men, and a National Library," in *QJLC*, v. 28, April 1971, p. 114–136, John Y. Cole discusses the history of the 1870 law and its role in the development of the Library's collections.

Goff, Frederick R., "Almost Books," *The New Colophon* (Z1007.C72), v. 1, April 1948: 125–133.

Roberts, Martin Arnold, *Records in the Copyright Office Deposited by the United States District Courts Covering the Period, 1790–1870* (Washington: Govt. Print. Off., 1939. 19 p. Z642.R64 1939).

Tanselle, G. Thomas, "Copyright Records and the Bibliographer," in *Studies in Bibliography: Papers* of the Bibliographical Society of the University of Virginia (Z1008.V55), v. 22: 77–124.

*Map of Central Europe from* Liber Chronicarum *(Nuremberg Chronicle), published by Anton Koberger in 1493. The woodcut illustration is based on the 1454 map of Cardinal Nicolas of Cusa. Melville Eastham Collection, Geography and Map Division. Negative in division.*

# 68

## Melville Eastham Collection

Atlases, sixteenth and seventeenth centuries; papers of Melville Eastham

Geography and Map Division
Manuscript Division

Ten rare sixteenth-century atlases were presented to the Library in 1930 and 1938 by Melville Eastham (1805?–1964), cofounder of one of the first radio manufacturing companies and well-known collector of early printed maps. The volumes include the 1595 edition of Gerardus Mercator's *Atlas,* the publication which introduced the designation *atlas* for a bound map collection; *Theatrum Orbis Terrarum,* issued by Abraham Ortelius in 1571; Braun and Hogenberg's *Civitates Orbis Terrarum* (1572); and the atlas of England and Wales prepared by Christopher Saxton (1579). The atlases are described in the atlas catalog of the Geography and Map Division. In 1962 Mr. Eastham presented the balance of his collection to the American Geographical Society in New York City.

In 1974 Mrs. Eastham gave the Library her husband's personal papers and printed map collection. The 434 maps were derived chiefly from sixteenth- and seventeenth-century atlases and include examples by most of the important cartographers and atlas publishers of the period: Blaeu, Hondius, Janson, Lafreri, Mercator, Ortelius, Saxton, and Visscher. Approximately half of the maps depict regions in England, France, and Germany. A brief inventory prepared by Melville Eastham is filed with the collection.

The Melville Eastham papers in the Manuscript Division contain approximately fifty-eight hundred items—diaries, correspondence, financial records, technical notes, reports, and related material—and are listed in the division's master record of manuscript collections.

LeGear, Clara E., and Walter W. Ristow, "The Melville Eastham Gift of Atlases," *QJLC,* v. 15, August 1958: 218–227; reprinted as "Sixteenth Century Atlases Presented by Melville Eastham," on p. 51–61 of *A La Carte: Selected Papers on Maps and Atlases* (Washington: Library of Congress, 1972. 232 p. GA231.R5), compiled by Walter W. Ristow.

# 69

## Edison Laboratory Collection

Films by the Edison Company and for the various Edison industries

Motion Picture, Broadcasting, and Recorded Sound Division

In 1965, through a cooperative agreement with the National Park Service, the Library of Congress reproduced on safety film the motion pictures found at the Edison Laboratory in West Orange, New Jersey, shortly after its designation as a national historic site. With the assistance of W. K. L. Dickson, Thomas Alva Edison (1847–1931) developed a successful motion picture camera and projector between 1887 and 1894. The Edison film studio, "Black Maria," was completed in 1891, and those Edison films registered for copyright protection from 1893 to 1894 became the first motion pictures to be copyrighted in the United States. The collection preserves some of the Edison Company's earliest releases, promotional films for the various Edison industries, and footage (picture portion) from Edison's early sound experiments. Edison, who was unusually camera shy, is featured in newsreel clips from the 1920s. Reference prints are available for most of the seventy-five reels of film comprising the collection, and the material is recorded in the collection shelflist in the Motion Picture, Broadcasting, and Recorded Sound Division.

Spehr, Paul C., "Motion Pictures," *QJLC,* v. 23, January 1966: 70–74.

, "Some Still Fragments of a Moving Past: Edison Films in the Library of Congress," *QJLC,* v. 32, January 1975: 33–50.

# 70

## Harrison Elliott Collection

Paper specimens, personal papers and research material relating to the history of papermaking

Rare Book and Special Collections Division

Harrison G. Elliott (1879–1954), probably the most prominent producer of handmade paper of America during the early twentieth century, began his study of paper while employed by the International Paper Company. In 1925 he joined the Japan Paper Company, a New York importing firm which distributed fine handmade papers from fifteen European and Oriental countries. As advertising and direct mail promotion manager, Elliott designed and commissioned paper specimens and continued to write numerous articles on the history of papermaking. In 1954 Elliott donated to the Library of Congress the study collection which he had formed over a forty-year period. The collection includes twentieth-century paper specimens and sample books as well as trade journals, photographs, trade correspondence, and other secondary materials relating to the history and manufacture of paper. Of special interest is a sample collection of 300 early American papers and the correspondence and memorabilia of Dard Hunter, an authority on the history of paper and a personal friend of Elliott's. The collection contains approximately forty-five hundred specimens and fifty-eight hundred secondary sources and is listed in a subject index and shelflist.

Krill, John, "Harrison G. Elliott: Creator of Handmade Papers," *QJLC*, v. 35, January 1978: 4–26.

# 71

## English Year Book Collection

### Published reports of late medieval English court cases

Law Library

The Year Books, the reports of pleadings in cases decided in English courts during the reigns of Edward I through Henry VIII, are the foundation of English common law. In contrast to the formal Latin court records, the Year Books are written in contemporary Anglo-Norman and offer eyewitness accounts of the colloquy between judge and counsel. The Law Library has assembled a strong collection of printed Year Books published between the late fifteenth and late seventeenth centuries. Many of these "black letter editions" were purchased by the Library from Boston lawyer William Vail Kellen and listed in the *Annual Report of the Librarian of Congress* for 1905, p. 163–173. The collection includes almost two hundred works printed by Richard Tottell, the preeminent figure in sixteenth-century Year Book publishing; eleven publications by Richard Pynson, who dominated the field before Tottell; and all eleven parts of the standard edition issued between 1678 and 1680. Most regnal years are represented by at least one black letter edition. In addition, the collection contains the two major and two minor abridgments of Year Book cases published in the fifteenth and sixteenth centuries, including the rare Statham's *Abridgement of Cases* which was probably issued in the 1490s. The 500 volumes are arranged by the numbering system used in *A Bibliography of Early English Law Books* (Cambridge, Mass.: Harvard University Press, 1926. 304 p. Z6458.G7B36), compiled by Joseph Henry Beale.

Complementing these early printed sources are three modern series which reprint original Anglo-Norman texts with English translation and notes. Items are represented in the card catalog of the Law Library.

*Law Library,* p. 11–13.

# 72

## Ex-slave Narrative Collection

Transcribed interviews with former slaves and related WPA
research files and recordings

Archive of Folk Song
Rare Book and Special Collections Division

The interviewing of former slaves was begun in the Ohio River
Valley by the Federal Emergency Relief Administration in 1934 and
was extended to other areas between 1936 and 1938 by the WPA
Federal Writers' Project (FWP) under the direction of John A. Lomax.
Federal field workers met with informants who had been slaves in
households and plantations of varying sizes and had been trained in
many slave occupations. The ex-slaves had reportedly ranged in age
from one to over fifty at the time of the emancipation in 1865.

The Archive of Folk Song maintains interviews and documentation gathered in seventeen states, including particularly extensive files
compiled by the Alabama, Arkansas, Georgia, South Carolina, and
Texas projects. The research files (six drawers) contain narratives,
appraisal sheets, and photographs as well as copies of bills of sale,
advertisements for auctions, state laws pertaining to slavery, and related documents. Assisted by a grant from the National Science Foundation, a team from the University of the District of Columbia is now
organizing the collection. Recorded interviews with ex-slaves, acquired
from several sources, have been copied on tape and include material
from Alabama, Mississippi, Virginia, and Texas (AFS 14,415–14,418).

Subsequent to the transfer of WPA materials to the Library of
Congress which was begun in 1939, Benjamin A. Botkin, the FWP folklorist who later became head of the Archive of Folk Song, undertook
the editing and indexing of the narratives. Approximately two thousand
edited narratives prepared under his direction have been assigned to
the Rare Book and Special Collections Division. The multivolume set
has been microfilmed and published as *Slave Narratives: A Folk History
of Slavery in the United States, from Interviews with Former Slaves*
(St. Clair Shores, Mich.: Scholarly Press, 1976. 17 v. E444.F27
1976) and *The American Slave: A Composite Autobiography* (West-

port, Conn.: Greenwood Publishing Co. [1972] + E441.A58), edited by George P. Rawick. Anthologies containing selections from the collection include the Federal Writers' Project's *Lay My Burden Down: A Folk History of Slavery* (Chicago: University of Chicago Press [1945] xxi, 285 p. E444.F26), edited by B. A. Botkin, and *Voices from Slavery* (New York: Holt, Rinehart, and Winston [1970] 368 p. E444.Y42), edited by Norman R. Yetman.

Yetman, Norman R., "The Background of the Slave Narrative Collection," *American Quarterly* (AP2.A3985), v. 19, fall 1967: 534–553.

# 73

## George Fabyan Collection

Early editions of works of seventeenth-century English literature, publications relating to cryptography

Rare Book and Special Collections Division

George Fabyan (1867–1936), a member of the Chicago Stock Exchange and founder of the Riverbank Laboratories in Geneva, Illinois, was an accomplished cryptographer. During World War I he trained army intelligence officers in deciphering codes, winning the French Legion of Honor for his efforts. One of his areas of specialty was the Shakespeare-Bacon authorship controversy, and he published writings on the principles of Baconian ciphers and their application in sixteenth- and seventeenth-century books. The cryptographer's research collection was received by the Library of Congress in 1940 through his bequest. The Fabyan Collection incorporates the Francis Bacon material assembled by John Dane of Boston and includes thirty-three distinct editions of Bacon's works published between 1597 and 1640. In addition to many volumes of seventeenth-century English literature, the collection contains early cryptographic texts such as Johannes Trithemius's *Polygraphiae Libri Sex*, present in the first edition (1518) and seven subsequent printings. The collection numbers approximately 1,550 volumes and is listed in the catalogs of the Rare Book and Special Collections Division.

*ARLC,* 1940, p. 201–202.

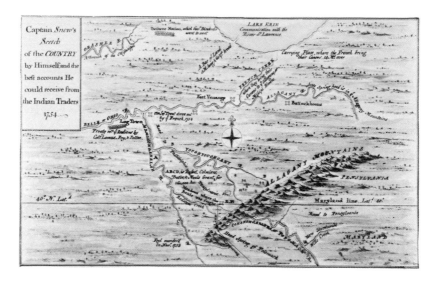

*Manuscript map by Captain Snow showing Western Pennsylvania, northern Virginia, and northern Maryland at the beginning of the French and Indian War (1754). The fort at the junction of the Allegheny and Monongahela Rivers marks the site of the present city of Pittsburgh. William Faden Collection, Geography and Map Division. Negative in division.*

# 74

## William Faden Collection

Maps of the French and Indian and revolutionary wars

Geography and Map Division

The Faden Collection contains manuscript and printed maps illustrating the campaigns of the French and Indian and revolutionary wars. These 101 maps, many of which were drawn by British military engineers, had formed part of the working collection of William Faden (1750?–1836), geographer to King George III and foremost British map publisher of the late eighteenth century. The maps and plans pertain chiefly to the activities of Sir William Howe and Generals Edward Braddock, John Burgoyne, Henry Clinton, and Charles Cornwallis and, in some cases, are annotated with corrections for revised editions. The maps are individually described in the Library's computerized map catalog. Edward Everett Hale prepared an inventory of the Faden collection before it was sold to the Library in 1864.

Faden, William, *Catalogue of a Curious and Valuable Collection of Original Maps and Plans of Military Positions Held in the Old French and Revolutionary Wars* (Boston: [J. Wilson] 1862. 13 p. Z6027.A5F2), compiled by E. E. Hale.

# 75

## Ethel M. Fair Collection

Illustrated maps, twentieth century

Geography and Map Division

The Ethel M. Fair Collection contains 879 illustrated maps published in the twentieth century by newspapers, magazines, government agencies, and educational institutions. Items range from advertisements to literary and historical theme maps (for example, the "Map of Sinclair Lewis' United States as it appears in his novels") and for the most part depicts regions in America and Europe. The collection was assembled and donated in 1972 by Ethel M. Fair, director of the Library School of the New Jersey College for Women from 1930 to 1950. The pictorial maps are indexed by subject.

Brown, Betty J., "Picture Maps," *Wilson Library Bulletin* (Z1217.W75), v. 11, February 1937: 385–389, 415, 426.

# 76

## Farm Security Administration Collection

Photographs of American life taken by FSA photographers, 1935–42

Prints and Photographs Division

Probably the most famous pictorial record of American life in the 1930s is the photographic collection produced by the Farm Security Administration (FSA). Roy E. Stryker, formerly an economics instructor at Columbia University, began this documentary project in 1935 under the auspices of the Resettlement Administration. The agency was reconstituted as the Farm Security Administration a year later and it continued Stryker's program. Some of the photographers included on the small staff at one time or another were Jack Delano, Walker Evans, Dorothea Lange, Russell Lee, Carl Mydans, Arthur Rothstein, Ben Shahn, John Vachon, and Marion Post Wolcott. The staff initially photographed the lives of sharecroppers in the South and migratory agricultural workers in the midwestern and western states. As the scope of the project expanded, the photographers documented rural conditions throughout the country, life in urban communities, and the domestic impact of the war effort. Avoiding sensational or sentimental shots, they worked largely from shooting scripts and compiled notes to accompany their images. The FSA photo archive was absorbed by the Office of War Information (OWI) in 1942. Approximately 164,000 original FSA negatives, 2,600 Kodachrome transparencies, 75,000 photoprints, and some photographers' notebooks were transferred to the Library of Congress in 1944 along with the photo files of the OWI (no. 177). Microfilm copies of the various photographers' assignments are recorded in the catalog of the Prints and Photographs Division by photographer, location, and subject. The photoprints are interfiled by geographic region and subdivided by subject.

Among the many recent publications that contain reproductions from the collection are: *In This Proud Land: America 1935–1943, as Seen in the FSA Photographs* (New York: Galahad Books, 1973. 191 p. TR820.5.S87) by Roy Emerson Stryker and Nancy Wood; *Walker Evans, Photographs for the Farm Security Administration, 1935–1938: A Catalog of Photographic Prints Available from the Farm Security*

*Migrant from Oklahoma holding her pieced quilt, photographed by Dorothea Lange in Kern County, California (1936). Farm Security Administration Collection, Prints and Photographs Division. LC–USF34–1780–C.*

*Administration Collection in the Library of Congress* (New York: Da Capo Press, 1973. 1 v. (unpaged) HN57.D22) ; and *Just Before the War: Urban America from 1935 to 1941 as Seen by Photographers of the Farm Security Administration* (Los Angeles: Printed by the Rapid Lithograph Co., 1968. [70] p. E169.J86). Chadwyck-Healey Ltd. is currently preparing a microfiche publication of the FSA photographs.

Adams, Elizabeth L., and Marion Lambert, "The Photographic Section of the Library of Congress," *Library Journal* (Z671.L7), v. 71, September 1, 1946: 1081–1087.

*Guide,* Vanderbilt, no. 219.

U.S., Library of Congress, Photograph Section, *Index of Microfilms, Series A, Lots 1–1737* ([Washington] 1945. 26 leaves. N4010.A53 1945; reprint, [Washington] 1946).

*Poster for* The Woman God Forgot *(1917). As Montezuma's daughter in this spectacular historical film, Miss Farrar falls in love with a Spanish soldier and delivers the Aztec capital to the conquistadores. Geraldine Farrar Collection, Music Division. LC–USZ62–67581.*

## Geraldine Farrar Collection

Papers, pictorial material, and recordings of soprano Geraldine Farrar

Music Division
Motion Picture, Broadcasting, and Recorded Sound Division

Between 1954 and 1964 the American soprano Geraldine Farrar (1882–1967) presented to the Library rich documentation of her stage, screen, and public service career. Following her Berlin debut in 1901 and three seasons with the Monte Carlo Opera, Miss Farrar joined the Metropolitan Opera, winning popular acclaim in the roles of Madame Butterfly, Carmen, Manon, Mignon, Mimi, and Tosca. She brought her portrayal of Carmen to the screen under the direction of Cecil B. De Mille and starred in six of his silent films. After her retirement from the stage in 1931, Miss Farrar served as commentator for the Metropolitan Opera broadcasts and became an active supporter of the American Red Cross, the Republican Party, and America First. Miss Farrar used the correspondence, scripts, contracts, programs, playbills, scrapbooks, posters, and photographs now in the Music Division as source material for *The Autobiography of Geraldine Farrar: Such Sweet Compulsion* (New York: Greystone Press [1938] 303 p. ML420.F27A2; reprint, 1970). The manuscript of this work is also in the collection. Correspondents include David Belasco, Sarah Bernhardt, Lucrezia Bori, Gustave Charpentier, Georg Droescher, Paul Dukas, Emma Eames, Olive Fremstad, Amelita Galli-Curci, Giulio Gatti-Casazza, Lilli Lehmann, Lotte Lehmann, Jules Massenet, Lily Pons, Rosa Ponselle, and Kate Douglas Wiggin. An alphabetical list of correspondents is kept on file. The collection occupies some eighteen linear feet.

The fifty disc recordings in the Farrar Collection include radio broadcast transcriptions and special pressings made by the Gramophone and Typewriter Company, Ltd., between 1904 and 1906. The inventory is on file in the Motion Picture, Broadcasting, and Recorded Sound Division.

Hill, Richard S., "Music," *QJLC*, v. 12, November 1954: 48.
*NUCMC*, 67–644.

# 78

## Federal Theatre Project Collection

Scripts, posters, photographs, production notebooks, and other "product materials" of the FTP, 1935–39

Research Center for the Federal Theatre Project, George Mason University

The Federal Theatre Project (FTP) was established in August 1935 as a part of the arts program of the Works Progress Administration (renamed Work Projects Administration in 1939). Supporting 150 separate units throughout the United States, the FTP produced over 830 major stage plays, 6,000 radio programs, and innumerable marionette plays, vaudeville shows, outdoor pageants, and circuses. At the conclusion of the project in June 1939, the "product materials" generated by the FTP were sent to the Library of Congress, and the administrative records to the National Archives. The Library's FTP collection was placed on deposit at George Mason University in Fairfax, Virginia, in 1974. Occupying over eight hundred cubic feet of shelf space, the collection is the largest single gathering of original FTP materials and contains documentation for many FTP productions, particularly those which originated in the New York City, San Francisco, and Los Angeles areas. Included are 5,000 playscripts, 2,500 radio scripts, 25,000 photographs, forty blueprints, 1,000 posters, over sixteen hundred costume designs, 350 scene designs, 750 production notebooks, 1,700 programs and heralds, musical scores for twenty-six productions, and eighteen cubic feet of research materials and play readers' reports. With the support of the National Endowment for the Humanities, the Research Center for the Federal Theatre Project at George Mason University has organized the collection and is preparing a register for publication. In addition, the center has conducted over 250 interviews with actors, producers, directors, and designers formerly affiliated with the project. The center also publishes a newsletter, *Federal One,* which highlights material in the collection. Many items are reproduced in *Free, Adult, Uncensored: The Living History of the Federal Theatre Project* (Washington: New Republic Books, 1978. 228 p. PN2266.-F66), edited by John O'Connor and Lorraine Brown, and in Lorraine Brown's article, "Federal Theatre: Melodrama, Social Protest, and Genius," in *QJLC,* v. 36, winter 1979, p. 18–37. Much of the sixth volume of *Performing Arts Resources* (P6935.P46) will be devoted to the FTP and the Library's FTP Collection.

Of related interest are the manuscript scores and printed music from the FTP and the Federal Music Project in the Music Division. Appointments are required to use this material. A few theater posters are included in the Work Projects Administration Poster Collection (no. 265) in the Prints and Photographs Division.

Walsh, Elizabeth D., "New Deal Theatre: The Best Art Is That Which Can Be Enjoyed by All the People . . .," *Dramatics,* v. 48, March/April 1977: 15–19.

———, and Diane Bowers, "WPA Federal Theatre Project," *Theatre News,* v. 8, April 1976: 1–3.

The wild gander leads his flock through the cool night,
Ya-honk! he says, and sounds it down to me like
an invitation;
The pert suppose it is ~~meaningless~~, but I listen closer,
I find ~~it has~~ its place and sign up there toward
the November sky.—

The ~~cloud~~ moose of the north, the cat on the housesill, the chickadee,
the prairie-dog,
The litter of the grunting sow as they tug at her teats,
The brood of the turkey-hen, and she with her
half-spread wings,
I see in them and myself the same old law.

The press of my foot to the earth springs a hundred
affections,
They scorn the best I can do to relate them.—

I am enamoured of growing outdoors,
Of men that live among cattle or taste of the
ocean or soil,
I can eat and sleep with them week in and week out.

What is commonest and cheapest is Me,
Me going in for my chances, spending
for vast returns,
Adorning myself to bestow myself on the first
that will take me,
Not asking the sky to come down to my
good will,
Scattering it freely forever.—

The pure contralto sings in the organ-loft,
The carpenter dresses his plank... the tongue of his fore-plane
whistles its wild ascending lisp,
The married and unmarried children ride home to their
thanksgiving dinner,
The pilot seizes the king-pin, he heaves down with a strong arm,

*The only page known to exist from Whitman's original manuscript of* Leaves of
Grass *(1855). On the back of the page Whitman made notes for a poem pub-
lished in the second edition, to which use the leaf probably owes its survival.
Feinberg-Whitman Collection, Manuscript Division. LCMSS–18630–3.*

# 79

## Feinberg-Whitman Collection

Papers and photographs of Walt Whitman, early editions of
his writings, and secondary research materials

Manuscript Division

The Feinberg-Whitman Collection, purchased by the Library over
the last decade with the assistance of anonymous benefactors, probably
is the largest and most important group of materials relating to American poet Walt Whitman (1819–1892) ever assembled. In building
this collection, Charles E. Feinberg noted in 1958 in the *Papers of the
Bibliographical Society of America* that he "tried to acquire all available letters, postcards, checks, bills, and documents, primarily to re-
construct Whitman's daily life and creative activity." Personal papers
form the core of the collection—more than one thousand of Whitman's
letters (about twenty-eight hundred are known to exist), approximately
two thousand letters received by him, and more than one thousand
manuscripts, ranging from an annotated clipping to a commonplace
book (March 1876–May 1889) of nearly four hundred pages. Also in
the collection are photocopies of many Whitman manuscripts held by
public repositories and of a large selection of those in private hands.
Among the printed items are many volumes from Whitman's personal
library; first editions and proofs of most of Whitman's publications,
including several copies of all editions of *Leaves of Grass* from 1855 to
1891, many of them inscribed or signed, and page and galley proofs of
*Specimen Days* (1882–83) ; early critical and biographical treatments;
and works of more recent scholarship. The collection also has numerous
photographs and pictorial materials relating to Whitman's life and
work and personal items such as the poet's walking stick, watch, and
pen. Mr. Feinberg, a retired Detroit business executive, has been actively involved with the quarterly *Walt Whitman Review* and has preserved correspondence relating to each issue, manuscript material
pertaining to various Whitman publications, and documentation of the
Whitman exhibits drawn from the collection.

A portion of the 20,000-item collection is described in the catalog
of the exhibition held at the Detroit Public Library. An unpublished
finding aid is available in the Manuscript Division. The Library's

extensive resources for the study of Walt Whitman include additional manuscript material in the Manuscript Division and a collection of early editions of Whitman's writings kept in the Rare Book and Special Collections Division (no. 261).

Broderick, John C., "The Greatest Whitman Collector and the Greatest Whitman Collection," *QJLC*, v. 27, April 1970: 109–128.

Feinberg, Charles E., *Walt Whitman: A Selection of the Manuscripts, Books and Association Items Gathered by Charles E. Feinberg: Catalog of an Exhibition Held at the Detroit Public Library, Detroit, Michigan, 1955* ([Detroit: 1955] 128 p. Z8971.5.F4).

White, William, "Charles E. Feinberg, Book Collector," *The Private Library* (Z990.P7), 2d ser., v. 1, summer 1968: 63–73.

# 80

## Roger Fenton Collection

Crimean War photographs by Roger Fenton

Prints and Photographs Division

Among the earliest documentary photographs in the Library of Congress are 265 original Crimean War photoprints by Roger Fenton (1819–1869). With the support of the Manchester publisher Thomas Agnew & Sons, Fenton went to the Crimea in 1855 to photograph the international forces that had taken arms against Russia. Fenton photographed battlefields, the harbor at Balaklava, leading British, French, and Turkish commanders, and men in the ranks. Using a horse-drawn van as a mobile darkroom, he prepared his wet collodion negatives in the field and printed his images when he returned to England. The original contact prints in the collection, purchased from the photographer's grandniece Frances M. Fenton in 1944, are on "salted paper" and include handwritten captions that may have been added by Fenton himself. The collection is kept with the master photographs in the Prints and Photographs Division and is represented in the division catalog. The division copy of Helmut and Alison Gernsheim's book *Roger Fenton, Photographer of the Crimean War* (London: Secker & Warburg, 1954. 106 p. DK214.F45) has been annotated to indicate items in the collection. Also in the division are Fenton's photographic studies of British cathedrals.

*Guide,* Vanderbilt, no. 230.

Milhollen, Hirst D., "Roger Fenton, Photographer of the Crimean War," *QJLC,* v. 3, August 1946: 10–12, reprinted in *A Century of Photographs, 1846–1946, Selected from the Collections of the Library of Congress* (Washington: Library of Congress, 1980. TR6.U62.D572), compiled by Renata V. Shaw.

# 81

## Austin E. Fife Collection

### Field recordings of Utah folklore and folk music, 1946–47

Archive of Folk Song

The Fife Collection of Mormon and Western folksongs was recorded in Utah from 1946 to 1947 under the joint auspices of the Utah Humanities Research Foundation and the Archive of Folk Song. Dr. Austin E. Fife and his wife Alta visited the southeastern and southwestern corners of the state and the valleys west of the Wasatch Range seeking secular and historical songs from the early days of Mormon settlement. To a lesser degree, the Fifes recorded Mormon superstitions, folk cures, frontier legends, religious stories, and traditional American and Danish folksongs. The 106 disc recordings (AFS 8,638–8,724 and 10,368–10,386) have been copied on tape and are accompanied by field notes and a concordance. Several songs have been published on a Library of Congress recording.

"Collectors and Collecting," *Western Folklore* (GR1.C26), v. 7, July 1948: 301.

Emrich, Duncan, comp., *Songs of the Mormons, and Songs of the West* (Library of Congress, Division of Music, Recording Laboratory [1952]   2 s. 12 in.  33⅓ rpm. AFS L30).

Fife, Austin E., and Alta S. Fife, "Folk Songs of Mormon Inspiration," *Western Folklore* (GR1.C26), v. 6, January 1947: 42–52.

# 82

## Millard Fillmore Collection

### Maps collected by Millard Fillmore

Geography and Map Division

The Fillmore Collection offers an excellent cross section of American map production during the middle of the nineteenth century. Embracing maps of cities, states, European countries, and Civil War battles, these 247 maps from the personal collection of Pres. Millard Fillmore (1800–1874) were purchased by the Library in 1916. They form the largest extant presidential map collection. While most are printed maps, the collection includes a manuscript copy of William Eddy's survey of San Francisco which, according to the inscription, was presented to Congress on December 31, 1849. Most pieces bear Fillmore's signature. The maps are listed in the purchase inventory and are recorded in a card file kept with the collection. A few items are described in the Library's computerized map catalog.

# 83

## Irving Fine Collection

Music manuscripts, papers, photographs, and sound recordings of composer Irving Fine

Music Division
Motion Picture, Broadcasting, and Recorded Sound Division

Through the generosity of Verna Fine Gordon, the Library of Congress has become the major repository of the music manuscripts of Irving Fine (1914–1962), the American composer who for many years headed the School of Creative Arts of Brandeis University. The collection comprises scores, sketches, and photocopies of works written throughout his career, including incidental theater music composed for a production of *Alice in Wonderland* (1942); *The Hour Glass* (1949), a cycle for unaccompanied chorus to texts by Ben Jonson; *Mutability,* a song cycle for contralto and piano originally commissioned by the Creative Concerts Guild, Inc., in 1952; *Serious Song* (1955), for orchestra; and *Symphony,* which was first performed by the Boston Symphony shortly before his death. Photographs, clippings, programs, scrapbooks, and a few letters, also donated by Mrs. Gordon since 1963, document the development of Fine's career from the mid-1930s to 1962. Many music manuscripts by Fine are listed in the catalog of the Music Division. The collection measures four linear feet and is complemented by commissioned works by Fine in the Elizabeth Sprague Coolidge Foundation Collection (no. 52) and the Koussevitzky Archives (no. 138).

Forty unpublished tapes presented by Mrs. Gordon in 1969 feature recordings of concert, broadcast, and private performances of the composer's works. Fine himself accompanies a number of songs on the piano, including the cycles *Mutability* and *Childhood Fables for Grownups.* The collection is represented in the catalog of the Motion Picture, Broadcasting, and Recorded Sound Division and listed in an inventory on file.

Waters, Edward N., "The Realm of Tone—Music," *QJLC,* v. 22, January 1965: 37–38.

——, "Variations on a Theme: Recent Acquisitions of the Music Division," *QJLC,* v. 27, January 1970: 53, 82.

# 84

## Peter Force Library

Manuscripts and maps relating to American history, early
American imprints, and incunabula

Manuscript Division
Geography and Map Division

The holdings of Americana in the Library of Congress owe much of
their strength to the collecting zeal of Peter Force (1790–1868). In the
course of preparing his "Documentary History of the American Revolution," a compilation better known today as *American Archives,* this
Washington publisher and politician assembled what was probably the
largest private collection of printed and manuscript sources on American history in the United States. The Peter Force Library was purchased by act of Congress in 1867. In one stroke, the Library of Congress established its first major collections of eighteenth-century
American newspapers, incunabula, early American imprints, manuscripts, and rare maps and atlases. Although no complete inventory
survives, many of the approximately 22,500 Force volumes are recorded
without source designation in the *Catalogue of Books Added to the
Library of Congress from December 1, 1866, to December 1, 1867*
(Washington: Govt. Print. Off., 1868. 526 p. Z881.U5 1868).

Manuscripts from the Force Library as well as personal papers
donated in 1875 by Peter Force's son, William Q. Force, and related
material acquired in the twentieth century are kept in the Manuscript
Division. While spanning the period from 1492 to 1961, the papers
date chiefly from the years 1750 to 1868. Personal papers cover Force's
work as a Washington printer and publisher, the genesis of his archival
project, and his military service, political career, and participation in
scientific and historical societies. Documentation compiled for *American
Archives* includes transcripts of official records, private papers, and
colonial publications; a twenty-five-volume Hispanic collection, consisting primarily of transcriptions of works concerning the New World
by various Spanish writers, notably Bartolomé de Las Casas; material
originating from the collections of Ebenezer Hazard and George Chal-
mers; and numerous original manuscripts, particularly from the colonial
period. The collection includes extensive resources for the study of

121

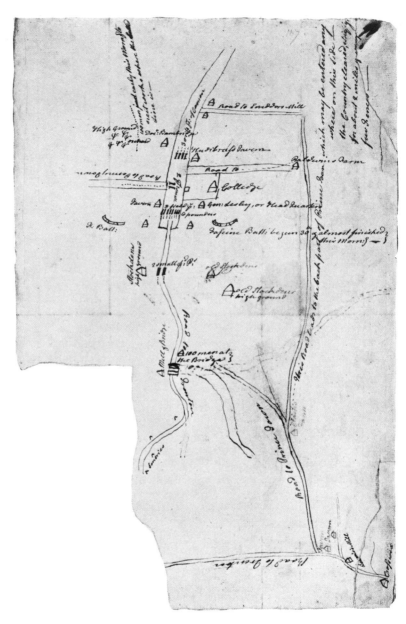

*Intelligence map sent by Gen. John Cadwalader to General Washington on December 31, 1776, showing British positions at Princeton, New Jersey, several days before the successful American attack. Peter Force Collection, Geography and Map Division. Negative in division.*

122

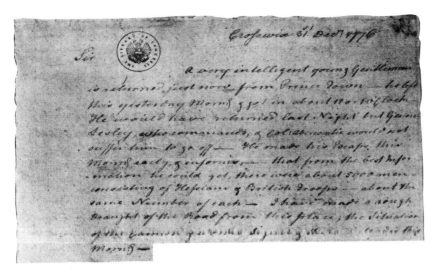

*General Cadwalader's letter of December 31, 1776, to General Washington which accompanied the reconnaissance sketch shown. It begins "A very intelligent young gentleman is returned just now from Prince Town . . . & informs, that from the best information he could get, there were about 5000 men—consisting of Hessians & British troops—about the same number of each—I have made a rough draught of the road from this place; the situation of the cannon & works begun & those intended this morn:g." George Washington Papers, Manuscript Division. LCMSS–44693–93.*

eighteenth-century American history in the papers of Ephraim Blaine, John Davis, Pierre Du Simitière, John Fitch, Nathanael Greene, Thomas Hamilton, John Paul Jones, Charles Simms, Edward Vernon, and others. The collection totals 150,000 items and is described in an unpublished finding aid. Some of the material has been reported to the *National Union Catalog of Manuscript Collections* and has been microfilmed. A small part of the papers has been indexed.

An inventory uncovered in 1970 has enabled the Geography and Map Division to pinpoint the Peter Force maps dispersed throughout the division's general collections. The approximately 768 manuscript and printed maps range in date from the seventeenth to the mid-nineteenth centuries and include maps relating to the French and Indian War and the American Revolution, and of the District of Columbia, various American cities, and the West Indies. All of the maps of America dating from 1759 to 1790 are listed in the Library's computerized map catalog and will be described in a bibliography now being prepared by the Library's American Revolution Bicentennial Office.

Incunabula, pre-1801 American imprints, and other rare publications from the Force Library have been absorbed into the collections of the Rare Book and Special Collections Division. The division holdings include important compilations of pamphlets that were assembled by such collectors as William Duane, Ebenezer Hazard, Jacob Bailey Moore, Israel Thorndike, and Oliver Wolcott. It is estimated that over eight thousand of the approximately forty thousand pamphlets purchased from Force were printed before 1800.

Goff, Frederick R., "Peter Force," *The Papers of the Bibliographical Society of America* (Z1008.B51P), v. 44, 1st quarter 1950: 1–16.

*Rare Bk. Div. Guide,* p. 5–6, 30.

Stephenson, Richard W., "Maps from the Peter Force Collection," *QJLC,* v. 30, July 1973: 183–204.

U.S., Library of Congress, *Special Report of the Librarian of Congress to the Joint Committee of the Library Concerning the Historical Library of Peter Force, Esq.* (Washington: 1867. 8 p. Z733.U57S 1867).

# 85

## Thaddeus M. Fowler Collection

Panoramic maps of American cities, late nineteenth and early
twentieth centuries

Geography and Map Division

In the years following the Civil War, the panoramic map became
a popular cartographic form for portraying American cities. Though
generally not drawn to scale, "bird's-eye views" were based on detailed
on-site study and provide an accurate picture of landscape features,
streets, and buildings of the period. Thaddeus M. Fowler (1842–1922),
whose panoramic maps are among the best represented in the Geography and Map Division collections, prepared views of towns in at least
eighteen states and Canada over a period of more than fifty years.
Between 1969 and 1972 the Fowler family presented to the Library
over one hundred panoramas executed by the mapmaker. These date
from after his move to Morrisville, Pennsylvania, in 1885 and include
numerous renderings of West Virginia and Pennsylvania towns. Of
special note is an unpublished panoramic drawing of Allentown, Pennsylvania, measuring twenty-eight by seventy-one inches. The gift joined
the many Fowler views acquired by the Library through copyright
deposit and brought the total number of separate panoramic maps by
Fowler in the division to over two hundred. The views are individually
described in the Library's computerized map catalog and listed by town
in John Hébert's checklist of 1,117 panoramic maps in the division.
Panoramas by Albert Ruger are discussed in entry number 213. There
are additional city panoramas in the custody of the Prints and Photographs Division.

Hébert, John R., "Panoramic Maps of American Cities," *Special Libraries*
(Z671.S72), v. 63, December 1972: 554–562.

U.S., Library of Congress, Geography and Map Division, *Panoramic Maps of
Anglo-American Cities: A Checklist of Maps in the Collections of the Library
of Congress, Geography and Map Division* (Washington: Library of Congress,
1974. 118 p. Z6027.U5U54), compiled by John R. Hébert.

*Panoramic map of Fairmont (west bank) and Palatine, West Virginia, drawn by Thaddeus M. Fowler and published in 1897. Thaddeus M. Fowler Collection, Geography and Map Division. Negative in division.*

# 86

## John Ross Frampton Collection

Commercial piano recordings, 1912 to the early 1930s

In 1960 John Frampton of Chippewa Falls, Wisconsin, presented to the Library of Congress the extensive collection of early piano recordings that had been assembled by his father, John Ross Frampton (1879–1955), professor of piano. The American and European releases collected by Professor Frampton feature performances by such leading pianists as de Greef, Hambourg, Hoffmann, Kempff, Moiseevich, Murdoch, and Rachmaninoff and date from 1912 to the early 1930s. The 747 discs were listed by performer in a card index before they were integrated with the other commercial recordings held by the Motion Picture, Broadcasting, and Recorded Sound Division.

Waters, Edward N., "Music," *QJLC*, v. 18, November 1960: 36–37.

# 87

## Benjamin Franklin Collection

Papers and publications of Benjamin Franklin

Manuscript Division
Rare Book and Special Collections Division

In 1882 the U.S. government purchased a portion of the papers Benjamin Franklin (1706–1790) had bequeathed to his grandson William Temple Franklin (1760–1823). The collection represents the material taken to London by William Franklin to prepare his three-volume work, *Memoirs of the Life and Writings of Benjamin Franklin* (London: 1817–18), and acquired in 1851 by Henry Stevens, an American bookdealer in London. At the time of purchase the books and pamphlets in the collection were sent to the Library of Congress and the manuscripts to the Department of State. The manuscripts were subsequently transferred to the Library in 1903 and 1922 and became the core of the Benjamin Franklin papers in the Manuscript Division. The Franklin papers date chiefly from the 1770s and 1780s and contain correspondence, journals, records, and articles. Much of the material relates to Franklin's diplomatic activities in France— letterbooks of the U.S. Legation in Paris (1779–82), negotiations in London (1775), records of the U.S. peace commissioners (1780–83), and correspondence with David Hartley (1775–81). Also in the collection is the original manuscript of "Articles of Belief and Acts of Religion" (1728), and correspondence with Mary Stevenson (1760–79) and Jan Ingenhousz (1777–85). William Temple Franklin, whose papers form a part of the 8,000-item collection, annotated some of the correspondence (1726–90). These papers have been microfilmed and described in a published register.

Approximately two hundred items from the Benjamin Franklin Collection in the Rare Book and Special Collections Division can be traced to the Stevens purchase and are described in Henry Stevens's *Benjamin Franklin's Life and Writings: A Bibliographical Essay on the Stevens' Collection of Books and Manuscripts Relating to Doctor Franklin* (London: Printed by Messrs. Davy & Sons, 1881. 40 p. Z8313.S84). The collection embraces 850 volumes that were written, printed, edited, or published by Franklin. Notable items include numerous early editions and translations of the *Autobiography*, Baroness Le Despencer's annotated copy of the *Abridgement of the Book of Common Prayer* (London: 1773) which Franklin edited, one of the four known surviving copies of *A Vindication of the New-North-Church in Boston* (Boston: 1720) which was printed during Franklin's apprenticeship at his brother's shop, and the first edition of Franklin's *Dissertation on Liberty and Necessity* (London: 1725). Items in the collection, along with Franklin material elsewhere in the division, are recorded in the author/title and shelflist card file. Of related interest are the few volumes once owned by Franklin that were purchased by Thomas Jefferson and acquired by the Library of Congress as part of the Thomas Jefferson Library (no. 130).

NUCMC, 72–1716.

U.S., Bureau of Rolls and Library, *Letter from the Secretary of State Transmitting a Report of Theodore F. Dwight on the Papers of Benjamin Franklin* (Washington: 1881. 99 p. 47th Congress, 1st session. Senate. Misc. doc. no. 21. Z6616.F83U5).

U.S., Library of Congress, Manuscript Division, *Benjamin Franklin: A Register and Index of His Papers in the Library of Congress* (Washington: Library of Congress, 1973. 27 p. Z6616.F83U66).

——, *List of the Benjamin Franklin Papers in the Library of Congress* (Washington: Govt. Print. Off., 1905. 322 p. Z6616.F83U7), compiled under the direction of Worthington Chauncey Ford.

# 88

## French Political Cartoon Collection

French political prints, 1789–1871

Prints and Photographs Division

The 200 prints forming the French Political Cartoon Collection in the Prints and Photographs Division were produced in France between 1789 and 1830 and pertain chiefly to the events and themes of the French Revolution and the reign of Napoleon Bonaparte. The collection, assembled by the Library over a number of years, contains many items which were published anonymously. Items are arranged by date of event and indexed by subject.

Supplementing this material is a group of approximately five hundred lithographs and relief cuts (many colored) from the period 1870 to 1871. Many prints relate to the Paris Commune. Among the major artists represented are André Gill and Alfred Le Petit.

# 89

## Sigmund Freud Collection

Papers of Sigmund Freud and early editions of Freud's writings

Manuscript Division
Rare Book and Special Collections Division

Since the early 1950s, the Library of Congress has been forming a large and extremely important collection of the papers of Sigmund Freud (1856–1939). The Sigmund Freud Collection in the Manuscript Division contains manuscripts of articles and books written by Freud and files of his incoming correspondence, much of which has been donated by the Freud family. Thousands of Freud's letters to fellow physicians, disciples, and friends, and copies of biographical documents from European archives have been acquired from a number of sources, including Sigmund Freud Archives, Inc., a New York organization established to collect and preserve Freud material. The Freud Collection, which at present contains approximately forty thousand items, is described in an unpublished finding aid. While a portion of the collection (some of this material has been microfilmed) is open to researchers, most papers are restricted for varying lengths of time.

In 1975, to augment the Library's collection of Sigmund Freud manuscripts, the Rare Book and Special Collections Division began collecting first editions of Freud's works in German and English and later editions containing textual revisions by the author. One hundred titles have been assembled already including an offprint of the early publication *Über Coca* (Wien: 1885) ; a presentation copy of Freud's first book, *Zur Auffassung der Aphasien* (Leipzig und Wien: F. Deuticke, 1891) ; and the first edition of *Die Traumdeutung* (Leipzig und Wien: F. Deuticke, 1900), a work which has come to epitomize Freud's contribution to psychiatry. Also available are more than fifty books from Freud's library, virtually all of which bear an inscription to Freud, his signature, or some other indication of ownership. The volumes from Freud's library are recorded in the division provenance file.

Matheson, William, "Microcosm of the Library: The Rare Book and Special Collections Division," *QJLC*, v. 34, July 1977: 234.

U.S., Library of Congress, Manuscript Division, "Recent Acquisitions of the Manuscript Division," *QJLC*, v. 26, October 1969: 250, 254.

———, "Recent Acquisitions of the Manuscript Division," *QJLC*, v. 28, October 1971: 297–304.

# 90

## Toni Frissell Collection

Photographs and papers of Toni Frissell

Prints and Photographs Division

In 1970 Toni Frissell donated to the Library a massive collection of photographs, negatives, and manuscripts documenting her distinguished career. Miss Frissell became interested in photography while assisting her brother Varick in making a documentary film and subsequently served overseas as a World War II news photographer. While Miss Frissell has photographed subjects as diverse as the 1968 Republican national convention and oil drilling teams, she is probably best known for her pioneering fashion photography and her informal portraits of Konrad Adenauer, the Astors, Charles Chaplin, Sir Winston Churchill, John Kennedy, the Mellons, Pope Pius XII, and other prominent figures. Her photographs have been published in such magazines as *Harper's Bazaar, Life, Sports Illustrated,* and *Vogue,* and used to illustrate *A Child's Garden of Verses* (1944) and *Mother Goose* (1948). The Frissell Collection in the Prints and Photographs Division contains 270,000 black and white negatives, 42,000 color transparencies, 25,000 enlargement prints, and proof sheets dating from 1935 to 1971. Images can be located by subject using the annotated scrapbooks, "book boards," and files of published assignments. Eventually the subject index, which now covers the period from 1965 to 1970, will be expanded to provide subject access to the entire collection. The accompanying personal papers will be transferred to the Manuscript Division when the collection has been processed. There is a special charge for reproducing material in the collection.

U.S., Library of Congress, Prints and Photographs Division, "Acquisition Notes," *LCIB*, v. 30, May 27, 1971: 303–304.

# 91

## General Foods Corporation Collection

Broadcast recordings and scripts of General Foods' radio shows, 1930s and 1940s

Motion Picture, Broadcasting, and Recorded Sound Division

In 1956 the General Foods Corporation donated to the Library of Congress sound recordings and scripts from radio series that had been sponsored by its products. The transcription discs feature broadcasts of twenty-one radio shows aired chiefly in the early 1940s, including *The Adventures of the Thin Man, Duffy's Tavern, The Fanny Brice Show, The Jack Benny Program, Lum and Abner, Portia Faces Life,* and *Young Dr. Malone.* Dating from 1932 to 1949, the scripts are stamped in many cases "as broadcast" or "master" and include handwritten revisions, timing notes, and commercials. The scripts document over 130 broadcasts, some of which are also represented by sound recordings. The nearly two hundred discs have been copied on tape and are recorded by series title in the catalog of the Motion Picture, Broadcasting, and Recorded Sound Division. The scripts are arranged in folders by series title.

# 92

## Arnold Genthe Collection

### Photographs by Arnold Genthe

### Prints and Photographs Division

In 1943 the Library of Congress purchased the photographic materials remaining in the studio of Arnold Genthe (1869–1942) at the time of his death. Originally trained as a classical scholar, Genthe taught himself photography soon after emigrating from Germany in 1895. The success of his photographs of San Francisco's Chinatown led him to establish a local portrait studio. He became famous for his impressionistic portrayals of society women, artists, dancers, and theater personalities. Moving to New York in 1911, Genthe experimented with the new Autochrome color process and executed one of the first documentary commissions in color. The Library's collection of approximately ten thousand negatives and eighty-seven hundred contact and enlargement prints is the largest single collection of Genthe's work and contains images from all periods of his career: the famed photographs of Chinatown, which are probably the only negatives from his early years to escape the 1906 San Francisco earthquake and fire; views taken during his travels in Europe and Asia; photographs of Yosemite and New Orleans; studies of dancers; and reproductions of painting and sculpture. The greater part of the collection relates to portrait commissions. Many sitters are listed in the division biographical card index and keyed to the original negatives through Genthe's logbooks. The original Genthe photoprints are kept with the master photographs and grouped by subject. Also in the collection are 375 original color transparencies, some of which were the gift of the Museum of Modern Art in 1947.

*Guide,* Vanderbilt, no. 260–261.

Vanderbilt, Paul, "The Arnold Genthe Collection," *QJLC,* v. 8, May 1951: 13–18; reprinted in *A Century of Photographs, 1846–1946, Selected from the Collections of the Library of Congress* (Washington: Library of Congress, 1980. TR6.U62.D572), compiled by Renata V. Shaw.

*Viewpoints,* no. 128–129, 181.

*Siegfried comes upon the dragon in part 1 of Fritz Lang's* Die Nibelungen *(1923–24), one of the feature films in the German Collection. This still was deposited for U.S. copyright protection before the film's American release. Prints and Photographs Division. LC–USZ62–66566.*

# 93

## German Collection

German films, 1930s and early 1940s

Motion Picture, Broadcasting, and Recorded Sound Division

After World War II several thousand films that had been produced in Germany chiefly from 1933 to 1945 were confiscated by the U.S. government and transferred to the Library of Congress. The collection in the Motion Picture, Broadcasting, and Recorded Sound Division contains approximately one thousand silent and sound features, over one thousand newsreels, including an extensive run of *Die Deutsche Wochenschau* (September 1939–March 1945), and numerous educational, entertainment, documentary, and propaganda shorts. Public Laws 87–846 and 87–861 returned the film copyrights to the original owners in 1963 and gave the Library screening privileges and permanent custody of the prints. The Library has reference copies of most newsreels, 80 percent of the features, and 60 percent of the shorts. Most films are not translated. Feature films are recorded in the collection shelflist, which lists all of the titles in the collection, and are indexed by director and year of release. Fact sheets, stills, scripts, and official censorship cards are available for many films.

# 94

# German Speech and Monitored Broadcast Collection

Speech and broadcast recordings made in Germany, 1930s and early 1940s

Motion Picture, Broadcasting, and Recorded Sound Division

Approximately twenty-five hundred German sound recordings were seized by American forces during and after World War II and transferred to the Library of Congress. The collection contains disc recordings of special events, public addresses by Nazi party officials, and foreign radio broadcasts that were monitored chiefly between 1939 and the end of the war. The radio transcriptions include news broadcasts and political speeches from over twenty European countries and governments in exile. British and American programs account for much of the collection and are identified in notes on file in the Motion Picture, Broadcasting, and Recorded Sound Division. Non-English-language recordings are listed chronologically by country of origin in a card index. Most disc recordings have been reproduced on tape, and selected items are listed in Gerhard L. Weinberg's *Guide to Captured German Documents* ([Maxwell Air Force Base, Ala.: Air University, Human Resources Research Institute, 1952] 90 p. Z2240.W4), p. 35–39.

# 95

## George and Ira Gershwin Collection

Music manuscripts, papers, pictorial material, and book and record collections of George Gershwin; papers of Ira Gershwin

Music Division
Motion Picture, Broadcasting, and Recorded Sound Division

The largest public collection of original source material for the study of the life and work of American composer George Gershwin (1898–1937) is the Gershwin Collection in the Music Division. The collection was begun in 1953 with Rose Gershwin's bequest of holograph scores of *Rhapsody in Blue*, *Concerto in F*, *An American in Paris*, *Second Rhapsody*, *Cuban Overture*, and *Porgy and Bess*. The two major manuscripts not in Mrs. Gershwin's possession, *George Gershwin's Song Book* and *"I Got Rhythm" Variations*, were subsequently donated by composer Kay Swift and George Gershwin's brother and lyricist, Ira Gershwin. Since the 1950s, Ira Gershwin has attempted to assemble for the Library complete documentation of his brother's career—holograph sketches and scores, student notebooks, scrapbooks, financial records, contracts, telegrams, books from his personal library, and scripts of Gershwin films and stage productions. For many items he has provided annotations. Ira Gershwin has also contributed drafts of his own lyrics and personal correspondence, including letters exchanged with Merle Armitage and Kurt Weill. Arthur Gershwin has donated portrait photographs made and collected by his brother George. The most recent addition to the collection, a 1977 gift from Betty Lasky in memory of her father Jesse L. Lasky, is a copy of the first edition of the piano-vocal score of *Porgy and Bess* autographed by individuals associated with the original 1935 production. The collection measures seventeen linear feet.

Approximately 250 disc recordings from the Gershwins are maintained in the Motion Picture, Broadcasting, and Recorded Sound Division. These include commercial recordings made by George Gershwin in London in 1926 and 1928 and several privately prepared transcriptions of broadcasts and rehearsals. The noncommercial recordings

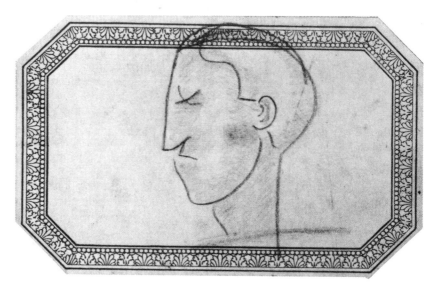

*Self-portrait of George Gershwin, sketched on the cover of a harmony exercise book used by the composer while studying under Joseph Schillinger in the early 1930s. George and Ira Gershwin Collection, Music Division. Courtesy of Ira Gershwin. Negative in division.*

are represented in the division catalog and fully described in notes on file. An inventory of the commercial releases is also available.

Campbell, Frank C., "The Musical Scores of George Gershwin," *QJLC*, v. 11, May 1954: 127–139.

———, "Some Manuscripts of George Gershwin (1898–1937)," *Manuscripts* (Z41.A2A925), v. 6, winter 1954: 66–75.

Jablonski, Edward, and Lawrence D. Stewart, *The Gershwin Years*, 2d ed. (Garden City, N.Y.: Doubleday, 1973. 416 p. ML410.G288J3 1975), p. 397–398, 403.

# 96

## Leopold Godowsky Collection

Music manuscripts and papers of pianist Leopold Godowsky

Music Division

In 1969 Leopold Godowsky, Jr., presented to the Library of Congress fifty-two of his father's music manuscripts. Leopold Godowsky (1870–1938), one of the great piano virtuosos at the turn of the century, wrote works of such technical difficulty that they have been mastered by few pianists. The collection includes his transcriptions of works by Bach, Schubert, and Weber, and ten pieces arranged for the left hand that were inspired by Chopin's *Etudes*. In 1975 and 1976 Mrs. Leonard S. Saxe, the widow of Godowsky's nephew and legal adviser, added to the collection business and financial papers, clippings, printed music, photographs, notes prepared by her husband for Godowsky's biography, and records of his legal disputes with recording companies and publishers. The letters, many of which have been translated into English, include correspondence conducted on concert tours. The holographs acquired in 1969 are listed in the Music Division catalog and in the *Quarterly Journal*. The papers measure approximately twelve linear feet.

Waters, Edward N., "Notable Music Acquisitions," *QJLC*, v. 28, January 1971: 46–48.

# 97

## Hermann Göring Collection

Biographical photographs of Hermann Göring

Prints and Photographs Division

The personal photo albums of Hermann Göring (1893–1946) were among the confiscated German materials transferred to the Library in 1947. These forty-seven albums form one of the most extensive biographical collections in the Prints and Photographs Division and provide detailed coverage of Göring's activities during World War I and the years 1933 to 1942. Depicted are official functions—meetings with foreign leaders, ceremonies, travels in southern Europe, air force inspection tours—as well as hunting trips, parties, and family gatherings. Göring apparently relied on no single photographer, since the collection includes pictures by Helmuth Kurth, Eitel Lange, and miscellaneous government and commercial agencies. For the most part, the chronologically arranged albums retain the original German captions and are marked "Photoarchiv Generalfeldmarschall Göring" or "Der Reichsmarschall des Grossdeutschen Reiches Photoarchiv." The contents of each album are summarized in the division catalog.

*Guide,* Vanderbilt, no. 289.

Vanderbilt, Paul, and Alice Lee Parker, "Prints and Photographs," *QJLC,* v. 6, November 1948: 38–39.

# 98

## Robert Winslow Gordon Collection

American folk music recordings and song texts collected by
Robert Winslow Gordon, late 1910s–early 1930s

Archive of Folk Song

When Robert Winslow Gordon (1888–1960) became the first
director of the Archive of American Folk Song in 1928, he brought to
the Library what was then probably the largest and most diverse collection of American folksongs assembled by a single collector. Gordon
began making wax cylinder recordings while teaching at the University
of California at Berkeley (1918–24). In 1925, assisted by a fellowship
from Harvard University, he began an extensive field trip which took
him to Asheville, North Carolina, where he recorded Bascom Lamar
Lunsford (no. 149), and to Darien, Georgia, where he researched black
folksong traditions. In addition to the 825 cylinder recordings generated by these projects, all of which have been transcribed on tape
(AFS 18,994–19,012), the Gordon Collection includes ninety-five instantaneous disc recordings (AFS 13,577–13,671) which were made at
the Library and on a pioneering field trip through Virginia, West
Virginia, and Kentucky with portable disc equipment in early 1932.
The recordings are listed in concordances and card files in the Archive
of Folk Song. Selections from the Gordon field recordings are featured
on a recent Library album.

In addition to recording folksongs, Gordon solicited song texts
for "Old Songs That Men Have Sung," a column he edited for *Adventure* magazine in the mid-1920s. Through this column Gordon
developed a nationwide network of folksong informants. The Archive
of Folk Song has many of Gordon's papers relating to his column and
other collecting activities. The collection contains Gordon's *Adventure*
correspondence (Debora G. Kodish, who has written a master's thesis
on Gordon at the Memorial University of Newfoundland, has prepared
a geographic and informant index to this material); correspondence of
the column's previous editor, Robert Frothingham; songsters, magazines, and reprints; songs collected by Gordon in California, North
Carolina, and Georgia; Gordon's "Inferno Collection" of bawdy folk
lyrics; and song collections in manuscript, typescript, carbon copy, or

photostat form. These include compilations written, collected, or sent to Gordon by T. B. Boyd, R. M. Davids, Nellie Galt, J. H. Hanford, Mellinger Edward Henry, Guy B. Johnson, Nettie F. McAdams, Joseph F. McGinnis, E. A. McIlhenny, Mabel E. Neal, Mary Newcomb, Howard W. Odum, R. M. Phillips, Margaret Purcell, and Betty Bush Winger. The 3,858 song texts derived from the *Adventure* letters are arranged in a bound set. These texts and the songs from the above collections are indexed in a card file by first line and title. The manuscripts and printed matter fill thirty-one file boxes. All manuscript material is represented in a container list and is available on microfilm in the Music Division. This division also has a microfilm of its autographed compilation of Gordon's *Adventure* columns.

Ms. Kodish discusses Gordon's work in her article, " 'A National Project with Many Workers': Robert Winslow Gordon and the Archive of Folk Song," in *QJLC,* v. 35, October 1978, p. 218–233. Gordon's activities as head of the Archive of Folk Song are reported in the *Annual Report of the Librarian of Congress* for the years 1928 to 1932.

Rosenberg, Neil V., and Debora G. Kodish, eds., *"Folk-songs of America":* *The Robert Winslow Gordon Collection, 1922–1932* (Library of Congress, Recording Laboratory [1978] 2 s. 12 in. 33⅓ rpm. AFS L68).

# 99

## Frederic W. Goudy Collection

Personal library, papers, and publications of type designer Frederic Goudy

Rare Book and Special Collections Division

American type designer Frederic W. Goudy (1865–1947) began experimenting with layout and printing while working as a book-keeper in Chicago in the 1890s. He created a total of 124 type designs, executing many from drawing to casting, and operated the Village Press with his wife Bertha from 1903 to 1939. The Goudy Collection in the Rare Book and Special Collections Division was purchased from Goudy himself in 1944 and consists largely of material that escaped a disastrous workshop fire of 1939. The collection includes Goudy's personal library on typography and numerous examples of fine printing (ca. 1890–1944), particularly from private American presses. The output of the Village Press is documented by over 150 items ranging from dummies and broadsides to finished books. The division copy of Melbert B. Cary's *A Bibliography of the Village Press* (New York: Press of the Woolly Whale, 1938. 205 p. Z232.G68C3) has been annotated to indicate collection holdings. In addition, the collection contains photographs of Goudy and his wife and drawings, rubbings, proofs, and posters illustrative of his commercial design work on *The Inland Printer* and for the Curtis Publishing Company, the Peerless Motor Car Company, and other clients. In 1975 a group of manuscripts was added to the original purchase, bringing the total number of manuscript items in the collection to 3,169. The acquisition includes correspondence largely from the years 1935 to 1945, papers relating to Goudy's *A Half-Century of Type Design and Typography, 1895–1945* (1946), and notes and galley proofs for an unpublished book by Paul Bennett entitled "Goudy: The Man and His Work." Howard Coggeshall, Richard Ellis, and Mitchell Kennerley are among the correspondents. Many of the 1,791 volumes and 708 pamphlets in the Goudy Collection are represented in author/title and shelflist files. Also available is a register describing nonbook materials and an inventory of the 1944 purchase.

Beske, Kurt, "Craftsman in a Machine Age," *QJLC*, v. 34, April 1977: 97–115.

Haykin, David Judson, "The Goudy Collection," *QJLC*, v. 1, January/March 1944: 63–65.

# 100

## John C. H. Grabill Collection

Photographs of frontier life in Colorado, South Dakota, and Wyoming, late nineteenth century

Prints and Photographs Division

The one hundred and sixty-one photographs sent by John C. H. Grabill to the Library of Congress for copyright protection (1888–91) are thought to be the largest surviving collection of this early Western photographer's work. The photographs document frontier life in Colorado, South Dakota, and Wyoming and include views of hunters, prospectors, cowboys, Chinese immigrants, and U.S. Army personnel as well as cattle and sheep ranches, mining operations, towns, natural landmarks, forts, railroads, mills, stagecoaches, and wagons. A number of the images pertain to Indians and their contact with the white man. According to the information printed on the photographic mounts, Grabill had studios in Deadwood and Lead City, South Dakota, and was "Official photographer of the Black Hills & F. P. [Fort Pierre] R. R. and Home State Mining Co." The photographs retain their original captions and are recorded in the catalog of the Prints and Photographs Division. A shelflist is kept in the division reference file.

*Guide,* Vanderbilt, no. 301.

*Viewpoints,* no. 42, 123–124.

# 101

## Percy Grainger Collection

Percy Grainger's field recordings of English and Danish folk songs, 1900s–1920s

Archive of Folk Song

The Australian composer and pianist Percy Grainger (1882–1961) was among the first collectors to make field recordings of English folksongs. Working in Lincolnshire and Gloucestershire from 1906 to 1909, Grainger recorded versions of "Brigg Fair," "The Old Ewe," and "Rufford Park Poachers" which have no counterparts in other collections, according to Patrick O'Shaughnessy in his article "Percy Grainger: The English Folk-Song Collection," in *Studies in Music* (ML5.S9255), no. 10, 1976, p. 19–24. In 1940 the composer authorized the Library to copy his wax cylinders for preservation on discs in the Archive of Folk Song. A few years later the Danish folksongs and tales recorded in Jutland with Evald Tang Kristensen in the 1920s were also duplicated with Grainger's permission. The ninety-three disc recordings (AFS 4,326–4,412 and 9,576–9,583) are available on tape and listed in a concordance.

# 102

## Graphic Design Collection

Specimens of commercial and ornamental printing, 1875–1925

Prints and Photographs Division

The Graphic Design Collection contains samples of commercial and ornamental printing produced in Europe and America between 1875 and 1925. The advertisements, tradecards, menus, publishers' prospectuses, postage stamps, type specimen books, and other printed items in the collection were chosen as examples of regional and international trends in graphic design and of such printing techniques as chromolithography, embossing, woodblock printing, and offset lithography. This study collection was apparently assembled in Germany in the 1930s and 1940s and was among the confiscated German materials transferred to the Library after World War II. The 5,000 specimens are arranged by country of origin. Of related interest in the division are propaganda materials assembled by the Rehse-Archiv für Zeitgeschichte und Publizistik and received by the Library in the 1940s.

*Guide*, Vanderbilt, no. 266.

# 103

## H. Vose Greenough Collection

Recordings of music performances in the Boston area, mid-twentieth century

Motion Picture, Broadcasting, and Recorded Sound Division

Acoustic consultant H. Vose Greenough, Jr., made recordings of music events in the Boston area for nearly twenty-five years. He recorded, initially on disc and later on tape, performances of the Boston Symphony Orchestra chiefly in the late 1930s and 1940s, the first seasons at Tanglewood, local recitals, and early concerts of E. Power Biggs, some which were issued under the label of Greenough's own company, Technicord Records. In 1977, through his bequest, the Library received his entire collection of 1,021 acetate discs, 793 tapes, and logbooks. The collection is being copied on tape and indexed by date of performance, artist, and composer.

# 104

## Woody Guthrie Collection

Recordings and papers of Woody Guthrie

Archive of Folk Song

Woody Guthrie (1912–1967) was recorded by Alan Lomax for the Archive of Folk Song in 1940, scarcely a month after he first arrived on the East Coast. During these recording sessions Guthrie talked about his life and musical development, the oil boom, the dust bowl, and the migration of the "Okies." He performed a number of songs and played the guitar and harmonica. The original seventeen disc recordings (AFS 3,407–3,423) have been copied on tape and listed in notes and in the catalogs of the Archive of Folk Song. Elektra Records has released a three-record set selected from the Lomax recording sessions. In addition to the recordings, the Archive of Folk Song has its correspondence with Guthrie (1940–50)—these forty items are listed in a finding aid—and three song collections received from him in the 1940s: "War-time Songs," "Alonzo M. Zilch's Own Collection of Original Songs and Ballads," and "Songs of Woody Guthrie."

The original manuscript of "Songs of Woody Guthrie," a collection of 200 songs which Guthrie performed on the radio in the late 1930s, was microfilmed by the Library of Congress under the title "Labor Songs." Guthrie also allowed the Library to reproduce the manuscript of "Book in Progress," an early version of Guthrie's autobiographical novel *Bound For Glory* (1943), and a collection of songs done in collaboration with Pete Seeger and Alan Lomax and later issued as *Hard Hitting Songs for Hard-Hit People* (New York: Oak Publications [1967] 368 p. M1629.L83H4). The microfilms are available in the Music Reading Room.

Reuss, Richard A., "Woody Guthrie and His Folk Tradition, *Journal of American Folklore* (GR1.J8), v. 83, July/September 1970: 283–284, 289, 290–291.

*Woody Guthrie Library of Congress Recordings* (Elektra [1964] 6 s. 12 in. 33⅓ rpm. EKL 271/272).

"A Woody Guthrie Record Discography," *The Little Sandy Review* (ML1.L565), no. 5, 1960: 28–33.

ALONZO M. ZILCH'S

own

COLLECTION

of

Original

SONGS and BALLADS

-------------------------------------------------
Every song in this book is an original
wording of above stated Author and all
persons are warned not to throw nor shoot
at said author under any circumstances
during hours or periods of performance.
All misunderstandings will be handled and
settled out of court by my personal and
secretarial lawyer now residing in Pots-
ville. All songs having non-beneficial
bearings, injurious exposing, etc., on any
person or group of persons will be omitted from book immediately. To which I
have this day set my foot with all my
might and main.

*Alonzo M. Zilch*

Alonzo M. Zilch

*Woody W. Guthrie*

Title page of song collection written by Woody Guthrie in the mid-1930s and
sent to Alan Lomax in 1941. Guthrie's faint note to Lomax (top) explains how
his cousin relocated the typescript. Woody Guthrie Collection, Archive of Folk
Song. Courtesy of Marjorie M. Guthrie. LC–USZ62–67582.

152

# 105

## Joseph S. Hall Collection

Folklore recordings made in the Great Smoky Mountains, late 1930s–late 1960s

Archive of Folk Song

Between 1937 and 1941, with the assistance of Columbia University and the National Park Service, Joseph S. Hall took portable disc recording equipment to remote communities of Tennessee and North Carolina. He studied the speech patterns of people who lived, or had formerly lived, within the boundaries of the Great Smoky Mountains National Park and presented his findings in his doctoral thesis *The Phonetics of Great Smoky Mountain Speech* (1942). Dr. Hall recorded folktales, local history, and descriptions of local customs and of traditional farming, hunting, weaving, and cooking practices as well as songs, ballads, hymns, square dance pieces, and fiddle tunes. In 1958 the Library of Congress duplicated the 161-disc collection for preservation in the Archive of Folk Song (AFS 11,412–11,426). Additional material taped by the folklorist between 1956 and 1967 was copied by the Library in 1969 (AFS 13,710–13,715). Microfilms donated by Dr. Hall reproduce field notes dating from the late 1930s through the 1960s, an inventory of the field recordings, and transcribed texts. The contents of the recordings are listed in notes on file in the Archive of Folk Song. Dr. Hall describes his field techniques in *Mountain Speech in the Great Smokies* ([Washington] U.S. Dept. of the Interior, National Park Service, 1941. 12 p. E160.U624, no. 5).

*Costume design by Lucinda Ballard for the New York revival of* Show Boat *in 1946. The sketch is inscribed to Dorothy Hammerstein. Oscar Hammerstein II Collection, Music Division. LC–USZ62–67583.*

# 106

## Oscar Hammerstein II Collection

Professional papers and sound recordings of Oscar Hammerstein II

Music Division
Motion Picture, Broadcasting, and Recorded Sound Division

Oscar Hammerstein II (1895 1960), grandson of the celebrated opera impresario, wrote the scripts and lyrics for some of the most popular musical comedies of the twentieth century. Among these are *Show Boat* (1927) and *Music in the Air* (1932) with Jerome Kern, and *Oklahoma* (1943), *Carousel* (1945), *South Pacific* (1949), *The King and I* (1951), and *The Sound of Music* (1959) with Richard Rodgers (no. 203). In the 1960s the Library received a large collection of Oscar Hammerstein's papers through the generosity of his widow, Dorothy Hammerstein. The collection relates directly to his musicals and contains scripts, notes, librettos, correspondence, printed music, pictorial material, playbills, press notices, and awards, as well as articles by or about Hammerstein. The productions *South Pacific, Flower Drum Song,* and *The Sound of Music* are particularly well documented. The material is arranged according to format and listed in a brief inventory. The collection measures approximately thirty-eight linear feet.

A few dictaphone belts on which Hammerstein recorded drafts for *The Sound of Music* and *Flower Drum Song* are kept in the Motion Picture, Broadcasting, and Recorded Sound Division. The recordings have been copied on tape and are represented in the division catalog.

Waters, Edward N., "Songs to Symphonies: Recent Acquisitions of the Music Division," *QJLC*, v. 25, January 1968: 86.

———, "Variations on a Theme: Recent Acquisitions of the Music Division," *QJLC*, v. 27, January 1970: 78.

# 107

## Harkness Collection

### Documents relating to colonial Mexico and Peru

Manuscript Division

In 1928 and 1929 Edward Stephen Harkness (1874–1940), American philanthropist, presented to the Library of Congress an important collection of documents from the first 200 years of Spanish rule in Mexico and Peru. The Mexican manuscripts (2,939 folios) fall into four categories. The majority were owned for many years by the descendants of the conquistador Hernando Cortés and pertain to the purported Cortés-Ávila conspiracy to overthrow the government of New Spain (1566) and to the affairs of Cortés and his family between 1525 and 1565. The other Mexican material consists of denunciations and judicial proceedings conducted by the Inquisition during the third quarter of the sixteenth century and miscellaneous manuscripts ranging in date from 1557 to 1609. The Mexican items are described in a published guide and have been reproduced on microfilm.

The Peruvian manuscripts (1,405 folios) are more varied in character. The greater part of the collection is composed of notarial instruments (1531–1618), original documents which were retained by notaries after copies had been sent to Spain. Other manuscripts include royal cédulas (1555–1610), viceregal decrees (1556–1651, 1740) and the minutes and acts of the town councils of Chachapoyas (1538–45) and San Juan de la Frontera de Guamanga (1539–47). Forty-eight documents relating to Francisco Pizarro and his kinsmen and Diego de Almagro and his son, key figures in the Spanish conquest of Peru, have been published with full Spanish texts, translations, and notes. The Peruvian manuscripts are described in a published register and have been reproduced for reference use as enlargement prints. Auxiliary finding aids are available in the Manuscript Division.

Two sixteenth-century manuscript maps donated by Mr. Harkness have been added to the Vellum Chart Collection (no. 252) in the Geography and Map Division.

*ARLC,* 1929, p. 45–46, 134–135.

U.S., Library of Congress, Manuscript Division, *The Harkness Collection in the Library of Congress: Calendar of Spanish Manuscripts Concerning Peru, 1531–1651* (Washington: Govt. Print. Off., 1932. 336 p. Z6621.U58H3).

——, *The Harkness Collection in the Library of Congress: Documents from Early Peru: The Pizarros and the Almagros, 1531–1578* (Washington: Govt. Print. Off., 1936. 253 p. F3442.U58).

——, *The Harkness Collection in the Library of Congress: Manuscripts Concerning Mexico, A Guide* (Washington: Library of Congress, 1974. 315 p. F1231.U54), with translations by J. Benedict Warren.

# 108

## Henry Harrisse Collection

Publications, papers, and maps pertaining to the early exploration of America

Rare Book and Special Collections Division
Geography and Map Division

Perhaps best known for *Bibliotheca Americana Vetustissima* (New York: G. P. Philes, 1866. 519 p. Z1202.H3 1866), a description of over three hundred writings on America published between 1492 and 1551, Henry Harrisse (1829–1910) wrote extensively on Christopher and Ferdinand Columbus, John and Sebastian Cabot, and the early voyages of American exploration. Through his bequest, the Library of Congress acquired in 1915 his personal copies of his publications, complete with marginal comments and interleaved notes. In addition to over two hundred volumes, the collection preserves correspondence pertaining to Harrisse's research, an original letter by Pietro Martire d'Anghiera, and a manuscript (ca. 1533) describing a voyage along the northern coast of South America. Publications are listed in a card file in the Rare Book and Special Collections Division.

The fourteen rare manuscript maps and one view from the Harrisse bequest in the Geography and Map Division include Samuel de Champlain's vellum map of the coast of New England and Nova Scotia (1607) and maps of North and South America (1639) by Joan Vingboons, cartographer of the prince of Nassau. The manuscript items are listed by cartographer in the division card catalog of rare materials and are not maintained as a collection. Harrisse's study collection of 600 photographs, facsimiles, and tracings of early maps is also in the division.

*ARLC,* 1915, p. 31–35.

*G&M Div. Guide,* p. 10–11.

Goff, Frederick R., "Henry Harrisse, Americanist," *Inter-American Review of Bibliography* (Z1007.R4317), v. 3, January/April 1953: 3–10.

# 109

## Hauslab-Liechtenstein Collection

Maps collected by military geographer Franz Ritter von Hauslab

Geography and Map Division

The largest remaining portion of the map collection assembled by the Austro-Hungarian military geographer Feldzeugmeister Franz Ritter von Hauslab (1798–1883) was transferred to the Library of Congress in 1975 from the library of the Air Force Cambridge Research Laboratories (AFCRL) in Bedford, Massachusetts. This collection had been purchased after Hauslab's death by Prince Johann II of Liechtenstein and acquired in the mid-1940s by a New York book dealer along with items from the princely library. Aside from the materials dispersed in the nineteenth century and the rarities sold to Harvard University in 1951, the collection preserves much of the geographer's original cartographic library and reflects his varied interests and activities. Many of the 3,600 maps (9,735 sheets) depict Hauslab's native Austria, Russia, Turkey, the Middle East, Italy, and Germany. Especially numerous are multisheet topographical series from the late eighteenth and early nineteenth centuries, such as the 180-sheet Cassini survey of France (1789), represented in the collection by a hand-colored, uncreased copy. The collection also includes thematic maps pertaining to geology, geodesy, vulcanism, ethnography, linguistics, and military science, several hundred military maps and plans dating from the sixteenth through the nineteenth centuries, city maps and plans, and a few cartographic sketches by Hauslab, Alexander von Humboldt, Karl Ritter, and anonymous draftsmen. The partial title checklist begun by the AFCRL Library may be consulted in the Geography and Map Division.

Of related interest is an album bearing the Hauslab bookplate that was purchased by the Library in 1950 for the collections of the Prints and Photographs Division. The album's 257 copper engravings date from the sixteenth to the early eighteenth centuries and depict battles, cities under attack, and army encampments. Renata Shaw discusses fifty-five of the prints in her article, "Broadsides of the Thirty Years War," in *QJLC*, v. 32, January 1975, p. 2–24.

ITALIA

*Perspective map of Italy, anonymously published about 1850. Franz Ritter von Hauslab introduced a color gradient technique for showing elevations on small- and medium-scale maps and collected examples of relief maps issued by European publishers. Hauslab-Liechtenstein Collection, Geography and Map Division. LC–USZ62–63690.*

Ristow, Walter W., "The Hauslab-Liechtenstein Map Collection," *QJLC,* v. 35, April 1978: 108–138.

# 110

## Hawaiian Imprint Collection

### Hawaiian publications, nineteenth century

Rare Book and Special Collections Division

Among the volumes originally assigned to the Rare Book Room when it was established in 1927 was a group of Hawaiian publications selected from the Library's general collections. The 353 books and pamphlets forming the Hawaiian Imprint Collection consist largely of nineteenth-century government documents, schoolbooks, and religious texts and include some of the earliest works printed in Oahu. From the missionary press of Elisha Loomis, the Islands' first printer, are copies of a sixteen-page anthology of word lists and readings in the Hawaiian language produced in September 1822 and a four-page primer captioned KA BE-A-BA (1824). Roger J. Trienens describes the two texts in *Pioneer Imprints from Fifty States* (Washington: Library of Congress, 1973. 87 p. Z208.T75). Approximately half of the collection is represented in the division's dictionary catalog.

# 111

## Wally Heider Collection

Popular music recordings, mid-twentieth century

Motion Picture, Broadcasting, and Recorded Sound Division

In 1973 Wally Heider, the founder of Wally Heider Recording in Los Angeles, presented to the Library of Congress an important collection of popular music tapes and radio transcription discs. The tapes feature concert and night club performances by famous swing and jazz groups that were recorded under contract by Mr. Heider in the 1950s and 1960s. For the most part, the tapes were made in the western states and remain unpublished. Slightly over half of the radio transcription discs donated by Mr. Heider were originally distributed by the Armed Forces Radio Service (AFRS) between 1943 and 1960 for broadcast on military stations overseas (no. 9). The AFRS recordings include programs of *Command Performance, The Tommy Dorsey Show, The Woody Herman Show, Spotlight Bands,* and other well-known series. The remaining transcription discs in the collection are commercial recordings leased to domestic radio stations on a subscription basis and were unavailable to the general public. The recordings preserve the sounds of many dance bands popular between the mid-1930s and 1950. The approximately nineteen hundred discs and 1,350 tapes are indexed by performer or band following the system used by the donor. In 1970 Mr. Heider published a discography of jazz and pop music issued on sixteen-inch transcription discs.

Hickerson, Joseph C., and James R. Smart, "All That Is Audible: Recent Recorded Sound Acquisitions in the Music Division," *QJLC,* v. 32, January 1975: 53–54, 67–69.

*Page from* Petit solfège illustré *(1893?), a sight-reading text for children illustrated by the French artist Pierre Bonnard. Heineman Foundation Collection, Music Division. Negative in division.*

# 112

## Heineman Foundation Collection

Rare music publications and manuscripts

Music Division

Since 1960 the Heineman Foundation for Research, Educational, Charitable, and Scientific Purposes has assisted the Library of Congress in purchasing rare books and manuscripts for the collections of the Music Division. Established in 1947 by Dannie N. Heineman (1872–1962), head of the international public utilities and engineering firm SOFINA and a noted bibliophile, the foundation actively supports higher education, medical and mathematical research, and special libraries. The foundation's donations have been used to acquire music manuscripts and letters of Franz Liszt, correspondence (1914–40) of the singer John McCormack, autographed compositions by Eugen d'Albert, the early music dictionary *Terminorum Musicae Diffinitorium* (ca. 1494) by Johannes Tinctoris, a copy of the first published libretto of Handel's *Messiah* (1712), and other rarities. Acquisitions are recorded in the division catalog and reported in the *Quarterly Journal*. The Heineman Foundation Collection measures approximately sixteen linear feet. Mr. Heineman's personal collection of books and manuscripts is on deposit at the Pierpont Morgan Library in New York City.

U.S., Library of Congress, Music Division, "Music Treasures Obtained Through the Heineman Foundation," *LCIB*, v. 28, October 30, 1969: 570–571.

# 113

## Victor Herbert Collection

Music and music manuscripts of Victor Herbert

Music Division

The Library's extensive Victor Herbert Collection was formed largely in the 1950s and 1960s through gifts of the composer's daughter, Ella Herbert Bartlett. Victor Herbert (1859–1924), born in Ireland and educated in Germany, came to the United States in 1886 and became famous as a cellist, conductor, and operetta composer. The Herbert Collection in the Music Division contains major music manuscripts from every period of his American career, from *The Captive,* a cantata written in 1891 for the Worcester Festival, to *The Dream Girl,* which was first performed shortly before his death. Included are holographs of the popular operettas *Babes in Toyland* (1903), *Eileen* (1917), *The Enchantress* (1911), *The Lady of the Slipper* (1912), *Naughty Marietta* (1910), *The Only Girl* (1914), *The Princess Pat* (1915), *The Red Mill* (1906), and *Sweethearts* (1913), as well as of orchestral works, the score for the film *The Fall of a Nation* (1916), theater music, choral pieces, compositions for cello, piano, and violin, and arrangements of works by other composers. The collection also embraces orchestral and band parts, published piano-vocal scores, and items from Herbert's personal music library. The collection is arranged according to format and measures approximately fifty-five linear feet. Acquisitions have been reported regularly in the *Quarterly Journal.*

*ARLC,* 1935, p. 134–135.

Waters, Edward, N., "Music," *QJLC,* v. 17, November 1959: 25–26.

# 114

## Jean Hersholt Collections

Early editions of Hans Christian Andersen's writings and his papers; first editions of the writings of Hugh Walpole and Sinclair Lewis and related papers

Rare Book and Special Collections Division

In the early 1950s Mr. and Mrs. Jean Hersholt presented to the Library their collection of Anderseniana, probably the most comprehensive collection in America of first editions, manuscripts, letters, presentation copies, and pictorial material relating to Hans Christian Andersen (1805–1875). The Hersholt Collection, formed by the collectors over a thirty-year period, chronicles Andersen's publications beginning with his first book, *Ungdoms-forsøg* (Youthful Attempts), which was issued in Copenhagen in 1822 under the pseudonym William Christian Walter. Among the first editions in the collection are the six pamphlets published by C. A. Reitsel of Copenhagen between 1835 and 1842 with the title *Eventyr, fortalte for børn* (Fairy Tales Told for Children). These contain the earliest printings of nineteen of the fairy tales, among them "The Emperor's New Clothes" and "Thumbelina." The collection also includes manuscripts of several fairy tales, Andersen's correspondence (1868–74) with his American publisher Horace E. Scudder, volumes inscribed by Andersen, early translations, significant posthumous editions, and works about Andersen. Items in the collection are listed in author/title and shelflist files as well as in a published catalog.

To a lesser degree, Jean Hersholt collected letters, literary manuscripts, and first editions of the writings of two of his friends, Sir Hugh Walpole (1884–1941) and Sinclair Lewis (1885–1951). Walpole is represented by sixty inscribed publications and holograph manuscripts of *The Duchess of Wrexe, The Captives,* and *Wintersmoon.* Twenty-eight of the thirty-two first editions of Sinclair Lewis's works in the collection are inscribed to Hersholt. Of particular interest is Lewis's personal copy of his 1930 Nobel Prize acceptance speech with his numerous revisions. Both collections were donated in the early 1950s and are listed in author/title and shelflist files. Hersholt, who was knighted by King Christian X of Denmark in 1946 for his war relief work, also assembled a small collection of Danish underground publications from World War II. The four collections contain a total of 963 items.

Goff, Frederick R., "The Hersholt Collection of Anderseniana," *QJLC*, v. 9, May 1952: 123–127.

——, "The Hersholt Gift of Works of Hugh Walpole and Sinclair Lewis," *QJLC*, v. 11, August 1954: 195–198.

——, "Rare Books," *QJLC*, v. 10, May 1953: 172–175.

U.S., Library of Congress, *Catalog of the Jean Hersholt Collection of Hans Christian Andersen: Original Manuscripts, Letters, First Editions, Presentation Copies, and Related Materials* (Washington: 1954. 97 p. Z8035.3.U5).

# 115

## John Hills Collection

Maps of British army operations in New Jersey during the
American Revolution

Geography and Map Division

In 1882 the Library of Congress purchased a set of twenty manuscript maps that had been found among the papers of Sir Henry Clinton, commander in chief of the British forces in America between 1778 and 1781. Prepared by military engineer John Hills (fl. 1767–1817), these manuscripts depict British army operations in New Jersey during the American Revolution and comprise the most comprehensive provincial cartographic survey of the period. The maps were originally used as an atlas and include a title page and table of contents. The items are described in the Library's computerized map catalog and have been reproduced in facsimile by Portolan Press. Other maps by Hills are included in the William Faden Collection (no. 74) and the Peter Force Library (no. 81).

Guthorn, Peter J., *John Hills, Assistant Engineer* (Brielle, N.J.: Portolan Press [1976] 85 p. TA533.H54G87).

U.S., Library of Congress, Map Division, *A List of Geographical Atlases in the Library of Congress,* v. 1 (Washington: Govt. Print. Off., 1909. 1208 p. Z6028.U56, v. 1; reprint, Amsterdam: Theatrum Orbis Terrarum, 1971), compiled under the direction of Philip Lee Phillips, no. 1339.

# 116

## John L. Hines Collection

Papers and World War I maps of General Hines

Manuscript Division
Geography and Map Division

In 1945 Gen. John L. Hines (1868–1968) presented to the Library of Congress papers from the period 1881 to 1944. The core of the collection reflects his later military career: his service with the Mexican Punitive Expedition (1916–17) and American Expeditionary Forces (1917–20), his appointment as deputy chief (1922) and chief of staff of the army (1924), and his subsequent commands (1926–32). World War I material consists of training and operations reports, memoranda, orders and intelligence summaries (many with maps attached), unit histories, and related reports; postwar papers pertain largely to the internal affairs of the War Department and legislation affecting the army. The Manuscript Division has compiled a finding aid for the 13,000-item collection.

One hundred eighty-seven maps from the Hines papers were transferred to the Geography and Map Division in 1970. These printed maps relate to Hines's World War I operations on the French and Belgian fronts and bear annotations on troop placement and battery positions. The maps are briefly listed in the division's card catalog of rare materials.

*NUCMC,* 71–1363.

# 117

## Historic American Buildings Survey

Measured drawings, photographs, and data sheets documenting works of American architecture

Prints and Photographs Division

The Historic American Buildings Survey (HABS) is the largest
and most important architectural collection in the Prints and Photographs Division. The survey was begun in 1933 "as a work relief project under the Civil Works Administration, to aid unemployed architects and draftsmen and at the same time to produce a detailed record
of such early American architecture as was in immediate danger of
destruction," stated Leicester B. Holland, chief of the Library's Fine
Arts Division, in 1935. Reaching its peak activity from 1934 to 1935,
the project was discontinued during World War II and resumed in
1957. The project records buildings in all fifty states, the District of
Columbia, Puerto Rico, and the Virgin Islands, and involves the cooperation of the National Park Service, which administers the program,
the American Institute of Architects, which serves in an advisory
capacity, and the Library of Congress, which receives the HABS records and makes them available to the public. To date, the Library has
received documentation in the form of measured drawings, photographs, and typed pages of historical and architectural information for
approximately 13,000 of the 17,000 structures and sites surveyed by
HABS since 1933. The original emphasis of HABS was on individual
monuments of historic and architectural importance. In recent years,
however, the project has also traced the development of historic dis-
tricts and complexes, such as Coral Gables, Florida, and Nantucket,
Massachusetts.

The collection is extensively indexed by location, building type,
and characteristic architectural detail. HABS records are also listed in a
published national catalog, issued in 1941 and updated by a supplement
in 1959, and in a new series of revised state and local catalogs. Complementing the official HABS documents are inventories (HABSI)
compiled by volunteers in the late fifties and early sixties. The complete
set of measured drawings received by the Library between 1933 and
1976 is available on microfilm or electrostatic prints. The records for
individual states can also be purchased. Chadwyck-Healey Ltd. is plan-

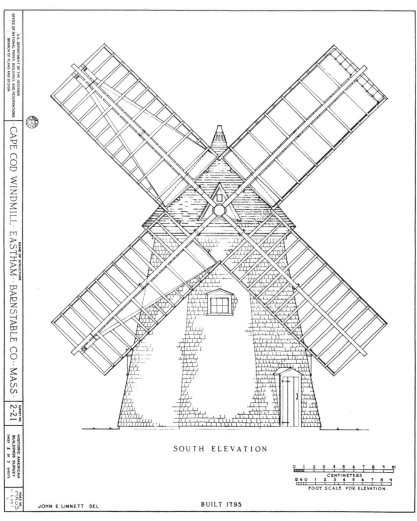

SOUTH ELEVATION

CENTIMETERS

FOOT SCALE FOR ELEVATION

JOHN E LINNETT DEL

BUILT 1793

*Cape Cod windmill, measured architectural drawing by John E. Linnett. Originally built in Plymouth, Massachusetts, in 1793, this octagonal, shingle-covered structure was floated across Massachusetts Bay in the 1820s and moved to Eastham, Barnstable County, in 1850. Historic American Buildings Survey, Prints and Photographs Division. LC–USZ62–67584.*

ning to publish the HABS photographs and data sheets as a microfiche set. C. Ford Peatross discusses HABS and its relation with other research materials in the division in his article, "Architectural Collections in the Library of Congress," in *QJLC*, v. 34, July 1977, p. 249–284; reprinted in *Graphic Sampler* (Washington: Library of Congress, 1979. NE400.-G7), compiled by Renata V. Shaw.

Historic American Buildings Survey, "Documenting a Legacy: 40 Years of the Historic American Buildings Survey," *QJLC*, v. 30, October 1973: 268–294; issued also as an offprint (NA705.H56 1973).

——, *Historic American Buildings Survey: Catalog of the Measured Drawings and Photographs of the Survey in the Library of Congress, March 1, 1941,* 2d ed. ([Washington, Govt. Print. Off., 1941] 470 p. NA707.H45 1941; reprint, New York: B. Franklin, [1971]); and its *Catalog Supplement* comprising additions since March 1, 1941 (Washington: National Park Service, Division of Design and Construction, Historic American Buildings Survey, 1959. 1 v. (unpaged) NA707.H45 1941 Suppl.).

——, "Preservation through Documentation: An Exhibition," *QJLC*, v. 25, October 1968: 272–289; issued also as an offprint (NA705.H56 1968).

# 118

## Historic American Engineering Record

Measured drawings, photographs, and data sheets documenting works of American engineering

Prints and Photographs Division

Through the cooperative effort of the National Park Service, the Library of Congress, and the American Society of Civil Engineers, the Historic American Engineering Record (HAER) was established in 1969 to document significant examples of American engineering. HAER focuses its large-scale research on regional studies which identify engineering landmarks within a limited area, and on industrial studies which isolate structures associated with a specific production or service industry. HAER also documents individual monuments of importance, particularly those threatened by demolition. Like the Historic American Buildings Survey (no. 117), which served as a model for the program, HAER sends its documentary material to the Prints and Photographs Division, where it is organized by location (state, county, city) and recorded in the division's architectural card catalog. To date, the collection contains measured drawings, photographs, and typed pages of historical and technical information for twenty-nine of the over five hundred sites which have been surveyed by HAER since 1969 in the United States and its territories and possessions. The sites are listed in the national HAER catalog published in 1976.

Historic American Engineering Record, *The Historic American Engineering Record Catalog, 1976* (Washington: National Park Service, U.S. Dept. of the Interior [1976] 193 p. T21.H53 1976), compiled by Donald E. Sackheim.

# 119

## Oliver Wendell Holmes Library

Book and print collection of the Holmes family

Rare Book and Special Collections Division
Prints and Photographs Division

The book and print collection of Chief Justice Oliver Wendell Holmes (1841–1935), received through his bequest in 1935, represents the combined libraries of several generations of the Holmes family. In addition to the hundreds of works on jurisprudence, constitutional law, philosophy, history, economics, political science, education, oriental art, science, and bibliography assembled by Justice Holmes, the collection contains the books of Holmes's great-grandfather, the revolutionary war patriot Jonathan Jackson; his grandfather, Judge Charles Jackson; and his paternal grandfather, the Rev. Abiel Holmes, an early collector of Americana. Possibly the most outstanding feature, however, is the American literature collected by Justice Holmes's father, Dr. Oliver Wendell Holmes (1809–1894), author of *The Autocrat of the Breakfast Table*. Noteworthy are presentation volumes inscribed by James Russell Lowell, Henry Wadsworth Longfellow, and Ralph Waldo Emerson and rare nineteenth-century publications, such as *Illustrations of the Athenaeum Gallery of Paintings* (1830) and the New York edition of *Alice's Adventures in Wonderland* (1866) bound with sheets of the suppressed English edition of the previous year. Approximately seventeen hundred volumes from the Holmes Library are housed in the Rare Book and Special Collections Division. As cataloging is completed, the works are recorded in author/title and shelflist card files.

Many of the several hundred European and American prints received through Holmes's bequest have been integrated with the fine print collections of the Prints and Photographs Division and are listed by artist in the division catalog. As yet there is no card index for the 230 Japanese woodcuts from the Holmes bequest.

*ARLC,* 1935, p. 270–274.

Matheson, William, "Recent Acquisitions of the Rare Book Division," *QJLC,* v. 31, July 1974: 170.

# 120

## Theodor Horydczak Collection

### Photographs of the Washington, D.C., area, 1920s–1950s

Prints and Photographs Division

Theodor Horydczak worked as a professional photographer in Washington, D.C., from 1923 to 1959 and became a specialist in architectural and scenic views. In addition to his commercial assignments, Horydczak took less formal photographs showing local neighborhoods, construction work, and scenes of daily life. Horydczak's studio files, presented to the Library in 1973 by the photographer's daughter and son-in-law, Norma and Francis Reeves, record the life and growth of Washington over a forty-year period. The files contain 14,000 black-and-white negatives, 1,500 color transparencies, and 16,300 photoprints. To date, 400 sample prints from the 1920s, 1930s, and 1940s have been filed by subject. Horydczak's logbook provides copyright information and has been microfilmed.

Brannan, Beverly W., "Discovering Theodor Horydczak's Washington," *QJLC*, v. 36, winter 1979: 38–67; reprinted in *A Century of Photographs, 1846–1946, Selected from the Collections of the Library of Congress* (Washington: Library of Congress, 1980. TR6.U62.D572), compiled by Renata V. Shaw.

# 121

## Jedediah Hotchkiss Collection

Papers and Civil War maps of Major Hotchkiss

Geography and Map Division
Manuscript Division

In 1948 an outstanding collection of American Civil War maps was purchased by the Library from Mrs. R. E. Christian, granddaughter of Major Jedediah Hotchkiss (1828–1899), a topographical engineer in the Confederate Army. Working principally in West Virginia and Virginia, areas he had toured during his earlier geological studies, Hotchkiss made detailed battle maps which were used, as annotations demonstrate, by Generals Lee and Jackson in planning their campaigns. He also filled several notebooks with topographic and strategic drawings. Hotchkiss's masterpiece, prepared at the request of Stonewall Jackson and presented to the Library by Mrs. Christian in 1964, shows the offensive and defensive points of the Shenandoah Valley from the Potomac to Lexington, Virginia. Many of the maps were used to compile the definitive *Atlas to Accompany the Official Records of the Union and Confederate Armies* (Washington: Govt. Print. Off., 1891–95. 2 v.). The collection also includes maps made or used by Hotchkiss during his postwar career as a consulting engineer in Staunton, Virginia. The 341 sketchbooks, manuscripts, and annotated printed maps are described in the Hotchkiss catalog compiled by Clara Egli LeGear and will be listed in the second edition of *Civil War Maps* now being prepared by Richard W. Stephenson.

Also acquired through the 1948 purchase were Major Hotchkiss's diaries (1845–99), notebooks, correspondence, and related papers. The greater part of the 27,000-item collection in the Manuscript Division consists of business papers, research files, writings, lectures, and other material dating from after the Civil War. From the war years are diaries and letters including requests for position maps and occasional topographic sketches. Additional papers were acquired in 1958. The papers have been described in a finding aid and microfilmed.

LeGear, Clara Egli, "The Hotchkiss Map Collection," *QJLC,* v. 6, November 1948: 16–20; reprinted as "The Hotchkiss Collection of Confederate Maps" on

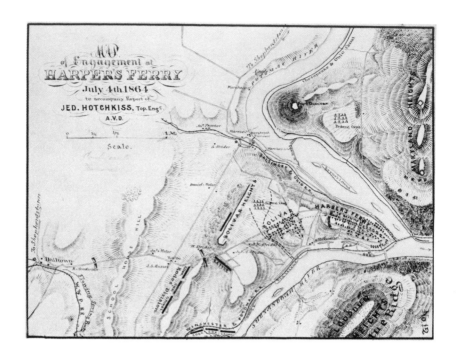

*Engagement at Harper's Ferry, West Virginia, from the manuscript atlas of the Confederate campaign in northern Virginia, 1864 to 1865, prepared by Jedediah Hotchkiss. After testing the strength of the Union forces at Harper's Ferry on July 4, 1864, General Early's Confederates crossed the Potomac at Shepherdstown and advanced to within a few miles of Washington, D.C. Jedediah Hotchkiss Collection, Geography and Map Division. Negative in division.*

p. 183–188 of *A La Carte: Selected Papers on Maps and Atlases* (Washington: Library of Congress, 1972. 232 p. GA231.R5), compiled by Walter W. Ristow.

U.S., Library of Congress, Map Division, *The Hotchkiss Map Collection: A List of Manuscript Maps, Many of the Civil War Period, Prepared by Major Jed. Hotchkiss, and Other Manuscript and Annotated Maps in His Possession* (Washington: 1951. 67 p. Z6027.U5H6; reprint, Falls Church, Va.: Sterling Press, 1977), compiled by Clara Egli LeGear.

Webb, Willard, "The Hotchkiss Papers: An Additional Note," *QJLC,* v. 7, November 1949: 23–24.

# 122

## Harry Houdini Collection

Publications, scrapbooks, and other material relating to spiritualism and magic

Rare Book and Special Collections Division

Harry Houdini (1874–1926), master magician and escape artist, wrote in *A Magician Among the Spirits* (1924) that he had "accumulated one of the largest libraries in the world on psychic phenomena, Spiritualism, magic, witchcraft, demonology, evil spirits, etc., some of the material going back as far as 1489." In 1927, through Houdini's bequest, the Library received 3,988 volumes from his collection. While strongest in nineteenth- and twentieth-century publications on spiritualism—Houdini doubted "if any one in the world has so complete a library on modern Spiritualism"—the Houdini Collection contains a number of magic books inscribed or annotated by well-known magicians. Leonard N. Beck discusses significant items in "Things Magical in the Collections of the Rare Book Division," *QJLC*, v. 31, October 1974, p. 208–234. Also in the collection are prints, playbills, printed ephemera, periodicals, and many volumes of pamphlets on such topics as card tricks, mediums, hypnotism, handcuff escape methods, and chalk-talking. Of special note are over one hundred unannotated scrapbooks containing theater notices and news clippings on subjects of personal interest. Houdini's scrapbooks are currently being microfilmed. Bound volumes are listed in a card file by author or title; periodicals and boxed materials, by title; and scrapbooks, by shelf number. Houdini's theatrical collection was sold after his death to Messmore Kendall and later donated to the University of Texas.

*ARLC*, 1927, p. 29–31.

# 123

## Richard Howe Collection

Maps of the American colonies, 1750s–1770s

Geography and Map Division

In 1905, the Library acquired from the descendants of Adm. Lord Richard Howe (1726–1799) manuscript maps of the North and South American coastline, the West Indies, and the Philippine Islands. The seventy-two maps and charts were produced in the 1750s, 1760s, and 1770s and include items that may have been consulted by Admiral Howe as commander in chief of the British fleet in North America during the first two years of the American Revolution. Map 12, for example, entitled "Sketch of the River Elk, at the Head of Chesapeak Bay," shows the site of British headquarters and the "Landing of the Kings troops" and was apparently drawn in August and September of 1777 by "Mr Hunter, Master of the Eagle." The Howe Collection is recorded in the Library's computerized map catalog and the majority of its items are listed in the 1905 *Annual Report of the Librarian of Congress.*

*ARLC,* 1905, p. 60–61, 189–198.

# 124

## Gardiner Greene Hubbard Collection

### Fine prints

The Library's first major collection of fine prints was donated in 1898 by Mrs. Gardiner Greene Hubbard shortly after the completion of the new Library building. The collection had been assembled by her late husband, Gardiner Greene Hubbard (1822–1897), first president of the National Geographic Society and an important figure in the development of the telephone industry, and included works by Dürer, Rembrandt, Callot, and other major printmakers, historical prints pertaining to Napoleon Bonaparte and Frederick the Great, and numerous portraits. Through her bequest, Mrs. Hubbard provided the Library with a special fund for the purchase of additional prints. A catalog published in 1905 describes the 2,700 items donated by Mrs. Hubbard and includes indexes for engravers, artists, and portrait subjects. In a card file in the Prints and Photographs Division are listed 300 items relating to Napoleon. The collection has been integrated with the division's fine print holdings.

"The Galleries, the Gardiner-Greene-Hubbard Collection," *The Scrip* (N1.S4), v. 3, May 1908: 261–268.

U.S., Library of Congress, Prints and Photographs Division, *Catalog of the Gardiner Greene Hubbard Collection of Engravings, Presented to the Library of Congress by Mrs. Gardiner Greene Hubbard* (Washington: Govt. Print. Off., 1905. xxiii, 517 p. NE53.W3A5), compiled by Arthur Jeffrey Parsons.

# 125

## Arthur W. Hummel Collection

Rare maps of China

Geography and Map Division

Arthur W. Hummel (1884–1975), distinguished sinologist who headed the Orientalia Division of the Library of Congress from 1928 to 1954, was instrumental in forming the Library's collection of rare Chinese maps. The first segment of the Hummel Collection came to the Geography and Map Division in 1930 when Andrew W. Mellon purchased for the Library maps and atlases Dr. Hummel obtained while living in China. On an official procurement mission in 1934, Dr. Hummel acquired additional rare material for the division and in 1962 he donated manuscript maps from his personal collection. The eighty-five printed and manuscript maps and atlases date from the Ming period (1368–1644) through the nineteenth century and include examples showing military defenses, roads, tombs, and navigable coastline as well as general maps of China and its geographical divisions. The maps are presented in several formats: scrolls, wall maps, folded maps, and sets in portfolios. The maps are described in the Library's computerized map catalog. The atlases are listed in the division atlas catalog and reported without collection designation in *A List of Geographical Atlases in the Library of Congress* (Washington: Library of Congress, 1963. lxxii, 681 p. Z6028.U56, v. 6), compiled by Clara Egli LeGear.

*G&M Div. Guide,* p. 31–32.

Ristow, Walter W., and Catherine I. Bahn, "Maps," *QJLC,* v. 19, September 1962: 186.

*Russian outpost in eastern Siberia under attack by Manchu forces. The painting is one of four on a late seventeenth-century scroll map depicting frontier regions held by the Ch'ing emperors at the peak of their military power. Arthur W. Hummel Collection, Geography and Map Division. Negative in division.*

# 126

## Italian Collection

Italian films, 1930s and early 1940s

Motion Picture, Broadcasting, and Recorded Sound Division

Five hundred documentary, newsreel, feature, educational, and propaganda films produced in Italy between 1930 and 1943 were transferred to the Library following World War II. Public Laws 87–846 and 87–861 returned the copyrights to the original owners in 1963 and gave the Library screening privileges and permanent custody of the prints. The Library has untranslated reference prints for most of the 275 Istituto Luce newsreels (1938–43), 100 Luce shorts (1930–43), and several of the forty features (1934–40). All films are recorded by title in the collection shelflist in the Motion Picture, Broadcasting, and Recorded Sound Division. Fact sheets have been compiled for most newsreels.

# 127

## Andrew Jackson Collection

Papers and maps of Andrew Jackson

Manuscript Division
Geography and Map Division

Andrew Jackson (1767–1845) collected his correspondence and official papers long before he became president. Although he took the precaution of designating Francis P. Blair custodian of this material, the Jackson manuscripts were scattered after the president's death. The Library of Congress has painstakingly reconstructed the collection through 100 separate accessions, building upon the important body of correspondence, transcripts, speeches, and orders donated by Blair's grandchildren in 1903. The published index for the Jackson papers prepared by the Manuscript Division traces the provenance of the 26,000-item collection and provides an alphabetical list of writers and recipients of letters. The collection has been microfilmed.

The Geography and Map Division has eleven manuscript maps acquired through the Blair gift that pertain chiefly to General Jackson's operations in the lower Mississippi River Valley and the Gulf Coast during the War of 1812 and his campaign against the Creek Indians (1813–14). One drawing, dated January 28, 1815, shows the American encampment in the New Orleans area. The maps are listed as the Blair Collection in the division card catalog of rare materials.

*NUCMC,* 63–363.

U.S., Library of Congress, Manuscript Division, *Index to the Andrew Jackson Papers* (Washington: 1967. xxvi, 111 p. Z8443.U53).

# 128

## Henry James Collection

Early editions of Henry James's writings

Rare Book and Special Collections Division

In 1922, through the bequest of Mrs. Clarence W. Jones of Brookline, Massachusetts, the Library received a collection devoted to the writings of the American novelist, Henry James (1843–1916). Around this nucleus, the Library formed the Henry James Collection, adding books selected from the general collections and proof pages of several James novels which were deposited for copyright protection. The James Collection in the Rare Book and Special Collections Division contains first English and American editions of James's writings, significant later editions of books he revised, publications to which James contributed prefaces, stories, or essays, and critical studies by James scholars. One of the rarest items in the collection is a dramatization of *Daisy Miller* that was privately printed in 1882. The 132 volumes are represented in the collection card index and the dictionary catalog of the division.

# 129

## Japanese Collection

### Japanese films, 1930s and early 1940s

Motion Picture, Broadcasting, and Recorded Sound Division

The Japanese Collection contains 1,400 motion pictures produced in Japan primarily in the 1930s and early 1940s. Like the confiscated German and Italian films also in the Motion Picture, Broadcasting, and Recorded Sound Division, these motion pictures were transferred to the Library of Congress following World War II. Laws enacted in 1962 returned the foreign copyrights to their original claimants in January 1963 and gave the Library permanent custody of the prints as well as the right to screen and copy them for official use. The collection includes 200 features, 450 newsreels, and 750 educational, documentary, and propaganda shorts, all of which are listed by romanized title in the shelflist. The Library has untranslated reference prints for most films. Descriptive sheets are available for many titles.

# 130

## Thomas Jefferson Library

### Book collection of Thomas Jefferson

#### Rare Book and Special Collections Division

The book collections of the Library of Congress were reestablished, after their destruction in 1814, by the purchase of the private library of Thomas Jefferson (1743–1826). At the time of purchase, Jefferson's collection contained 6,487 volumes in the fields of politics, history, science, law, literature, fine arts, and philosophy and was recognized as one of the finest private libraries in the United States. While several members of Congress objected that the collection "was too philosophical, had too many books in foreign languages, was too costly, and was too large for the wants of Congress," as Librarian of Congress Ainsworth Rand Spofford wrote many years later, the purchase was authorized on January 26, 1815, for the sum of $23,950. The Jefferson Library forms the nucleus around which the present collections of the Library of Congress have been assembled. For nearly a century the subject arrangement that Jefferson developed from Sir Francis Bacon's division of knowledge was used to organize the Library of Congress book collection. Jefferson's statement, "There is, in fact, no subject to which a member of Congress may not have occasion to refer," is still the guiding principle for Library acquisitions.

While many of the Jefferson books were lost in the Library fire of 1851, the remaining volumes have been assembled as a unit in the Rare Book and Special Collections Division. Many books bear Jefferson's ownership markings as well as the original Library of Congress bookplates and classification. The contents of the entire 1815 purchase were reconstructed by E. Millicent Sowerby and described in a five-volume catalog. Shelved with the collection are a small number of books from Jefferson's third and final library which was sold at auction in 1829. The 2,465 Jefferson volumes are represented in an author/title card file.

Goff, Frederick R., "Jefferson, the Book Collector," *QJLC,* v. 29, January 1972: 32–47.

Nothing remains but the landed intereſt; and this in a political view, and particularly in relation to taxes I take to be perfectly united from the wealthieſt landlord to the pooreſt tenant. No tax can be laid on land which will not affect the propietor of millions of acres as well as the proprietor of a ſingle acre. Every land-holder will therefore have a common intereſt to keep the taxes on land as low as poſſible; and common intereſt may always be reckoned upon as the ſureſt bond of ſympathy. But if we even could ſuppoſe a diſtinction of intereſt between the opulent land-holder and the middling farmer, what reaſon is there to conclude that the firſt would ſtand a better chance of being deputed to the national legiſlature than the laſt? If we take fact as our guide, and look into our own ſenate and aſſembly we ſhall find that moderate proprietors of land prevail in both; nor is this leſs the caſe in the ſenate, which conſiſts of a ſmaller number than in the aſſembly, which is com-poſed of a greater number. Where the qualifications of the electors are the ſame, whether they have to chooſe a ſmall or a large number their votes will fall upon thoſe in whom they have moſt confidence; whether theſe happen to be men of large fortunes or of moderate property or of no property at all.

It is ſaid to be neceſſary that all claſſes of citizens ſhould have ſome of their own number in the repreſen-tative body, in order that their feelings and intereſts may be the better underſtood and attended to. But we have ſeen that this will never happen under any arrangement that leaves the votes of the people free. Where this is the caſe, the repreſentative body, with too few exceptions to have any influence on the ſpirit of the government will be compoſed of land-holders, merchants, and men of the learned profeſſions. But where is the danger that the intereſts and feelings of the different claſſes of citizens will not be underſtood or attended to by theſe three deſcriptions of men? Will not the land-holder know and feel whatever will

T. ꝑ.                                        promote

Johnston, William Dawson, *History of the Library of Congress,* v. 1, *1800–1864* (Washington: Gov't. Print. Off., 1904. 535 p. Z733.U57), p. 65–104.

Malone, Dumas, *Thomas Jefferson and the Library of Congress* (Washington: Library of Congress, 1977. 31 p. Z733.U57M27); from the forthcoming v. 6 of *Jefferson and His Time,* by Dumas Malone, to be published by Little, Brown, and Company.

U.S., Library of Congress, Jefferson Collection, *Catalogue of the Library of Thomas Jefferson* (Washington: Library of Congress, 1952–59. 5 v. Z881.U5 1952j), compiled with annotations by E. Millicent Sowerby.

# 131

## Frances Benjamin Johnston Collection

Photographs and papers of Frances Benjamin Johnston

Prints and Photographs Division
Manuscript Division

The Library of Congress is the principal repository of the writings and photographs of Frances Benjamin Johnston (1864–1952), one of the first American women to achieve prominence as a photographer. Trained at the Académie Julian in Paris, she studied photography on her return to Washington, D.C., in 1889 and later opened a studio. Her family's social position gave Miss Johnston access to the First Family and leading Washington political figures and launched her career as a photojournalist and portrait photographer. One of her scoops as a correspondent for the Bain News Service (no. 22) was to board Admiral Dewey's flagship with a letter of introduction from Theodore Roosevelt and interview the "Hero of Manila Bay" en route from the Philippines. Miss Johnston turned to garden and estate photography in the 1910s. She was one of the first contributors to the Library's Pictorial Archives of Early American Architecture (no. 186) and executed a comprehensive survey of southern architecture with the support of the Carnegie Corporation (no. 39).

Through the gifts of the photographer and the purchase of material from her estate, the Prints and Photographs Division has formed an extensive collection of Miss Johnston's documentary assignments and architectural studies. Among the nearly twenty-nine hundred negatives from her early career are her commercial projects on the American world's fairs, coal mining, such minority educational institutions as the Hampton Institute and the Tuskegee Institute, the White House, and Admiral Dewey. Photoprints are being listed in the division catalog as they are processed. The architectural material is kept separately. *A Talent for Detail: The Photographs of Miss Frances Benjamin Johnston, 1889–1910* (New York: Harmony Books [1974] 182 p. TR140.-J64A34 1974), by Pete Daniel and Raymond Smock, is illustrated with photographs from the collection.

Miss Johnston's personal papers in the Manuscript Division span the years 1885 to 1953 and consist primarily of correspondence. Also included are memoranda, articles, notes, the manuscript of her book *Early Architecture of North Carolina* (1941), and miscellaneous material relating to her photography of southern architecture. The division has prepared an unpublished finding aid for the 17,000-item collection.

*Guide,* Vanderbilt, no. 390, 391.

*NUCMC,* 66–1426.

*Cartoon drawing by Fred Packer. Columbia and Victor were the last major companies to settle with James Caesar Petrillo, president of the American Federation of Musicians, in the dispute over the distribution of record royalties in the early 1940s. Jack Kapp Collection, Motion Picture, Broadcasting, and Recorded Sound Division. Negative in Music Division.*

# 132

## Jack Kapp Collection

Cartoon drawings pertaining to the recording industry

Motion Picture, Broadcasting, and Recorded Sound Division

On display in the Motion Picture, Broadcasting, and Recorded Sound Division is the Jack Kapp Collection, a group of over sixty-five original cartoon drawings relating to the history of the recording industry and the phonograph record. Assembled in the 1940s by Jack Kapp (1901–1949), president of Decca Records, the collection was presented to the Library in 1950 by his widow, Mrs. Jack Kapp. The drawings date mostly from the 1930s and 1940s and include works by syndicated cartoonists such as Rube Goldberg and George McManus. Many items are personally inscribed to Jack Kapp. A large number of cartoons satirize James Caesar Petrillo, president of the American Federation of Musicians, who fought the growing use of recorded music in restaurants and on radio. The collection is uncataloged.

*Guide,* Vanderbilt, no. 402.

# 133

## Kern County Survey Collection

Photographs of agriculture and industry in Kern County, California, 1880s

Prints and Photographs Division

One of the last commissions of Carleton E. Watkins (1829–1916), early American landscape photographer, was a series of views of Kern County, California, executed in the late 1880s. As part of an effort to publicize this southern California region and encourage new settlement, local land developers asked Watkins to photograph Kern County agriculture, industry, and resources. In 1929 the Library received 415 original photoprints from the survey by transfer from the Bureau of Reclamation. The photographs depict ranch buildings, livestock, the propagation and processing of fruit and ground crops, methods of irrigation, and antimony mining operations, and include views of Bakersfield, the county seat. Captions provide extensive geographical, historical, and commercial information for each scene and key photographs to the four accompanying maps. The collection is represented in the catalog of the Prints and Photographs Division.

# 134

## Rudyard Kipling Collections

Early editions of Rudyard Kipling's writings; related papers
and research materials

Rare Book and Special Collections Division

Two complementary collections in the Rare Book and Special
Collections Division richly document the life and works of the British
author, Rudyard Kipling (1865–1936). The William Montelle Carpenter Collection, presented to the Library by Mrs. Lucile Russell
Carpenter in 1941, contains autograph manuscripts of Kipling's stories
and poems, original letters, drawings, corrected galley proofs, photographs, magazine articles, and an unusually large collection of early
editions. Among the manuscripts is the earliest known draft of "Mow-
gli's Brothers," the first story of *The Jungle Book,* which Kipling inscribed to Susan Bishop. The collection also includes such items of
associational interest as a copy of *Euclid's Elements* which Kipling
annotated while studying at the United Services College at Westward
Ho, North Devon, and a set of dessert plates on which Kipling painted
fruit and wrote verse. The Carpenters based their biographical sketch,
*Rudyard Kipling, a Friendly Profile* (Chicago: Argus Books, 1942.
72 p. PR4856.C3), on material in their 1,675-item collection. Some
material is described in William Montelle Carpenter's *A Few Significant
and Important Kipling Items!* ([Chicago: Special Book Co., 1930]
53 p. PR4856.C33).

The Kipling collection of Rear Adm. Lloyd H. Chandler, given to
the Library in 1937 and 1938, is known through his publication *A
Summary of the Work of Rudyard Kipling, Including Items Ascribed
to Him* (New York: Grolier Club, 1930. xxvii, 465 p. PR4856.A219).
Chandler secured texts of 846 prose and 1,103 verse pieces written or
attributed to Kipling and annotated them in preparation for a special
edition of Kipling's works. He located items, particularly from Kipling's
years as a journalist in India, that had not been collected previously.
The research materials are arranged alphabetically by title in looseleaf
notebooks, cross-indexed, and accompanied by volumes by Kipling or
Kipling scholars. These two gifts are joined by early editions of Kipling writings (476 volumes) that have been selected from the Library's

general collections. The contents of each collection are listed in card files in the division.

*ARLC,* 1938, p. 348–349; 1941, p. 137–138.

# 135

## George Kleine Collection

Film library and business papers of early film distributor
George Kleine

Motion Picture, Broadcasting, and Recorded Sound Division
Manuscript Division

The personal film library and business papers of George Kleine (1864?–1931) were purchased by the Library in 1947. In 1903, using his optical company in Chicago as a base of operation, Kleine became one of the first American distributors of European films. The Kalem Company, which Kleine founded in 1907 with Samuel Long and Frank J. Marion, gradually acquired exclusive control of the distribution of major English, French, and Italian motion pictures in the United States and Canada. Kleine later became actively involved in the Motion Picture Patents Company and the General Film Company.

The Kleine Collection in the Motion Picture, Broadcasting, and Recorded Sound Division contains comedy, drama, documentary, and educational films, serials, and actuality footage from the period 1898 to 1926. Many of the 456 motion pictures were produced by Thomas A. Edison, Inc., chiefly between 1914 and 1917. Also represented are approximately fifty films produced by the foreign companies Gaumont, Pathé, Cines, and Ambrosio and released by Kleine in the United States. The films are recorded by title in the collection shelflist and will be described and indexed in a published catalog. Reference prints are available for most of the collection. Pressbooks and other printed material relating directly to individual films are kept in the division.

The Kleine papers in the Manuscript Division consist of business correspondence, financial and legal papers, newspaper clippings, printed matter, and related material generated by Kleine's business activities. Papers are most numerous for the period from 1900 to 1930 and cover such topics as Kleine's association with Thomas A. Edison, litigation against the Motion Picture Patents Company, efforts to establish a nontheatrical film distribution system, and Kleine's importing of foreign films. A register for the 26,000-item collection will be published.

*NUCMC*, 79–1795.

U.S., Library of Congress, Motion Picture, Broadcasting, and Recorded Sound Division, *The George Kleine Collection of Early Motion Pictures in the Library of Congress, a Catalog* (Washington: Library of Congress, 1980. PN1998.-A1U57), prepared by Rita Horwitz and Harriet Harrison, with the assistance of Wendy White.

[Register in press]

# 136

## Johann Georg Kohl Collection

Maps and papers of Johann Georg Kohl relating to the early history of America

Geography and Map Division
Manuscript Division

When Johann Georg Kohl (1808–1878) came to the United States in 1854, he brought with him an important collection of facsimile drawings of maps relating to the discovery and exploration of the New World. The product of years of research in European libraries and archives, Kohl's drawings represented the most comprehensive collection of cartographic reproductions existing in America at that time. In 1856 Congress commissioned Kohl to duplicate his drawings for a proposed catalog of early maps of America. These remained in the custody of the Department of State until their transfer to the Library in 1903. A catalog, compiled by Justin Winsor in 1886 and reprinted with an index in 1904, describes 474 Kohl facsimiles now in the Geography and Map Division.

Another of Kohl's American projects, undertaken between 1855 and 1857 at the request of the U.S. Coast Survey, was a monumental study of the early history and exploration of the North American coastline. The twenty-nine-part manuscript included hydrographic and orthographic descriptions, route charts and narrative accounts of expeditions, catalogs of related maps, and bibliographies of historical source material. Some 101 facsimiles of maps of the West Coast and pertinent manuscripts were transferred to the division in 1912 and briefly described in the Lowery catalog. In 1925 the Coast and Geodetic Survey transferred to the Library five portions of the manuscript dealing with the Gulf Stream, the hydrography of the Gulf of Mexico, and harbors of the Atlantic Coast. The collection is partially listed in a card inventory in the Geography and Map Division. Fergus J. Wood discusses Kohl's work in America in his article "J. G. Kohl and the 'Lost Maps' of the American Coast," in *The American Cartographer* (GA101.A49), v. 3, October 1976, p. 107–115.

Other sections of the Kohl manuscript were transferred to the Manuscript Division in 1912: a "Historical List of Names" treating points on the Atlantic Coast from Maine to Long Island; a bibliography on the history of the East Coast from 1519 to 1885; and part of the historical study of the Gulf of Mexico. The Kohl material is listed in the division's master record of manuscript collections and is available on microfilm.

Lowery, Woodbury, *The Lowery Collection: A Descriptive List of Maps of the Spanish Possessions Within the Present Limits of the United States, 1502–1820* (Washington: Govt. Print. Off., 1912. 567 p. Z6027.A5U6), edited with notes by Philip Lee Phillips, p. vii–x.

Winsor, Justin, *The Kohl Collection (Now in the Library of Congress) of Maps Relating to America* (Washington: Govt. Print. Off., 1904. 189 p. Z6027.-A5W8).

# 137

## George Korson Collection

Field recordings of the music of American coal miners, mid-twentieth century

Archive of Folk Song

George Gershon Korson (1899–1967), one of the first collectors and interpreters of American industrial folklore, became interested in the folk culture of Pennsylvania coal miners in 1924 while a reporter for the *Pottsville Republican*. His initial collection of mining songs and ballads appeared in the *United Mine Workers Journal* and was probably the first folklore study to be published in an American trade union periodical. Korson continued as a journalist for eastern newspapers and for the American Red Cross and wrote an influential series of books, pamphlets, and articles drawn from field research. In 1946 Korson collected for the Archive of Folk Song over fifty mining songs, ballads, and fiddle tunes in the anthracite regions of Pennsylvania (AFS 7,978–8,017). In addition, the Library of Congress has duplicated recordings deriving from two of Korson's field studies. The first group (AFS 12,010–12,012) consists of 100 songs and ballads largely from the bituminous coal regions of Appalachia that were gathered for *Coal Dust on the Fiddle: Songs and Stories of the Bituminous Industry* (Philadelphia: University of Pennsylvania Press, 1943. xvi, 460 p. PS508.M5K57; reprint, Hatboro, Pa.: Folklore Associates, 1965) and the second (AFS 11,345) contains songs recorded near Pottsville, Pennsylvania, in preparation for his last book *Black Rock: Mining Folklore of the Pennsylvania Dutch* (Baltimore: Johns Hopkins Press, [1960] 453 p. GR900.K65). Notes and concordances are kept on file in the Archive of Folk Song. Korson has edited two Library of Congress albums based on his field recordings.

George Korson donated his original recordings, field notes, correspondence, manuscripts, and other personal papers to King's College, Wilkes-Barre, Pennsylvania, where they now comprise the George Korson Folklore Archive.

Korson, George, comp., *Songs and Ballads of the Anthracite Miners* (Library of Congress, Music Division, Recording Laboratory [1959]  2 s.  12 in.  33⅓ rpm.  AFS L16).

————, *Songs and Ballads of the Bituminous Miners* (Library of Congress, Music Division, Recording Laboratory [1965]   2 s.   12 in.   33⅓ rpm.   AFS L60).

Lowens, Irving, "Music," *QJLC*, v. 21, January 1964: 47–48.

# 138

## Koussevitzky Archives

Music manuscripts, twentieth century; papers of Natalie, Olga, and Serge Koussevitzky

Music Division

Serge Koussevitzky (1874–1951), conductor of the Boston Symphony from 1924 to 1949, was recognized for his encouragement of contemporary composers and his use of new works in symphony programs. In 1950 he established a permanent endowment at the Library of Congress to commission new musical compositions and continue the annual programming of commissions begun by the original Koussevitzky Foundation formed in Brookline, Massachusetts, in 1942. All original scores commissioned by both foundations as well as a small number of pieces owned or written by the conductor have been brought together at the Library of Congress in the Koussevitzky Archives. This important collection contains manuscripts of nearly 150 twentieth-century composers, some of whom are represented by several works. Included are the compositions listed below.

| | |
|---|---|
| Béla Bartók | *Concerto for Orchestra* |
| Benjamin Britten | *Peter Grimes* |
| Benjamin Britten | *Spring Symphony* |
| Aaron Copland | *Symphony no. 3* |
| George Crumb | *Madrigals* |
| Henri Dutilleux | *Symphony no. 2* |
| Arthur Honneger | *Symphony no. 5* |
| Serge Koussevitzky | *Concerto for Double Bass,* op. 3 |
| Olivier Messiaen | *Turangalîla-symphonie* |
| Darius Milhaud | *David* |
| Douglas Moore | *The Ballad of Baby Doe* |
| Francis Poulenc | *Gloria* |
| Wallingford Riegger | *Concerto for Piano and Woodwind Quintet* |
| Arnold Schoenberg | *A Survivor from Warsaw* |

| William Schuman | *Symphony no. 7* |
| Roger Sessions | *Symphony no. 3* |
| Karlheinz Stockhausen | *Mixtur* |
| Igor Stravinsky | *Ode* |
| Michael Tippett | *King Priam* |
| Heitor Villa-Lobos | *Symphony no. 11* |
| Iannis Xenakis | *Akrata* |

The holographs are individually cataloged. Commissions published by Boosey and Hawkes as of 1966 are listed in the 1967 catalog and subsequent acquisitions have been reported in the *Quarterly Journal*.

In 1978 through the bequest of Olga Naumoff Koussevitzky (1901–1978), who married the conductor in 1947, the Library received the papers of Serge and Olga Koussevitzky and of Natalie Ushkov Koussevitzky (1880–1942), Koussevitzky's first wife. The collection documents Koussevitzky's activities with the Boston Symphony Orchestra, the Berkshire Music Festival, the Berkshire Music Center at Tanglewood (Koussevitzky became its founding director in 1940), and the Koussevitzky Foundations and includes correspondence, financial and business records, concert programs, and other personal papers. Among the important correspondents represented are Samuel Barber, Leonard Bernstein, John Alden Carpenter, Aaron Copland, David Diamond, Vladimir Dukelsky, Lukas Foss, Howard Hanson, Roy Harris, Edward Burlingame Hill, Paul Hindemith, Nicolai Lopatnikoff, Bohuslav Martinů, Darius Milhaud, Nicolas Nabokov, Sergei Prokofiev, Albert Charles Paul Roussel, William Schuman, Igor Stravinsky, and Alexandre Tansman. The collection measures 201 linear feet.

Boosey and Hawkes, Inc., New York, *The Koussevitzky Music Foundations* ([New York: Boosey and Hawkes, 1967] 23 p.).

*NUCMC,* 67–650.

Waters, Edward N., "Music," *QJLC,* v. 9, November 1951: 35–36.

# 139

## Hans P. Kraus Collection

Documents relating to colonial Spanish America

Manuscript Division

In 1969 Hans P. Kraus, New York publisher and rare book dealer, presented to the Library of Congress a collection of 162 manuscripts relating to the history of Spanish America during the colonial period, 1492 to 1819. Focusing on colonial Mexico, the Kraus Collection brings together material on exploration, government, activities of the Inquisition, taxation and economic conditions, relations with the Indians and the French, and the impending loss of land to Anglo-American settlers. From the archives begun by Juan de Zumárraga, first bishop of Mexico, there are royal decrees and related papers dating from 1527 to 1660 that include the signatures of Emperor Charles V, his wife Isabella of Portugal, their children King Philip II and Juana, and Cardinal Garcia de Loaysa. Another set of documents pertains to the sixteenth-century civil administration of the Spanish Indies and throws light on the preparation of the New Laws of 1542 and the career of Bartolomé de Las Casas. The Kraus Collection also contains material on various aspects of the viceregal administration, items concerning the history of Spanish Florida, Tezozomoc's chronicle on the history of the Aztecs, and manuscripts describing the explorations of Amerigo Vespucci, Giovanni da Verrazzano, Alvar Núñez Cabeza de Vaca, Pedro de Ursúa, and Lope de Aguirre. A published catalog complete with name, place, and chronological indexes describes and summarizes documents in the collection. The Kraus Collection has been microfilmed.

*NUCMC,* 70–955.

U.S., Library of Congress, Manuscript Division, "Acquisition Notes," *LCIB,* v. 29, January 22, 1970: 29–31.

——, *Hans P. Kraus Collection of Hispanic American Manuscripts: A Guide* (Washington: Library of Congress, 1974.   187 p.   Z6621.U58K7), by J. Benedict Warren.

——, "Recent Acquisitions of the Manuscript Division: Private Papers of Public Men," *QJLC,* v. 27, October 1970: 349–352.

*Fritz Kreisler's most famous violin, made in 1733 by Giuseppe Guarneri of Cremona, Italy, and embellished with distinctive carving on the tailpiece and pegs. Fritz Kreisler Collection, Music Division. Photograph by David Finclair, courtesy of Jeanne Finclair. LC–USZ62–67586.*

# 140

## Fritz Kreisler Collection

Music manuscripts and papers of violinist Fritz Kreisler

Music Division

In 1955 Fritz Kreisler (1875–1962), one of the most celebrated violinists of the twentieth century, presented to the Library of Congress an extensive collection of his music manuscripts. The holographs include several brilliant pieces such as *Caprice viennois* and *Tambourin chinois* which Kreisler featured at solo recitals, and a number of the famous "classical manuscripts" which had been published as newly discovered works by Vivaldi, Pugnani, and Couperin before Kreisler revealed them to be his own compositions. Additional holographs were donated in 1971 by Eileen Conroy, Anthony Scovasso, and Sylvia Voorhees, the business associates of Kreisler's close friend and publisher Charles Foley. These later gifts have enriched the collection with original compositions by Kreisler; arrangements of works by Debussy, Ravel, and Schubert; and music manuscripts of Elgar, Bruch, and Grechaninov. Of biographical interest are Kreisler's medals, awards, radio scripts, concert itineraries, programs, clippings, photographs, a small amount of correspondence, and printed music (some with handwritten annotations). Many of the music manuscripts are recorded in the catalog of the Music Division. The collection measures four linear feet.

Kreisler's famous Guarneri violin (1733) and the violin he played as a child are kept with the division instrument collections.

Waters, Edward N., "Music," *QJLC*, v. 13, November 1955: 23–24.

——, "Notable Acquisitions of the Music Division," *QJLC*, v. 29, January 1972: 50–51.

# 141

## A. F. R. Lawrence Collection

Speech, popular music, and broadcast recordings, 1920s and 1930s

Motion Picture, Broadcasting, and Recorded Sound Division

A. F. R. Lawrence (1922–1972), the historian who organized the archive of CBS Records and helped found the International Piano Library, formed an outstanding collection of historical speech, radio broadcast, and popular song recordings that included preservation copies of many rare items he had personally rescued from destruction. In 1974 the Library of Congress purchased approximately 2,320 test pressings and 745 instantaneous disc recordings from his estate. Much of the collection consists of music recordings from the 1920s and 1930s. These range from performances and rehearsals of the Philadelphia Orchestra to issued and unissued "takes" by such popular singing stars as Connie Boswell, the Carter Family, Bing Crosby, Cliff Edwards, Annette Hanshaw, and Josh White. Radio broadcasts are represented by commercials probably made between 1926 and 1932 for CBS stations and excerpts from programs featuring Jack Benny, Ed Wynn, and other leading performers. While the greater portion of Dr. Lawrence's historical speech collection was acquired by the New York Public Library, many important published and unpublished items were part of the 1974 purchase, including a number of voice transcriptions of political figures made for the Columbia Graphophone Company series "Nation's Forum." Instantaneous disc recordings have been transcribed on tape and are described in notes on file. A partial list of test pressings is published in the January 1975 issue of the *Quarterly Journal*. Also received through the 1974 purchase were forty-two looseleaf notebooks containing Dr. Lawrence's notes, photocopied record catalogs, and matrix lists.

Hickerson, Joseph C., and James R. Smart, "All That Is Audible: Recent Recorded Sound Acquisitions in the Music Division," *QJLC,* v. 32, January 1975: 54–56, 69–73.

# 142

## George S. Lawrence and Thomas Houseworth Collection

Photographs of California and Nevada, mid-nineteenth century

Prints and Photographs Division

In 1866 Lawrence and Houseworth of San Francisco, "opticians, [and] importers of optical, mathematical, and philosophical instruments, stereoscopic goods, and Jos. Rodgers and Son's celebrated cutlery," issued the third edition of *Gems of California Scenery*. The Library acquired a set of these gold-toned stereographic halves one year after publication. Illustrated are major settlements, boom towns, placer and hydraulic mining operations, shipping and transportation routes, and such points of scenic interest throughout northern California and western Nevada as the Yosemite Valley and the Calaveras Redwoods. The collection includes an extensive pictorial survey of mid-nineteenth-century San Francisco. The captioned stereographic halves have been reproduced as 860 reference prints and are filed by subject. Kept with the stereos is the original Lawrence and Houseworth catalog for *Gems of California Scenery*. The collection is represented in the catalog of the Prints and Photographs Division.

*Guide,* Vanderbilt, no. 437.

# 143

## Lewis and Clark Collection

Maps thought to have belonged to explorer William Clark

Geography and Map Division

In 1925 the Office of Indian Affairs transferred to the Library of Congress thirteen manuscript maps which are thought to have belonged to William Clark (1770–1838), coleader of the Lewis and Clark Expedition. The treasure of the collection is the 37½ by 28¾ - inch manuscript map of the Missouri River Basin that was prepared by Scottish explorer and cartographer James Mackay and carried on the expedition. The remaining items pertain to the regions of official interest to Clark during his years as superintendent of Indian affairs. The maps are listed in the division card catalog of rare materials and discussed in the first two volumes of Carl I. Wheat's *Mapping the Transmississippi West, 1540–1861* (San Francisco: Institute of Historical Cartography, 1957–60. 4 v. GA405.W5).

*ARLC,* 1925, p. 84–86.

# 144

## Charles Martin Tornov Loeffler Collection

Music manuscripts and papers of composer Charles Martin Loeffler

Music Division

Charles Martin Tornov Loeffler (1861–1935), the American composer who shared the position of concertmaster of the Boston Symphony Orchestra with Franz Kneisel for nearly twenty years, is best known for his songs, chamber works, and orchestral poems. Through the gift and bequest of his widow, Elsie Fay Loeffler, the Library received between 1935 and 1938 the composer's papers and the publication and performance rights for his compositions. The Loeffler Collection encompasses correspondence, music holographs, manuscripts for literary works, programs, and news clippings covering the period 1882 to 1935. The holographs, some of which were added by Loeffler's publisher, G. Schirmer, Inc., represent the major portion of his creative work. The music manuscripts are recorded in the catalog of the Music Division and have been reproduced on microfilm. The letters include correspondence with Pablo Casals, Elizabeth Sprague Coolidge, Gabriel Fauré, Isabella Stewart Gardner, Lawrence Gilman, Philip Hale, Edward Burlingame Hill, Vincent d'Indy, Amy Lowell, Pierre Monteux, Henri Rabaud, Carlos Salzedo, John Singer Sargent, and Edgard Varèse. The collection measures six linear feet.

*ARLC,* 1936, p. 140–141.

*NUCMC,* 67–651.

Waters, Edward N., "New Loeffleriana," *QJLC,* v. 1, April/June 1944: 6–14.

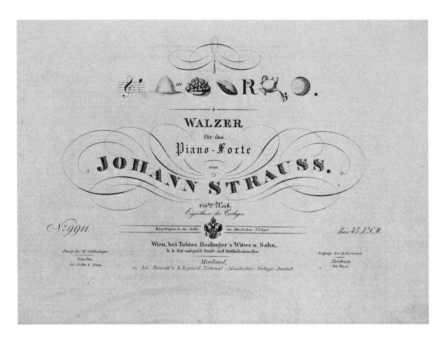

Cover from the piano score of Geheimnisse aus der Wiener-Tanzwelt *(title given in rebus form),* a waltz written by Johann Strauss the elder in 1845. Paul Löwenberg Collection, Music Division. *LC–USZ62–67587.*

# 145

## Paul Löwenberg Collection

Viennese dance music, second half of the nineteenth century

Music Division

The Löwenberg Collection, purchased in 1938, contains first editions of nearly all the works of the Lanner and Strauss families, the nineteenth-century "waltz kings" of Vienna. These rival families produced six composers who excelled in the writing and conducting of dance music: Josef Lanner (1801–1843), August Lanner (1834–1855), Johann Strauss the elder (1804–1849), Johann Strauss the younger (1825–1899), Josef Strauss (1827–1870), and Eduard Strauss (1835–1916). Paul Löwenberg of Vienna assembled the over sixteen hundred published piano scores in the collection and meticulously compiled four volumes of lists and clippings as background information. The unbound sheet music is broken down by composer and type (such as waltzes, polkas, quadrilles, and marches) and filed by title within each category. Löwenberg's indexes list items in the collection by title and opus number. The collection measures four linear feet and has been microfilmed.

*ARLC*, 1938, p. 169–170.

# 146

## Francis Longe Collection

Published theatrical works in English, 1607–1812

Rare Book and Special Collections Division

The Francis Longe Collection, purchased by the Library in 1908, contains early editions of theatrical works published in English between 1607 and 1812. Assembled by the Longe family of Norfolk, England, the collection includes original plays, theatrical adaptations, and translations credited to over six hundred playwrights. The Longe Collection is particularly rich in the works of lesser known seventeenth-century dramatists. The 2,105 plays are bound as a 331-volume set and listed by author or title in a card index. Among the librettos from the Library's collections listed in *Catalogue of Opera Librettos Printed before 1800* (Washington: Govt. Print. Off., 1914. 2 v. ML136.U55C45), prepared by Oscar George Theodore Sonneck, are approximately four hundred works from the Longe Collection. Arrangements are being made to microfilm the collection.

# 147

## *Look* Magazine Collection

Photographs taken for *Look* publications, 1940s to 1971

Prints and Photographs Division

In 1971 Cowles Communications, Inc., presented to the Library of Congress the photographic archives of *Look* magazine. Inspired by reader interest surveys conducted by George Gallup, John and Gardner Cowles planned *Look* as a magazine that would cover a broad variety of topics using interrelated pictures and text. The first issues appeared in 1937. Following World War II, *Look* systematically upgraded its photojournalistic and printing techniques, winning numerous awards for visual excellence and greatly expanding its circulation. By 1971, the magazine's final year of publication, the firm had a huge archive of pictures dating from as early as the 1940s that had been assembled for *Look, Flair, Quick,* and other *Look*-produced publications. The *Look* Collection in the Prints and Photographs Division contains over 3.5 million black-and-white negatives, one million color transparencies, four hundred thousand contact prints, and thirty thousand movie stills. Treated in the collections are innumerable subjects of interest to the American public in the mid-twentieth century, such as sports, movie and television personalities, food, fashion, national politics, and fads. Inquiries are limited to images published in the magazine between 1950 and 1971 which can be located by using annotated copies of the magazine that are housed with the collection and citations found in *The Readers' Guide to Periodical Literature.* A sampling of the photographs in the *Look* Collection appears in *The Look Book* (New York: H. N. Abrams [1975] 397 p. AC5.L84), edited by Leo Rosten. *Look* photographs cannot be reproduced for trade or commercial purposes. Appointments are required to use the collection.

U.S., Library of Congress, Prints and Photographs Division, "Look Magazine Photograph Files Given to LC," *LCIB,* v. 30, December 30, 1971: 733–734.

*Coretta and Martin Luther King at a convention of integration groups. This photograph by James H. Karales originally appeared in the* Look *article, "A Visit with Martin Luther King" (February 12, 1963).* Look Magazine *Collection, Prints and Photographs Division. LC–L9–B32237.*

# 148

## Woodbury Lowery Collection

Woodbury Lowery's maps and papers relating to Spanish colonies in North America

Geography and Map Division
Manuscript Division

In 1907, through the bequest of Woodbury Lowery (1853–1906), Washington patent lawyer and historian, the Library acquired a study collection of 300 original and facsimile maps relating to former Spanish possessions within the United States. Notes compiled by Lowery on 750 manuscript and printed maps in American and European archives were later assembled as a catalog by Philip Lee Phillips. The Library has added copies or reproductions of most of the items described in this bibliography. Seventy-six of the maps dating from 1750 to 1790 are recorded in the Library's computerized map catalog.

The Manuscript Division has eighteen volumes of Lowery's notes and transcripts. Over half the material pertains to the early history of Florida—the subject of the second of the two published volumes of Lowery's *The Spanish Settlements Within-the Present Limits of the United States* (New York: G. P. Putnam's Sons, 1905. 500 p. F314.L91)—and the remainder to New Mexico, California, Texas, and Louisiana. The collection is recorded in the division's master record of manuscript collections.

*Handbook of MSS. in LC*, p. 230.

Lowery, Woodbury, *The Lowery Collection: A Descriptive List of Maps of the Spanish Possessions Within the Present Limits of the United States, 1502–1820* (Washington: Govt. Print. Off., 1912. 567 p. Z6027.A5U6), edited with notes by Philip Lee Phillips.

# 149

## Bascom Lamar Lunsford Collection

Recordings of Appalachian musician Bascom Lamar Lunsford, 1935 and 1949

Archive of Folk Song

Largely through the influence of Robert W. Gordon, the first head of the Archive of Folk Song, Bascom Lamar Lunsford (1882–1973) abandoned his law practice and became a full-time performer and collector of southern Appalachian music. Lunsford participated in folk events throughout the United States, organizing the first Mountain Dance and Folk Festival in Asheville, North Carolina, in 1928. In 1935 Columbia University invited Lunsford to record selections from his personal repertory for its collections. These recordings are discussed by Anne Beard in her master's thesis for Miami University (1959) and have been duplicated for the Archive of Folk Song (AFS 1,778–1,841 and 15,727–15,820). A second major recording session was held at the Library of Congress in 1949. Over a seven-day period Lunsford performed over three hundred songs and ballads. The forty-five instantaneous disc recordings (AFS 9,474–9,518) have been duplicated on tape and are listed in a concordance and in card catalogs. Several ballads from the collection concerning Presidents Lincoln, Garfield, and McKinley have been issued on a Library of Congress recording *Songs and Ballads of American History, and of the Assassination of Presidents* (Library of Congress, Music Division, Recording Laboratory [1952] 2 s. 12 in. 33⅓ rpm. AFS 29). Also in the archive are early field recordings of Lunsford made by Robert W. Gordon (no. 98) and Frank C. Brown (no. 36). A list of these related collections is kept on file.

# 150

## Edward and Marian MacDowell Collection

Music manuscripts, papers, and photographs of composer
Edward MacDowell; papers of his wife Marian MacDowell

Music Division
Manuscript Division

A rich collection of primary source materials relating to the
American composer Edward MacDowell (1861–1908) has been assembled over the years in the Music Division. A purchase in 1972 from
the estate of Nina Maud Richardson, longtime companion of Marian
Nevins MacDowell (1857–1956), brought to the Library what appears
to be the entire corpus of extant letters from MacDowell to his wife.
While ranging in date from 1880 to 1903, most of these 138 letters were
written to Mrs. MacDowell in 1892 and 1893 while she was receiving
medical treatment in Philadelphia. Other MacDowell material in the
division includes 130 letters and eleven holographs donated in 1930
by Templeton Strong (1856–1948), emigré American composer and
student roommate of MacDowell in Germany; 300 photographs by or
relating to MacDowell; correspondence of Mrs. MacDowell pertaining
to musical personalities and the affairs of the MacDowell Colony; an
early self-portrait drawing; and holographs presented by the composer
and his wife. Music holographs are listed in the division card catalog.
Letters are organized by correspondent and many are recorded in inventories on file. The combined collections measure ten linear feet.

The Manuscript Division maintains the greater part of the Marian
MacDowell and Nina Maud Richardson papers acquired in 1972. Most
of the correspondence, writings, clippings, memorabilia, and related
material date from 1908 to 1938 and concern Mrs. MacDowell's activities with the MacDowell Colony in Peterborough, New Hampshire,
which she founded in memory of her husband as a retreat for artists,
writers, and composers. Major correspondents include Hamlin Garland, Edwin Arlington Robinson, and Thornton Wilder. The 2,000-
item collection is described in a finding aid. The records of the Mac-
Dowell Colony in the Manuscript Division, a collection of more than
twenty thousand items acquired in 1969, also include Mrs. MacDowell's
personal correspondence.

*ARLC,* 1930, p. 189–190.

NUCMC, 76–168

U.S., Library of Congress, Manuscript Division, "Recent Acquisition of the Manuscript Division," *QJLC,* v. 30, October 1973: 310–311.

U.S., Library of Congress, Music Division, "Recent Acquisitions of the Music Division," *QJLC,* v. 31, January 1974: 32, 34, 41–42, 63–64.

# 151

## C. P. MacGregor Company Collection

Broadcast recordings and scripts of radio programs distributed by C. P. MacGregor

Motion Picture, Broadcasting, and Recorded Sound Division

The C. P. MacGregor Company had its origins in the San Francisco sound recording studio founded in 1929 by Charles P. MacGregor (1897–1968) and Sigurd A. Sollie. The firm moved to Los Angeles in 1936 and began providing music and dramatic programs to subscribing radio stations. These recordings, like those leased to radio stations by similar services such as World, Langworth, Associated, and Standard, were for broadcast use only and were not sold to the public. In the 1930s and 1940s C. P. MacGregor distributed electrical transcription discs featuring such popular performers as the King Cole Trio, Stan Kenton and his Orchestra, Red Nichols and his Five Pennies, Jimmie Grier and his Orchestra, Peggy Lee, Anita Boyer, and Mel Torme. With the death of Mrs. MacGregor, the company ceased operation, and its sound recordings, scripts, and miscellaneous papers were given to the Library of Congress by Mrs. MacGregor's heirs, Mr. and Mrs. Paul Rice. Included among the over forty-two hundred discs and fifteen hundred tape recordings in the C. P. MacGregor Collection are 1,140 half-hour radio programs of *Heartbeat Theatre* which were donated in 1977. This dramatic series sponsored by the Salvation Army was broadcast weekly from 1956 to 1977 from recordings made in the MacGregor studio. The instantaneous discs have been copied on tape and the collection is currently being indexed.

*Erich Von Stroheim (left) and C. P. MacGregor recording a radio program in the C. P. MacGregor Studios (ca. 1945). C. P. MacGregor Company Collection, Motion Picture, Broadcasting, and Recorded Sound Division. Courtesy of Mr. and Mrs. Paul Rice. LC–USZ62–67588.*

# 152

## *McGuffey Reader* Collection

Rare Book and Special Collections Division

The *McGuffey Readers,* a series of textbooks which fused moral instruction with the teaching of language skills, are credited with revolutionizing elementary school education in the United States. A major collection of *McGuffey Readers* cited in Harvey C. Minnich's *William Holmes McGuffey and his Readers* (New York, Cincinnati: American Book Co [1936] 203 p. PE1117.M23M5) was assembled by M. ude Blair, a Detroit educator. In 1937 Miss Blair donated to the Library 195 different editions of readers, primers, spellers, and the *New Eclectic Speaker,* most of which show signs of classroom use. The Blair gift has been joined with items taken from the Library's general collections and forms the nucleus of the *McGuffey Reader* Collection in the Rare Book and Special Collections Division. The 1938 *Annual Report of the Librarian of Congress* describes the collection as including copies of all the first editions except the *First Reader* (1836) and *McGuffey's Rhetorical Guide* (1841). The 314 volumes are arranged in a numerical sequence based on title and imprint date. Many items donated by Miss Blair are listed in the appendix of Minnich's book and in the published catalog *Children's Books in the Rare Book Division of the Library of Congress* (Totowa, N.J.: Rowman and Littlefield, 1975. 2 v. Z1038.U5U54 1975).

# 153

## Leonora Jackson McKim Collection

Music manuscripts of contemporary chamber works for violin and piano, papers of Leonora Jackson McKim

Music Division

Under her maiden name of Leonora Jackson, Mrs. W. Duncan McKim (1879–1969) achieved international recognition as a concert violinist shortly after the turn of the century. Mrs. McKim donated many items to the music collections of the Library of Congress and, through her bequest, established a fund in the Library for the support of music for violin and piano. The McKim Fund commissions chamber works for violin and piano and arranges for their premieres at the Library of Congress. In order to bring these new compositions to a larger audience, the McKim Fund assists in the publication of recordings of these performances. Holographs acquired through McKim commissions include works by Leslie Bassett, Gordon W. Binkerd, Elliott Carter, Ulysses Simpson Kay, Meyer Kupferman, Ezra Laderman, Benjamin Lees, Ned Rorem, and Elie Siegmeister and are listed in the Music Division catalog. Also received through bequest were Mrs. Mc-Kim's literary works and music compositions, printed music, pictorial material, clippings, and concert programs. The McKim Collection measures twelve linear feet.

U.S., Library of Congress, Music Division, "McKim Fund Established at LC," *LCIB,* v. 29, April 2, 1970: 147–148.

———, "Recent Acquisitions of the Music Division," *QJLC,* v. 31, January 1974: 35.

# 154

## McManus-Young Collection

Publications and pictorial material relating to magic, magical apparatus

Rare Book and Special Collections Division
Prints and Photographs Division

John J. and Hanna M. McManus and Morris N. and Chesley V. Young jointly presented their magic collection to the Library of Congress in 1955. The collectors had become acquainted through their shared interests and together had developed the 20,000-item collection. John McManus, New York attorney and president of Rolls-Royce's American affiliate, and his wife also assembled a collection of magic paraphernalia which they donated to the Ringling Museums in Sarasota, Florida. Since the death of John McManus in 1955, Dr. Young, a New York ophthalmologic surgeon, and his wife have added material to the Library's collection.

The McManus-Young Collection provides a rich survey of the literature of what Dr. Young terms "illusion practices," the magician's manipulation of the imagination of others, and includes works on conjuring, ventriloquism, fortune-telling, spiritualism, witchcraft, gambling, hypnotism, automata, and mind reading. Rare volumes and pamphlets from the collection are kept as a unit in the Rare Book and Special Collections Division. While strongest in nineteenth- and twentieth-century publications, the collection embraces significant older works such as Reginald Scott's *The Discoverie of Witchcraft* (London: 1584), Thomas Ady's *A Candle in the Dark* (London: 1656), and many editions of Henry Dean's *Hocus Pocus*. Also included is an extensive file of explanations of magic tricks, the scrapbooks of mentalist C. A. George Newman, and the famous card-rise box designed by Austrian magician Dr. Johann N. Hofzinser. Leonard N. Beck's article, "Things Magical in the Collections of the Rare Book Division," in *QJLC*, v. 31, October 1974, p. 208–234, describes many McManus-Young items. Most volumes are represented in the author/title and shelflist card files for the collection.

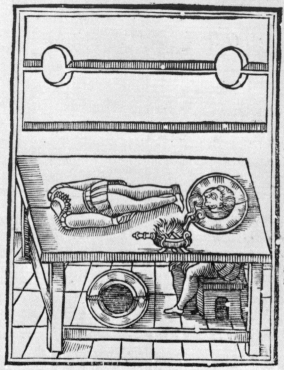

*The "decollation of John Baptist," one of the magic tricks explained in Reginald Scot's* The Discoverie of Witchcraft *(1584). McManus-Young Collection, Rare Book and Special Collections Division.*

Among the pictorial materials from the collection maintained by the Prints and Photographs Division are dust jackets from magic books, portraits of magicians, carnival photographs, Houdiniana, and miscellaneous printed ephemera. Aside from the theater advertisements which are kept with the posters, the McManus-Young itms are described in the division catalog.

Young, Morris N., "The Art and Craft of Magic: An Exhibit in the Library of Congress, Washington, D.C.," *The Linking Ring* (GV1541.L5), v. 37, March 1957: 41–53.

# 155

## Sheikh Maḥmūd al-Imām al-Manṣūrī Collection

Arabic books and manuscripts pertaining to Islamic studies

Near East Section, African and Middle Eastern Division

In 1945 the Library purchased a collection of Arabic manuscripts and printed books from Sheikh Maḥmūd al-Imām al-Manṣūrī, professor of religion at al-Azhar University in Cairo. Assembled by the collector from sources in the Middle East, Africa, and Europe, the collection deals with virtually every aspect of Islamic studies and includes commentaries, biographies, dictionaries, and works of religious law, literature, and philosophy. Of particular interest among the 1,400 manuscripts are ten works by the Syrian scholar, 'Abd al-Ghanī al-Nābulusī (1641–1731). One text, transcribed by the scholar's grandson, is thought to be unique. The manuscripts and 3,600 printed books are shelved in their original numerical sequence and recorded in a photographic reproduction of the collection inventory. Manuscripts are also listed by author in a separate bound catalog.

# 156

## Alfred Marie Collection

Drawings (copies) of French Renaissance and baroque architecture

Prints and Photographs Division

In 1951 the Library of Congress acquired much of the study collection of Alfred Marie, prominent authority on French Renaissance and baroque architecture. Bringing together copies of documents scattered in various French archives, the collection consists of tracings of architectural drawings, garden plans, and theatrical designs, and typed transcripts of contemporary accounts and archival records. Most of the material relates to topics discussed in Marie's publications: the gardens, pavilions, and apartments of Versailles; the palaces of Marly-le-Roi and Saint-Germain-en-Laye and related royal building projects; and seventeenth- and eighteenth-century garden design. The 2,800 items are filed by monument and, in some cases, by architectural type. Inventories in each file indicate the provenance of the original records. The collection is recorded in the catalog of the Prints and Photographs Division.

*Guide,* Vanderbilt, no. 480.

# 157

## Matson Photo Service Collection

### Photographs of the Middle East, 1896–1946

Prints and Photographs Division

G. Eric Matson (1888–1977) and his family joined the American Colony in Jerusalem in 1896. This religious commune operated a large photo department which in 1934 became the Matson Photo Service, owned and managed by Mr. Matson and his wife Edith. The Matson Photo Service Collection, the gift of Mr. and Mrs. Matson in 1966, embraces the photo files of both operations. Covering the years 1896 to 1946, the photographs illustrate the dramatic changes that occurred in the Middle East during World War I and the following mandate period. The collection includes black-and-white series devoted to the ceremonies of various religious sects, Zionist activities and colonies, natural resources of Palestine, archaeological expeditions, and the locust plagues of 1915 and 1930, as well as two pioneering color projects executed by Mr. Matson for the National Geographic Society in the 1930s. The 20,000 negatives fall into three categories. Approximately five thousand negatives (1900–34) have been reproduced as reference prints and mounted in albums (Arno Press has published a facsimile edition of the albums). The prints are represented in the card catalog of the Prints and Photographs Division and the published Matson Photo Service catalog. Eight thousand unprinted negatives from the period 1934 to 1946 are listed in a manuscript catalog. The remaining 7,000 negatives, most of which are either duplicates or water-damaged, were retrieved from East Jerusalem in 1970 and are not yet cataloged. The three bound catalogs of the collection have been microfilmed.

Hobart, George S., "The Matson Collection: A Half Century of Photography in the Middle East," *QJLC*, v. 30, January 1973: 19–43; reprinted in *A Century of Photographs, 1846–1946, Selected from the Collections of the Library of Congress* (Washington: Library of Congress, 1980. TR6.U62.D572), compiled by Renata V. Shaw.

Matson, G. Eric, *The Middle East in Pictures: a Photographic History, 1898–1934* (New York: Arno Press, 1979. 4 v. DS44.5.M37 1979).

# 158

## *Meet the Press* Collection

Recordings, videotapes, and films of *Meet the Press;* papers
of its producer Lawrence E. Spivak; and related pictorial
material

Manuscript Division
Motion Picture, Broadcasting, and Recorded Sound Division
Prints and Photographs Division

*Meet the Press,* begun in 1945 by Martha Rountree and Lawrence
E. Spivak as a joint venture of the Mutual network and *American
Mercury* magazine, introduced a new kind of public affairs program
to American radio. The show brought controversial figures such
as John L. Lewis and Fiorello La Guardia to face the questions
of a panel of journalists. The series soon became a newsmaker in its
own right and was covered by the major wire services. *Meet the Press*
moved to television in the late 1940s and has continued providing a
national forum for political discussion for the past three decades.

Since 1965 Lawrence E. Spivak, the program's producer and permanent panelist, and the National Broadcasting Company have donated
to the Library ongoing *Meet the Press* documentation. The greater
part of the Lawrence E. Spivak papers in the Manuscript Division
relates to *Meet the Press* and *American Mercury* magazine, published
by Spivak between 1939 and 1950. *Meet the Press* documentation
includes letters from viewers typifying audience reaction to telecasts
(1956–75), autographs of various newsworthy individuals, transcripts
of radio and television broadcasts, scrapbooks, news clippings, and
lists of participants. The Spivak papers totaled 63,800 items in 1979 and
are described in an unpublished finding aid.

The Motion Picture, Broadcasting, and Recorded Sound Division
maintains *Meet the Press* programs, beginning with its first year on
radio (1945), and continues to receive audio tapes, kinescope negatives
or prints, and videotapes of the television programs (1949–present).
Viewing prints of approximately one hundred shows are available.
Material is indexed by broadcast date and guest. The division reference

collection includes a copy of the *Meet the Press* transcripts (1957–71) and the guest roster (1956–71) published by the Kraus Reprint Company in 1973.

Seven hundred photographs and cartoon drawings relating to *Meet the Press* programs from the years 1945 to 1970 have been transferred to the Prints and Photographs Division and recorded in the division catalog.

*NUCMC,* 74–1074.

# 159

## Dayton C. Miller Flute Collection

Flutes and books, manuscripts, music, and pictorial material
relating to the flute's history and performance

Music Division

The Dayton C. Miller Flute Collection is one of the world's most
extensive collections devoted to the history and performance of a single
instrument. Dayton Clarence Miller (1866–1941), professor of physics
at the Case School of Applied Science in Cleveland and a leading
authority on acoustics, was an accomplished amateur flutist and used
the instrument in many of his experiments. To further his studies, he
assembled material relating to the historical development of the flute
and flute playing. In 1941, through Dr. Miller's bequest, the Library of
Congress received his entire collection. The Miller Collection is actually
several collections in one. With 1,500 flutes and related instruments of
all types, ancient and modern, occidental and oriental, it is an unparalleled collection for studying the technical development of the
flute in the work of such leading instrument makers as Theobald Böhm
and H. F. Meyer. Dr. Miller's 3,000-volume library contains virtually
every publication on the flute and flute playing issued between 1488
and 1940 and it was the basis of his authoritative bibliography. Other
flute-related material accumulated by Dr. Miller includes printed music
(approximately four thousand titles): portraits and autographs of
flutists and composers of flute music; concert programs; clippings,
pamphlets, and articles; patent specifications; prints and photographs;
sales catalogs and price lists; and eight file drawers of correspondence
with musicians, dealers, and instrument makers. The instruments are
described in a published checklist which is indexed by type, maker,
trade name, and country of origin. The books are treated in Dr. Miller's bibliography. The collection's woodwind instructional books
(tutors) published before 1830 as well as those in the general collections
of the Music Division have been microfilmed and are available as a
seventeen-reel set, complete with index. Dr. Miller's card files list
many of the manuscripts and prints in the collection. Appointments
are required to study the instruments.

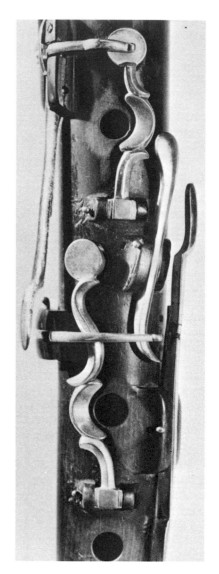

Engraved ivory, eighteenth-century sopranino recorder in F, anonymous. Dayton C. Miller Flute Collection, Music Division. Negative in division.

Detail of boxwood flute in C by Pentenrieder (Munich, 1837–47). Miller described this ten-key flute as having "unique keys equivalent to eight keys with several extra touch-pieces and cross G-sharp." Dayton C. Miller Flute Collection, Music Division. Negative in division.

Miller, Dayton C., *Catalogue of Books and Literary Material Relating to the Flute and Other Musical Instruments* (Cleveland: Priv. Print., 1935. 120 p. ML128.F7M44).

Shorey, David, "Dayton C. Miller Collection," *The National Flute Association Newsletter*, v. 2, August 1977: 13.

U.S., Library of Congress, Music Division, *The Dayton C. Miller Flute Collection: A Checklist of the Instruments* (Washington: Library of Congress, 1961. 115 p. ML128.W5U5), compiled by Laura E. Gilliam and William Lichtenwanger.

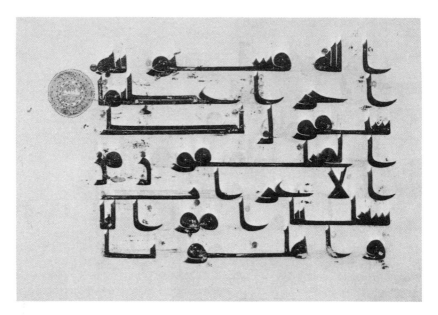

*Tenth-century vellum manuscript leaf from the eastern Mediterranean. This passage from the Koran is written in Kufic, an early Arabic script that was gradually replaced by more rounded, cursive styles. Kirkor Minassian Collection, Near East Section, African and Middle Eastern Division. LC–USZ62–67593.*

# 160

## Kirkor Minassian Collection

Islamic bookbindings, manuscripts, and related material

Near East Section, African and Middle Eastern Division
Rare Book and Special Collections Division

In the late 1920s and the 1930s the Library acquired from Kirkor Minassian (1874?–1944), New York art dealer and authority on Near Eastern manuscripts, over two hundred items relating to the development of writing and the book arts in the Middle East. The Minassian Collection encompasses Islamic and Armenian manuscripts, Islamic bookbindings, textiles, leaves of calligraphy, cuneiform tablets, and related material gathered by the collector in the Near East, Persia, Afghanistan, and India. The approximately seventy calligraphy samples are written chiefly in North African, old Turkish, Persian, and Kufic script and date from the tenth through the nineteenth centuries. The twenty Persian illuminations, by and large, illustrate scenes from the *Shāhnāmah* (Book of the Kings). Most of the ceramic and metal objects are decorated with writing. The majority of the collection is kept in the Near East Section.

Seventy-one Islamic bookbindings donated by Minassian, including one rare fourteenth-century example, are presently housed in the Rare Book and Special Collections Division. Most of these Turkish- and Persian-style bindings appear to date from the seventeenth and eighteenth centuries. No finding aids have been prepared for the collection.

*ARLC*, 1929, p. 32, 64; 1937, p. 27–28.

Selim, George Dimitri, "Arabic Calligraphy in the Library of Congress," *QJLC*, v. 36, spring 1979: 140–177.

# 161

## James T. Mitchell Collection

American book illustrations and portrait prints, 1770–1840s

Prints and Photographs Division

The Mitchell Collection in the Prints and Photographs Division contains American book illustrations and portraits from the late eighteenth and early nineteenth centuries. Ranging from technical diagrams to genre scenes, these 4,000 small-scale prints were apparently acquired by the Library in 1921 and were part of the collection assembled by James T. Mitchell (1834–1915), justice of the supreme court of Pennsylvania, to illustrate the techniques and styles of early American engraving. Many American printmakers active between the 1770s and 1840s—William Ralph, Benjamin Tanner, and Cornelius Tiebout, among others—are represented by examples of their work. The prints are filed alphabetically by artist. The collection was formerly identified as the Stauffer Collection.

# 162

## William ("Billy") Mitchell Collection

Papers and photographs of General Mitchell

Manuscript Division
Prints and Photographs Division

The papers of Gen. William ("Billy") Mitchell (1879–1936) were presented to the Library in 1949 by his widow, Mrs. Thomas Bolling Byrd, and two children, William Mitchell, Jr., and Mrs. Kenneth N. Gilpin, Jr., and supplemented by additional material given in 1960 by his sister, Mrs. Martin Fladoes. Spanning the period 1888 to 1946, the papers include correspondence, diaries, clippings, reports, and notes and form a comprehensive record of General Mitchell's military career and the early days of American aviation. Of particular interest are transcripts of General Mitchell's testimony before congressional committees, material relating to his court-martial (1925–26), correspondence with Franklin D. Roosevelt (1932–33), and typescripts of his books on aviation in World War I, the strategic importance of Alaska, and the Pacific as a probable arena for a second world war. The Manuscript Division has prepared an unpublished finding aid for the 20,000-item collection.

The photographs in the Prints and Photographs Division document roughly the same period as Mitchell's papers. The collection illustrates the history of U.S. Army aviation from its infancy as the Aeronautical Division of the Army Signal Corps (1907) through the formation of the Army Air Service (1918) and the Army Air Corps (1926). General Mitchell, who began his army career as a Signal Corps photographer, took many of the nearly forty-eight hundred photographs himself during tours of duty in the Philippines (1898–99), Alaska (1901–3), China, Korea, and Manchuria (1919–24), and during disaster relief operations after the San Francisco earthquake and fire (1906). The majority of the photographs are captioned, mounted in albums, and recorded in the division catalog.

*Guide,* Vanderbilt, no. 506.

*NUCMC,* 59–154.

U.S., Library of Congress, Aeronautics Division, "Aeronautics," *QJLC,* v. 6, August 1949: 39–43.

# 163

## *Modern Music* Archives

Business papers of the periodical *Modern Music,* 1924–46

Music Division

The business papers of *Modern Music,* a journal that championed the cause of contemporary music, were presented to the Library in 1975 by its editor Mrs. Mell Daniel, formerly Minna Lederman. *Modern Music* was published quarterly by the League of Composers of New York City from 1924 to 1946, initially under the title *The League of Composers' Review.* The archives contain business correspondence, typescripts of articles, photographs, two scrapbooks, a few original drawings of composers, and a significant number of letters (some present in photocopies) by George Antheil, Theodore Chanler, Aaron Copland, Frederick Jacobi, Lincoln Kirstein, and Lazare Saminsky. Of particular interest is an article by Bertolt Brecht entitled "The Usage of Music in the Epic Theatre," which was written for the journal and not printed. A list of correspondents and an introductory essay by Mrs. Daniel are kept with the collection. The *Modern Music* Archives measure four linear feet.

*NUCMC,* 78–392.

U.S., Library of Congress, Music Division, "15th Festival of Chamber Music Set for October 30–November 1: Gift of *Modern Music* Archives Announced," *LCIB,* v. 34. September 5, 1975: 349, 352.

# 164

## Ferdinand ("Jelly Roll") Morton Collection

Recordings of jazz musician Jelly Roll Morton, 1938

Archive of Folk Song

In a series of recording sessions begun at the Library of Congress in May 1938, Ferdinand ("Jelly Roll") Morton (1885–1941) unfolded to Alan Lomax his life story and his thoughts on the origins and development of jazz. His monolog focused on his early years in New Orleans before the formation of his Red Hot Peppers band in Chicago and his move to New York City. Jelly Roll Morton played the piano while he talked, breaking the narrative to perform versions of many of his famous compositions: "Original Jelly Roll Blues," "Kansas City Stomp," "Wolverine Blues," "The Pearls," and "State and Madison." The original fifty-four disc recordings (AFS 1,638–1,688 and 2,487–2,489) have been duplicated on tape and listed in a concordance. Some of the typed transcriptions of the sessions have been microfilmed. Alan Lomax used information from the Library's recordings for his biography *Mister Jelly Roll: The Fortunes of Jelly Roll Morton, New Orleans Creole and "Inventor of Jazz"* (New York: Duell, Sloan, and Pearce [1950] xvii, 318 p. ML410.M821.6), which has been reprinted by various publishers. Abridged versions of the Library's recordings have been published as 78-rpm discs by Circle Sound Studio and reissued by Riverside Records.

*Jelly Roll Morton: The Library of Congress Recordings* (Riverside [1957] 24 s. 12 in. 33⅓ rpm. RLP 9001–9012).

*The Saga of Mr. Jelly Lord* (Circle Sound Studio [1947?] 90 s. 12 in. 78 rpm).

# 165

## Daniel Murray Pamphlet Collection

Pamphlets on Afro-American history, 1850–1920

Rare Book and Special Collections Division

One of the official duties of Daniel Murray (1852–1925), a Library of Congress employee from 1871 to 1923, was to "secure a copy of every book and pamphlet, in existence, by a Negro author" for the Exhibit of Negro Authorship at the 1900 Paris Exposition. These volumes were returned to the Library and formed the nucleus of the "Library of Congress Collection of Books by Colored Authors." In 1926, through Murray's bequest, the Library received 1,448 books and pamphlets Murray had privately assembled for his projected "Historical and Biographical Encyclopedia of the Colored Race"; these were added to the Colored Author Collection. While the Colored Author Collection has been integrated with the Library's general collections (duplicates were transferred to Howard University in Washington, D.C.), 384 pamphlets from Murray's library have been retained as a unit in the Rare Book and Special Collections Division. These bound pamphlets were issued between 1850 and 1920 and pertain chiefly to slavery and the abolitionist movement. The pamphlets are recorded in a shelflist. The division also has card files listing the Murray volumes added to the general collections and material sent to Howard University.

U.S., Library of Congress, "American Blacks Collection Cataloged and Indexed," *LCIB,* v. 33, January 18, 1974: 13–15.

# 166

## Music Cover Collection

Illustrations from printed sheet music, 1830s–1870s

Prints and Photographs Division

The Prints and Photographs Division maintains a collection of 1,400 American music covers produced from the 1830s through the 1870s. Like the manufacturers of luxury goods, popular sheet music publishers found that illustrations enhanced the appeal of their product and became one of the principal users of commercial lithography during the mid-nineteenth century. The Music Cover Collection, bringing together materials acquired through copyright deposit and gift, includes designs by George Loring Brown, Benjamin Champney, Frederick Grain, William Keesey Hewitt, Winslow Homer, David Claypoole Johnston, Fitz Hugh Lane, and other well-known artists employed by American lithographic firms. Depicted are innumerable subjects of interest to contemporaries such as historical events, fashions, educational institutions, ships, railroads, theater personalities, exotic places, and sentimental scenes. For the most part, the illustrations are detached from the music and arranged by subject. The collection is represented in the division catalog. Nineteenth-century sheet music, complete with covers, can be consulted in the Music Division.

Parker, Alice Lee, and others, "Prints and Photographs Division," *QJLC*, v. 19, December 1961: 51–55.

# 167

## NBC Radio Collection

Broadcast recordings of NBC radio programs, 1933–70

Motion Picture, Broadcasting, and Recorded Sound Division

The NBC Radio Collection, deposited at the Library through an agreement with the Museum of Broadcasting and the National Broadcasting Company in September 1978, is one of the largest single collections of broadcast recordings in the United States. Documenting the broadcasting efforts of NBC from its earliest days through the advent and domination of television, the collection preserves a large percentage of NBC radio programs from the years 1933 to 1970 and is thought to contain a total of approximately 175,000 radio transcription discs (over 80,000 hours of programming). Included are 7,500 to 8,000 hours of war-related broadcasts from the World War II period; more than three hundred Metropolitan Opera broadcasts; most of the concerts and rehearsals of the NBC Symphony Orchestra; many recordings from the Salzburg Music Festival; speeches broadcast by presidents and national political figures; comedy and variety programs featuring Fred Allen, Amos and Andy, Jack Benny, Burns and Allen, Eddie Cantor, Bob Hope, Will Rogers, and other leading entertainers; and detailed news coverage of such events as the national political conventions (1936–48), the 1939 World's Fair, the Olympic Games, and the founding of the United Nations. This rich and varied collection will be cataloged and made available for research as the discs are copied on tape.

# 168

## National Association for the Advancement of Colored People Collection

Noncurrent records and photographs of the NAACP

Manuscript Division
Prints and Photographs Division

Since 1964 the National Association for the Advancement of Colored People (NAACP) has donated its noncurrent records to the Library of Congress. Numbering over 2.5 million items, the records consist of correspondence, clippings, legal briefs, trial transcripts, speeches, articles, memoranda, resolutions, reports, and other printed and manuscript material which provide detailed documentation of the association's growth and activities, particularly after 1919. The greater portion of the collection in the Manuscript Division is arranged in general office, administrative, financial, legal, crisis, youth, and branch files. Among the many topics of concern are discrimination and segregation in business, government, and education; lynchings and the association's antilynching campaign; mob violence; race riots; suppression of the black vote in the South; labor disputes; the association's efforts to assist government agencies in combating discrimination in World War II; and problems of returning World War II veterans. While focused on the welfare of black Americans in the United States, the records include files dealing with Haiti, the Virgin Islands, and the Pan-African Congress. Represented are correspondence by four of the five founders of the association, Mary White Ovington, Charles E. Russell, Oswald Garrison Villard, and William English Walling; papers of James Weldon Johnson and Walter White, the executive secretaries during the 1920s and 1930s; letters from literary figures associated with the Harlem Renaissance; records of the Scottsboro Defense Committee; and material related to W. E. B. Du Bois, A. Philip Randolph, and Paul Robeson. Also included are correspondence and memoranda by various staff members such as Robert Bagnall, Charles Houston, Addie Hunton, Daisy Lampkin, Thurgood Marshall, E. Frederic Morrow, Roy Nash, William Pickens, Herbert Seligmann, John R. Shillady, Arthur and Joel Spingarn, Moorfield Storey, and Roy Wilkins. Records dating from 1909 to 1970 are described in finding aids, and additions to the collection are anticipated. The use of material from the last thirty years is restricted. The NAACP records together with the over five hundred thousand-item collection of National Urban League records make up part of the division's growing resources for the study of black history.

As the NAACP records are processed, pictorial material is transferred to the Prints and Photographs Division. As of September 1978 the Prints and Photographs Division had received approximately five hundred black-and-white photographs produced before 1940. The majority portray staff members or events of interest to the NAACP. Many images relate to the association's antilynching campaign. The photographs are arranged by subject.

McDonough, John, "Manuscript Resources for the Study of Negro Life and History," *QJLC,* v. 26, July 1969: 126–129.

*NUCMC,* 68–2057.

U.S., Library of Congress, Manuscript Division, *The National Association for the Advancement of Colored People: A Register of Its Records in the Library of Congress,* v. 1, 1909–1939 (Washington: Library of Congress, 1972. 99 p. CD3065.N37U5. v. 1).

# 169

## National Child Labor Committee Collection

Records and photographs of the National Child Labor
Committee, 1904–53

Manuscript Division
Prints and Photographs Division

In 1954, to commemorate its fiftieth anniversary, the National
Child Labor Committee presented to the Library official records, correspondence, speeches, reports, press releases, and clippings from the
period 1904 to 1953. The collection includes field notes and unpublished studies on child labor conditions in various industries, sixty
scrapbooks documenting the organization's campaign for child welfare
legislation, minutes of the meetings of the board of trustees (1904–45)
and of the National Aid to Education Committee (1916–18), and
proceedings of the annual conferences (1905–16). The records are
supplemented by correspondence (forty-eight items) of Dr. Alexander
J. McKelway, secretary for the southern states of the committee, which
was given to the Library in 1947. The Manuscript Division has prepared an unpublished finding aid for the 2,800-item collection.

Housed in the Prints and Photographs Division are approximately
five thousand photographs and 350 original glass negatives taken by
Lewis Hine (1874–1940) for the National Child Labor Committee
which were also part of the 1954 gift. Between 1908 and 1924, Hine
investigated the industrial exploitation of children in American mills,
glass factories, mines, canneries, agriculture, street trades, and tenement
sweatshops. Many of Hine's images document the problems faced by
immigrant children in the United States. Photographs in the collection,
many of which were reproduced in the committee's publications, are
grouped in albums by type of employment and keyed to the original
caption files. The captions incorporate Hine's careful notes and often
record the subject's age, name, and work duties and the place and
date of the photograph. Some of the images are reproduced in Judith
M. Gutman's *Lewis W. Hine and the American Social Conscience* (New
York: Walker [1967] 156 p. TR140.H52G8). The collection is represented in the division catalog.

*Spinner in the Payne Cotton Mill, Macon, Georgia; one of the series of photographs by Lewis Hine published in National Child Labor Committee pamphlet 138, Child Labor in Georgia (1910). At the time of Hine's "photographic investigation," Georgia was the only state which permitted children under thirteen to work a sixty-six-hour week. National Child Labor Committee Collection, Prints and Photographs Division. LC–H5–545.*

*NUCMC,* 59–34.

U.S., Library of Congress, Manuscript Division, "Manuscripts," *QJLC,* v. 12, May 1955: 134–135.

# 170

## National Photo Company Collection

### News photographs of Washington, D.C., 1910s–1930s

Prints and Photographs Division

The photographic files of the National Photo Company were acquired by the Library from its proprietor Herbert E. French in 1947. During the administrations of Presidents Wilson, Harding, Coolidge, and Hoover, the National Photo Company supplied photographs of current news events in Washington, D.C., as a daily service to its subscribers. It also prepared sets of pictures on popular subjects and undertook special photographic assignments for local businesses and government agencies. The firm's files contain an estimated twenty thousand images and include chronological albums covering events of the period 1919 to 1930 and thematic groups of photographs on the four presidents, inaugurations, sports, landmarks, conventions, and topics of local interest. The original card indexes of the National Photo Company list by subject the 73,500 glass plate negatives which French donated to complement the captioned photoprints purchased by the Library. A large portion of the collection has been integrated with the division's self-indexing subject, geographical, and biographical files. The collection is currently being reorganized.

*Guide,* Vanderbilt, no. 534.

# 171

## National Press Club Collection

Recordings of speeches given at the National Press Club, Washington, D.C., 1952–present

Motion Picture, Broadcasting, and Recorded Sound Division

Since 1969 the National Press Club of Washington has donated to the Library of Congress tape recordings of speeches delivered at its luncheons and evening functions. The recordings begin in 1952, the year the club instituted its taping program, and preserve addresses by newsmakers in national politics, diplomacy, literature, and the arts. Guest speakers include Presidents Hoover, Truman, Eisenhower, Kennedy, Johnson, Nixon, and Carter at different stages of their careers, congressmen, cabinet members, foreign leaders—Adenauer, de Gaulle, Sukarno, Khrushchev, and Castro, among others—and well-known cultural figures ranging from Arthur Rubinstein to Alex Haley. In addition to the full texts of speeches, the tapes contain the concluding question-and-answer periods which, as a rule, are omitted from the recently initiated National Public Radio broadcasts of these events. The entire collection—approximately 830 recordings as of 1978—is being reproduced on tape. Speakers are reported in the chronological list on file. The collection is being indexed by subject, name, and date.

Leavitt, Donald L., "Acquisition Notes," *LCIB*, v. 28, January 16, 1969: 27–28.

Waters, Edward N., "Variations on a Theme: Recent Acquisitions of the Music Division," *QJLC*, v. 27, January 1970: 83.

# 172

## National Public Radio Collection

Broadcast recordings of NPR's cultural programs

Motion Picture, Broadcasting, and Recorded Sound Division

Through an agreement announced in 1976, cultural broadcasts of the National Public Radio (NPR) are added to the collections of the Library of Congress on a five-year delay basis. As of September 1978, the collection contained an estimated fourteen hundred tapes from the first years of NPR transmissions, including programs from *Concert of the Week, Folk Music Americana, Folk Music and Bernstein, Composers' Forum,* and two discussion series, *Book Beat* and *Poet Speaks.* Computer-generated indexes supplied by NPR provide access to program tapes by shelf order, date of broadcast, series title, program title, proper name, and subject. Under the 1976 agreement, news and public affairs programs are transferred to the National Archives.

U.S., Library of Congress, Music Division, "NPR Transfer Agreement Signed," *LCIB,* v. 36, April 16, 1976: 235–236.

# 173

## Naval Historical Foundation Collection

Personal papers relating to American naval history

Manuscript Division

Between 1949 and 1978, the Naval Historical Foundation deposited in the Library of Congress the largest single collection in the United States of personal papers relating to American naval history. Consisting of over 250 groups of private papers acquired by the foundation since its establishment in 1926, the collection brings together original source material dating from the American Revolution to World War II. The papers complement official records held by the National Archives, the Navy's Operational Archives, and the Federal Records Centers and deal with such topics as military strategy, American diplomacy, public administration, domestic naval policy, and the development of naval architecture, ordnance, engineering, communications, submarines, and aviation. Among the many naval officers represented by significant holdings of personal papers are William F. Fullam, Stephen B. Luce, and William S. Sims, who worked to reorganize the Navy Department at the turn of the century; Washington Irving Chambers and John Lansing Callan, pioneers in naval aviation; Stanford C. Hooper, an electronics expert instrumental in developing naval radio communications; World War II commanders William F. Halsey and Ernest King; and Albert Gleaves, David Dixon Porter, John Rodgers, Thomas Selfridge, and Robert W. Shufeldt. The Manuscript Division has prepared a catalog describing the contents of the collection as of 1972 and registers for a number of the more significant groups of papers. Many are also listed in the *National Union Catalog of Manuscript Collections*. From other sources, the Library has acquired the papers of such important naval figures as John Barry, William S. Benson, George Dewey, John Paul Jones, William D. Leahy, Alfred Thayer Mahan, and Matthew Fontaine Maury.

U.S., Library of Congress, *Naval Historical Foundation Manuscript Collection: A Catalog* (Washington: 1974. 136 p. Z1249.N3U5 1974).

# 174

## New York World-Telegram and Sun Collection

News photographs, 1920–1960s

Prints and Photographs Division

In 1967 the complete picture files compiled by the *New York World-Telegram and Sun* were donated to the Library by the *World Journal Tribune*. These files had been used by the *New York World-Telegram*, the paper created in 1931 by the merger of the *World* and the *Evening Telegram*. In 1950 the Scripps-Howard newspaper chain, owners of United Press International, added the *Sun* to their *World-Telegram*. The paper ceased publication in 1966 and became a component of the short-lived *World Journal Tribune*. The picture files contain approximately 1.25 million glossy photographs dating from 1920 to the mid-1960s. While international in scope, the files are particularly extensive for such matters of local interest as New York politics, transportation, labor problems, housing, cultural developments, and celebrities. The material is organized alphabetically in two sequences: biographical (75 percent of the photos) and subject (25 percent), with cross references linking the two files. Photos are dated, captioned, and credited to the owners of the reproduction rights. Most images taken outside the New York area derive from the Associated Press and United Press International and are accompanied by the original wire service captions. This large collection is still in the process of being organized for service and will be made available to researchers, by appointment, after the opening of the James Madison Memorial Building.

# 175

## *The New Yorker* Collection

Drawings for *The New Yorker* magazine, mid-twentieth century

Prints and Photographs Division

Since the early 1960s the Library of Congress has collected original cartoons and cover illustrations from *The New Yorker* magazine. Begining with its first issue in 1925, *The New Yorker* has published caricatures and humorous sketches aimed at a cosmopolitan audience. *The New Yorker* Collection in the Prints and Photographs Division contains over twenty-nine hundred drawings in various media that have appeared in the magazine since the early 1930s. Peter Arno, Perry Barlow, Whitney Darrow, Jr., Chon Day, Mischa Richter, Charles D. Saxon, William Steig, and Gluyas Williams are among the over thirty artists who have donated items to the collection. The diversity of subjects treated by the drawings is suggested by the sampling listed in the exhibition catalog, *They Made Them Laugh and Wince and Worry and . . . : Drawings for Six American Magazines, an Exhibition in the Great Hall of the Library of Congress, March 13 through June 12, 1977* (Washington: Library of Congress, 1977. [32] p.). The drawings, some retaining the original editorial markings, are organized by artist and described in the division catalog. Reproduction rights for most items are retained by *The New Yorker*.

*Sheep, horse, and ox from an album of original sketches attributed to the Japanese printmaker Hokusai (1760–1849). The sketchbook is designed to teach elementary drawing techniques. Crosby Stuart Noyes Collection, Japanese Section, Asian Division. LC–USZ62–67595.*

# 176

## Crosby Stuart Noyes Collection

Japanese illustrated books, prints, and drawings, eighteenth and nineteenth centuries

Japanese Section, Asian Division
Prints and Photographs Division

In 1905, Crosby Stuart Noyes (1825–1908), editor and publisher of the *Washington Star*, presented to the Library his collection of late eighteenth- and nineteenth-century Japanese graphic art. Introduced to Japanese prints through their influence on European and American artists, Noyes became an enthusiast of Japanese culture and assembled his collection during several trips to the Orient. The 1906 *Annual Report of the Librarian of Congress* includes a collection catalog and states the original gift consisted of "12 water-colors, 145 original drawings, 331 wood engravings, 97 lithographs, 658 illustrated books, and 61 other items." Approximately 250 titles (432 volumes) are represented among the illustrated books in *gachō, gafu,* and similar formats in the custody of the Japanese Section. Included are albums of original drawings and first and later impressions of printed works by Beisen, Bunchō, Hiroshige, Hokusai, Kuniyoshi, and over one hundred other artists. The collection retains its original numerical arrangement.

The single prints and drawings from the collection were transferred to the Prints and Photographs Division and are awaiting cataloging.

*ARLC,* 1906, p. 51–52, 141–170.

Kuroda, Andrew Y., "A History of the Japanese Collection in the Library of Congress, 1874–1941" in *Senda Masao Kyōju koki kinen toshokan shiryō ronshū* (Tenri: Senda Masao Kyōju Koki Kinenkai, 1970. 327, 139 p. Z665.S394 Orien Japan), p. 296–297; separate reprint of article (Washington, 1970. Z733.U63O74 1970).

# 177

## Office of War Information Collection

Broadcast recordings, photographs, and research files assembled by the OWI, early 1940s

Motion Picture, Broadcasting, and Recorded Sound Division
Prints and Photographs Division
Archive of Folk Song

Between 1944 and 1947, the U.S. Office of War Information (OWI) transferred to the Library of Congress thousands of items which had been used in the agency's support of the war effort. OWI sound recordings, photographs, and a small number of research papers have been kept together as special collections. The Motion Picture, Broadcasting, and Recorded Sound Division holds nearly fifty thousand acetate disc recordings of foreign and domestic radio broadcasts English-language programs, which were usually recorded live off the air, include news, entertainment, and informational reports from 1942, 1944, and 1945. These, together with recordings in French and German, have been taped and listed chronologically in a descriptive file. Recordings in other languages are being taped.

Thousands of mounted and captioned photoprints, original negatives, and copy negatives that were assembled for use in OWI publications, exhibits, and filmstrips are kept in the Prints and Photographs Division. Like the recordings, the OWI photographs portray the war effort from the American point of view and, by and large, depict scenes that reflect the American way of life in a favorable light. Typical subjects treated by the photographs are the trucking industry, factory workers, construction projects, shipbuilding, educational institutions, housing, and railroads. The collection brings together material acquired from commercial photo agencies, industry, and government agencies as well as images taken by staff photographers. Most photographs of domestic scenes are interfiled with the Farm Security Administration reference prints (no. 76) and are arranged by geographic region and subject. In some cases, assignments executed by OWI photographers have been reproduced on microfilm and recorded in the division catalog by photographer, subject, and locality. Foreign scenes are listed in the catalog by subject and place. The greater part of the OWI picture files is in the custody of the National Archives.

The Archive of Folk Song has gathered OWI research material on the spread and classification of rumors, and on jokes told by students about the war effort. The five boxes of reports, correspondence, and data sheets retain their original geographic and topical organization.

*Guide,* Vanderbilt, no. 553–555.

U.S., Library of Congress, Photographic Section, *Index of Microfilm, Series A, Lots 1–1737* ([Washington] 1945. 26 leaves. N4010.A53 1945; reprint, 1946).

# 178

## J. Robert Oppenheimer Collection

Papers and voice recordings of physicist J. Robert Oppenheimer

Manuscript Division
Motion Picture, Broadcasting, and Recorded Sound Division

The personal papers of physicist J. Robert Oppenheimer (1904–1967) were presented to the Library of Congress in 1967 by his widow, Katherine Harrison Oppenheimer, and supplemented in 1971 by material transferred from the Atomic Energy Commission. Once described by Dr. Oppenheimer as "a hideously complete archive," the 74,000-item collection consists of correspondence, desk books, printed lectures, scientific notes, memoranda, photographs, and clippings. While the bulk of the material dates from the years 1947 to 1967, the period during which Oppenheimer served as director of the Institute for Advanced Study in Princeton, New Jersey, the papers document many aspects of his career and contain information on theoretical physics, the development of the atomic bomb, the control of atomic energy, its role in international affairs, security in scientific fields, disarmament, and related matters. Oppenheimer's hearing before the Personnel Security Board of the Atomic Energy Commission is covered in great detail. Correspondents include Hans A. Bethe, Niels Bohr, Vannevar Bush, Leslie R. Groves, George Kennan, Archibald MacLeish, Linus Pauling, Franklin and Eleanor Roosevelt, and Leo Szilard. The papers are described in a published register.

The Motion Picture, Broadcasting, and Recorded Sound Division maintains over seventy tape, wire, and disc recordings of Dr. Oppenheimer's lectures and interviews. These transcriptions date chiefly from the 1950s and 1960s and include a three-hour discussion between Niels Bohr and Dr. Oppenheimer taped in Denmark in 1958 and a conference held at Seven Springs Farm in Mount Kisco, New York, that featured addresses by Nicolas Nabokov and Robert Lowell. The recordings are available on tape, represented in the division catalog, and described in an inventory on file.

*NUCMC*, 71–1392.

Sifton, Paul G., "Oppenheimer Papers," *LCIB*, v. 27, March 7, 1968: 119–120.

U.S., Library of Congress, Manuscript Division, *J. Robert Oppenheimer: A Register of His Papers in the Library of Congress* (Washington: Library of Congress, 1974. 63 p. Z8645.16.U53 1974).

——, "Recent Acquisitions of the Manuscript Division," *QJLC*, v. 25, October 1968: 344–346.

# 179

## Pierre Ozanne Collection

Maps and views of French naval operations during the American Revolution

Geography and Map Division

In 1911 the Library purchased twenty-three pen-and-wash drawings attributed to Pierre Ozanne (1737–1813), a marine artist assigned to the French fleet during the American Revolution. These finely executed works show the departure of the French forces from the Mediterranean and engagements with British ships in the West Indies and along the North American coast. Of particular interest are a map and view depicting the unsuccessful attack on Savannah in October 1779 which was led by the fleet commander, comte Charles Henri d'Estaing. The eighteen views in the collection are described and reproduced in Donald H. Cresswell's publication; the five maps are recorded in the Library's computerized map catalog. The Ozanne Collection will be treated in the bibliography of American revolutionary war maps now being compiled by the Library's American Revolution Bicentennial Office.

*Guide,* Vanderbilt, no. 560.

U.S., Library of Congress, *The American Revolution in Drawings and Prints: A Checklist of 1765–1790 Graphics in the Library of Congress* (Washington: 1975. xvii, 455 p. E209.U54 1975), compiled by Donald H. Cresswell, no. 278–280, 282–285, 288–289, 291–294, 297–302.

# 180

## Paper Print Collection

Films registered for U.S. copyright protection, 1894–1915

Motion Picture, Broadcasting, and Recorded Sound Division

Before the amendment of the copyright law in 1912, motion pictures were registered for copyright protection following the procedures originally developed for still photographs. To obtain copyright protection, motion picture producers were required to deposit with the Library of Congress paper contact prints made directly from the film negatives. These paper prints ranged in length from a few frames to the entire motion picture. In the 1950s and 1960s paper prints of complete films were restored to projectable filmstock through the efforts of film historian Kemp Niver and a team of technicians. The collection preserves approximately three thousand comedy, drama, travelog, and news films from the period 1894 to 1915, among them releases of the Thomas A. Edison Company (1897–1904); films of the American Mutoscope and Biograph Company (renamed the Biograph Company) from the years 1899 to 1912, including over three hundred films directed or supervised by D. W. Griffith (1909–12); and thirty works by the French filmmaker Georges Méliès (1903–4). The films are recorded by title in the collection shelflist in the Motion Picture, Broadcasting, and Recorded Sound Division and indexed in the published catalog. Reference prints are available for the entire collection.

Niver, Kemp R., "From Film to Paper to Film: The Story of the Library of Congress Paper-Print Conversion Program," *QJLC,* v. 21, October 1964: 248–264.

————, *Motion Pictures from the Library of Congress Paper Print Collection, 1894–1912* (Berkeley: University of California Press, 1967. xxii, 402 p. Z5784.M9N58), edited by Bebe Bergsten.

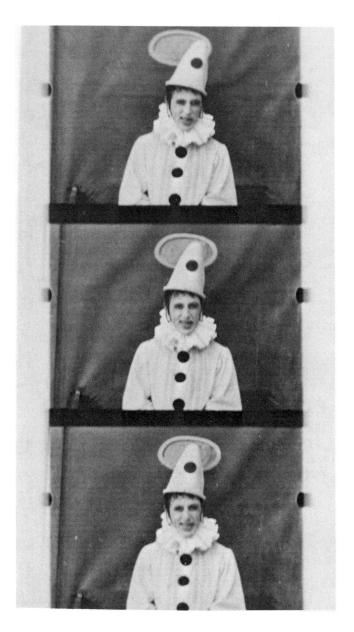

*D. W. Griffith as the duped husband in* At the French Ball *(1908). Griffith appeared in several early films of the American Mutoscope and Biograph Company before emerging as its leading director. Paper Print Collection, Motion Picture, Broadcasting, and Recorded Sound Division. Negative in division.*

# 181

## Peabody Museum Collection

Ethnological sound recordings, 1890s–1910s

Archive of Folk Song

The first documented use of mechanical recording equipment for ethnological research was by Jesse Walter Fewkes, an anthropologist affiliated with the Peabody Museum of Archaeology and Ethnology of Harvard University. Fewkes successfully recorded the speech and song of the Passamaquoddy Indians of Maine in March 1890 using a wax cylinder phonograph. He took the device on subsequent expeditions among the Zuñi and Hopi Indians of Arizona in 1890 and 1891 and published an influential series of articles on his work, beginning with "On the Use of the Phonograph in the Study of the Languages of American Indians," in *Science* (Q1.S35), v. 15, May 2, 1890, p. 267–269. In 1970 the Peabody Museum presented to the Library a collection of early ethnological recordings which included over fifty of these historic Fewkes cylinders. The collection also contains cylinders of Samoan, Javanese, Kwakiutl, Syrian, and Turkish music recorded by Benjamin Ives Gilman at the Chicago World's Fair in 1893, field recordings made by Herbert J. Spinden among the Nez Percé Indians in 1907, a Mexican *pastores* collection dating from the turn of the century, California Indian material collected by Roland Dixon around 1910, and recordings made by Washington Matthews approximately ten years earlier among the Navaho. The 264 wax cylinders have been duplicated on tape (AFS 14,737–14,754) and are described in notes and a concordance. The Peabody Museum has received tapes of the collection through exchange. One of the Passamaquoddy field recordings is reproduced on record LBC–15 of the Library's "Folk Music in America" series.

# 182

## Wilfrid Pelletier Collection

Broadcast recordings of music programs, late 1930s and 1940s

Motion Picture, Broadcasting, and Recorded Sound Division

In 1976, through exchange with Hobart and William Smith Colleges, the Library received a collection of recordings assembled by Wilfrid Pelletier, a conductor who began his career with the Metropolitan Opera in 1917. The collection contains sixteen-inch transcription discs of Metropolitan Opera performances and auditions dating from 1938 to 1949 and NBC Symphony Orchestra broadcasts, as well as transcriptions of *Ford Sunday Evening Hour, The Voice of Firestone,* and other radio shows that employed Pelletier as conductor, musical arranger, or composer. Rose Bampton, Pelletier's wife and a leading soprano of the Metropolitan Opera, is featured in many recordings. The 575 discs have been transcribed on tape and indexed by date, artist, composer, and title. An inventory of the collection is on file.

# 183

## Joseph and Elizabeth Robins Pennell Collection

Graphic art, papers, and cookbook collection of Joseph and Elizabeth Pennell

Prints and Photographs Division
Manuscript Division
Rare Book and Special Collections Division

Joseph Pennell (1857–1926) launched his career as an illustrator by selling picturesque drawings of south Philadelphia to *Scribner's Monthly* in 1881. Following the success of his sketches of New Orleans, published in George W. Cable's book *The Creoles of Louisiana* (1884), he married Elizabeth Robins (1855–1936), formerly his collaborator on a *Century* magazine article. The couple moved to London and became friends of the American artist James McNeill Whistler. Pennell, a prolific artist and writer, experimented with new graphic techniques and sought to draw critical attention to book illustration. His wife, a well-known columnist and biographer, frequently collaborated with the artist on travel writings. The couple returned to the United States in 1917, and Pennell taught for several years at the Art Students' League in New York City. Through the Pennells' bequest, the Library acquired their collection of books, manuscripts, and graphic art, some of which had been deposited as early as the 1910s. In addition, the Library was provided with a special fund for the acquisition of modern prints.

The Prints and Photographs Division has copies of virtually all of Pennell's published graphic work, approximately 1,885 prints. Included are his famous series on Philadelphia and the Panama Canal as well as "War Work in America," "War Work in England," and numerous depictions of industrial and urban scenes in Europe and America. The prints are listed in the fine prints card file and in *American Prints in the Library of Congress: A Catalog of the Collection* (Baltimore: Published for the Library of Congress by the Johns Hopkins Press [1970] xxi, 568 p. NE505.A47), compiled by Karen F. Beall and others. In addition, the division copies of Louis A. Wuerth's *Catalogue of the Lithographs of Joseph Pennell* (Boston: Little, Brown, 1931. xxii, 243 p. NE2415.P41) and *Catalogue of the Etchings of Joseph Pennell* (Boston: Little, Brown, 1928. xx, 312 p. NE1225.P4A4) are

*The Parthenon from the Gateway of the Acropolis, by Joseph Pennell. This drawing is for a lithograph from his series "Land of Temples" (1913). Joseph and Elizabeth Robins Pennell Collection, Prints and Photographs Division. LC–USZ62–67596.*

annotated to indicate collection holdings. Available upon request are several hundred original drawings, watercolors, etching plates, books illustrated by the artist, and miscellaneous works from the Pennells' private library.

The Pennell bequest also brought to the Library their personal papers, the papers of Mrs. Pennell's uncle Charles Godfrey Leland (1824–1903), and their compilation of Whistleriana (no. 184)—a total of 94,000 items. An additional 2,600 items were acquired from 1969 to 1979. The Pennell papers include correspondence with publishers, art dealers, and exhibitors; letters from leading writers and artists of the period such as Ford Madox Ford, Cass Gilbert, Henry James, Auguste Rodin, and John Singer Sargent; private exchanges between the couple written during the years 1883 to 1923; and a group of 400 letters from Whistler. The papers also contain manuscripts and galley proofs for their publications, research notes for their biography *The Life of James Mc-Neill Whistler* (1908), drafts for lectures, sketches and drawings, and legal papers. The Manuscript Division has prepared an unpublished finding aid for the Pennell material.

Writing extensively on gastronomy, Elizabeth Pennell amassed a large collection of European cookbooks. *My Cookery Books* (Boston and New York: Houghton, Mifflin, 1903. 171 p. Z5777.P41) is a personal account of her collecting activities and describes many of the 433 volumes on cookery from the Pennell bequest in the Rare Book and Special Collections Division. The collection is strongest in French and Italian cookbooks from the sixteenth through eighteenth centuries and includes such notable items as a fully illustrated edition of Bartolomeo Scappi's *Opera* (Venice: 1574?). Also in the division are 299 volumes on fine printing, bibliography, and literature from the Pennell library. Many works are listed in a separate author/title card file as well as the division catalog.

*ARLC,* 1926, p. 3–5, 335–341; 1936, p. 159–160.

Crutcher, Anne, "So You Think YOU'VE Got a Lot of Cookbooks," *The Washington Star,* October 27, 1976: D1, D4.

*NUCMC,* 66–1446.

U.S., Congress, House, Committee on the Library, *Accept Property Bequeated [sic] to United States by Joseph Pennell . . . Report, To Accompany H.J. Res. 526* ([Washington: Govt. Print. Off., 1936] 3 p. 74th Congress, 2d session. House. Rept. no. 2269. NC139.P4U6 1936).

U.S., Library of Congress, *Joseph Pennell Memorial Exhibition. Catalogue* (Washington: [Govt. Print. Off.] 1927. 46 p. NC139.P4U6 1927).

# 184

## Joseph and Elizabeth Robins Pennell Collection of Whistleriana

Graphic art and papers of James McNeill Whistler; photographs, publications, and research materials relating to his life

Prints and Photographs Division
Manuscript Division

Joseph and Elizabeth Pennell were introduced to James McNeill Whistler (1834–1903) after their move to London in 1884. As their friendship grew, the Pennells began collecting literary and biographical information on Whistler and were asked by the artist to write his biography. Whistler himself contributed notes and suggestions. *The Life of James McNeill Whistler* (Philadelphia: J. B. Lippincott Co.; London: W. Heinemann, 1908. 2 v. N237.W6P4 1908a) was issued following an unsuccessful suit by the executrix of Whistler's estate, Rosalind Birnie Philip, to prevent its publication. The Joseph and Elizabeth Robins Pennell Collection of Whistleriana was presented to the Library in 1917. The Pennells' bequest brought additional items to the collection and provided for its continued growth through an acquisition fund.

All nonmanuscript items from the Pennell gift are kept in the Prints and Photographs Division. The collection includes catalogs documenting exhibitions at which Whistler showed his work, reproductions of Whistler's paintings, biographical photographs, books, and pamphlets. The Pennells donated most of the 300 Whistler lithographs, etchings, and drypoints recorded in the fine prints card catalog and listed in *American Prints in the Library of Congress: A Catalog of the Collection* (Baltimore: Published for the Library of Congress by the Johns Hopkins Press [1970] xxi, 568 p. NE505.A47), compiled by Karen F. Beall and others. Also in the collection are twenty original pen and pencil sketches.

Kept as a separate unit within the Pennells' personal papers is their collection of Whistler manuscripts. Probably the most comprehensive archival record of Whistler's career, the collection includes autograph letters, typescript copies of correspondence, legal materials from the Whistler-Ruskin trial, plans for the proposed Whistler memorial, an extensive file of clippings from the period 1886 to 1937, and the diary (1850) and letters of Anna Mathilda Whistler, the artist's mother. Of particular interest are Whistler's letters to David Croal Thomson regarding the 1892 exhibition at the Goupil Gallery which brought Whistler international recognition. The Manuscript Division has prepared a finding aid which describes Whistler material within the 96,600-item collection.

*ARLC,* 1917, p. 21–22; 1926, p. 4, 336–339; 1936, p. 159–160.

*Guide,* Vanderbilt, no. 573.

*NUCMC,* 66–1446.

U.S., Library of Congress, Prints and Photographs Division, *The Joseph and Elizabeth Robins Pennell Collection of Whistleriana Shown in the Division of Prints, Library of Congress, Southwest Pavilion* (Washington: Govt. Print. Off., Library Branch, 1921. 65 p. ND237.W6U6), compiled by Joseph and Elizabeth Robins Pennell.

# 185

## Mary Pickford Collection

### Films of Mary Pickford

Motion Picture, Broadcasting, and Recorded Sound Division

In 1946 Mary Pickford (1893–1979), cofounder of United Artists and one of America's most popular film stars, donated to the Library approximately one hundred of her films. The Pickford Collection contains one-reel comedies and dramas made for the Biograph Company between 1909 and 1912 and such feature-length pictures from the period 1914 to 1931 as *Rebecca of Sunnybrook Farm* (1917), *Little Lord Fauntleroy* (1921), and *The Taming of the Shrew* (1929). The films are recorded by title in the collection shelflist in the Motion Picture, Broadcasting, and Recorded Sound Division, and reference prints are available for half of the collection. There are also reference prints of many of the Biograph films in the Paper Print Collection (no. 180).

# 186

## Pictorial Archives of Early American Architecture

Photographs of American architecture

Prints and Photographs Division

The Pictorial Archives of Early American Architecture (PAEAA) was the first photographic collection for the study of American architecture assembled at the Library of Congress. Initiated by a grant from the Carnegie Corporation in 1930, the PAEAA instituted a national campaign to acquire photographic negatives of seventeenth-, eighteenth-, and nineteenth-century buildings in the United States. During its most active period, 1930 to 1938, the PAEAA collected and cataloged approximately ten thousand negatives and photoprints, including series by John Mead Howells, Frances Benjamin Johnston, Delos Smith, Thomas T. Waterman, and Francis M. Wigmore. The architecture of Connecticut, Delaware, the District of Columbia, Maryland, Massachusetts, New Hampshire, New Jersey, New York, Pennsylvania, South Carolina, and Virginia is particularly well represented. Like the Historic American Buildings Survey (no. 117), which was established a few years later, the collection is organized by state, county, and city. Items are represented in the PAEAA card index and the master card catalog for the architectural collections.

*Guide,* Vanderbilt, no. 583.

"Pictorial Archives at Washington, D. C.: Records of Early American Architecture to Be Preserved," *The Architect* (NA1.A33), v. 14, July 1930: 361–362, 428.

# 187

## Playing Card Collection

Prints and Photographs Division

Two hundred and fifty decks of playing cards acquired by the Library of Congress over the years through gift, purchase, and copyright deposit have been organized as a unit in the Prints and Photographs Division. This heterogeneous collection contains cards produced in twenty-four countries during the eighteenth, nineteenth, and twentieth centuries and includes a few rare decks which are not found in other public collections in the United States. Of particular interest are depictions of prominent individuals, local costumes, and folklife that appear on some European decks. The decks are fully described on control cards kept with the collection. The material is filed alphabetically by country of origin.

# 188

## Portuguese Manuscript Collection

Manuscripts relating to Portuguese history and literature

Manuscript Division

Through purchases in 1927 and 1929, the Library of Congress acquired the nucleus of its general book collections in Portuguese history and literature and an important group of documents now in the custody of the Manuscript Division. Like the books and pamphlets, the majority of the 600 manuscripts can be traced to the private libraries of two Portuguese collectors, conde de Olivais e Penha Longa and Antonio Augusto de Carvalho Monteiro. A significant number of items are concerned with Sebastianism, the belief that King Sebastian, killed in North Africa in 1578, will return to restore Portugal to its former greatness; Luiz de Camões (1524?–1580), author of Portugal's epic poem *Os Lusíadas*; and the military orders of knighthood. Included are general historical works, histories of the Portuguese sovereigns, letters of seventeenth-century diplomatic figures, and a volume containing 201 letters (1774–79) of Manoel de Cunha Menezes, captain general of Pernambuco and Bahia. Also in the collection is material on the Peninsular Wars, the Miguelist civil strife, royal funeral ceremonies, the Inquisition, and genealogy. The manuscripts span a period of more than five centuries the earliest dates from 1438—and include original documents and copies. A guide to the Portuguese Manuscript Collection, now in press, contains an index listing names and places. While most of the Portuguese printed material acquired in the 1920s has been integrated within the general collections, a number of Portuguese pamphlets have been set aside for use in the Hispanic Society Room.

*ARLC,* 1928, p. 35; 1930, p. 54–55.

Ramalho, Américo da Costa, *Portuguese Essays,* 2d ed., rev. (Lisbon: National Secretariat for Information, 1968. 115 p. DP518.R38 1968), p. 87–98.

U.S., Library of Congress, Hispanic Division, *The Portuguese Manuscript Collection of the Library of Congress: A Guide* (Washington: Library of Congress, 1980), compiled by Mary Ellis Kahler and Christopher Lund.

*Thomas Jefferson's rough draft of the Declaration of Independence (1776). The manuscript includes textual changes made by Jefferson, by fellow Committee members John Adams and Benjamin Franklin, by the Committee of Five appointed to prepare the draft, and by the Continental Congress. Thomas Jefferson Papers, Manuscript Division. LC–USP6–187–A.*

# 189

## Presidential Papers Collection

Papers of twenty-three U.S. presidents

Manuscript Division

The Library's massive collection of presidential manuscripts and documents totals well over two million items and includes significant holdings for twenty-three U.S. presidents. The Library obtained the majority of the papers after 1900 through the donations of the families of former presidents and, in some cases, at the direction of the presidents themselves, and has continued to add manuscripts to these holdings. The individual collections range in size from 631 items (Zachary Taylor papers) to 700,000 items (William Howard Taft papers) and typically include correspondence, financial records, speeches, notes, and writings. Under the Presidential Papers Program authorized by Public Law 85–147, enacted August 16, 1957, the Library has organized, indexed, and microfilmed these papers and published guides in book form. Issued in the Presidents' Papers Index series, these guides describe provenance and contents and serve as an index to the microfilms. It is anticipated that additions to the papers will also be indexed and microfilmed. The presidents listed below are represented in the Manuscript Division by major groups of personal papers (the numbers in parentheses refer to the *NUCMC* entry).

| | |
|---|---|
| George Washington | (62-4608) |
| Thomas Jefferson | (77-1537) |
| James Madison | (63-375) |
| James Monroe | (60-428) |
| Andrew Jackson | (60-363) |
| Martin Van Buren | (60-2068) |
| William H. Harrison | (59-182) |
| John Tyler | (60-430) |
| James K. Polk | (73-902) |
| Zachary Taylor | (59-181) |
| Franklin Pierce | (60-429) |
| Abraham Lincoln | (59-183) |

| Andrew Johnson | (61-3688) |
|---|---|
| Ulysses S. Grant | (68-2038) |
| James A. Garfield | (76-159) |
| Chester A. Arthur | (60-427) |
| Grover Cleveland | (62-4985) |
| Benjamin Harrison | (62-889) |
| William McKinley | (62-891) |
| Theodore Roosevelt | (73-905) |
| William H. Taft | (62-4597) |
| Woodrow Wilson | (72-1779) |
| Calvin Coolidge | (62-4987) |

Presidential correspondence is included in other collections of personal papers held by the division. The Jackson manuscripts and maps are described in no. 127. The papers of former presidents beginning with Herbert C. Hoover are in the custody of presidential libraries, administered by the National Archives and Records Service. There is also a Rutherford B. Hayes Library in Fremont, Ohio.

U.S., Library of Congress, Manuscript Division, *The Presidential Papers Program of the Library of Congress* ([Washington: 1960] [4] p. CD3041.P7U54).

# 190

## Sergei Mikhailovich Prokudin-Gorskiĭ Collection

Photographs of Imperial Russia, early twentieth century·

Prints and Photographs Division

Sergei Mikhailovich Prokudin-Gorskiĭ (d. 1943) was one of the first Russians to experiment with color photography. Traveling in a specially equipped railroad car-darkroom provided by Nicholas II, he made color photographs of Russian art works and architecture, industry, agriculture, topography, and daily life. Prokudin-Gorskiĭ apparently completed surveys in seven regions: the area traversed by the Murman railroad, White Russia, the Ural Mountains, the Marinsky Canal system, the Volga River basin, the Caucasus, and Turkestan. At the outbreak of the Russian Revolution, the photographer escaped to Paris with glass plate negatives dating chiefly from the period 1909 to 1911. The Library purchased the material from Prokudin-Gorskiĭ's sons in 1948. Each of the 1,900 negatives in the collection consists of three separate images exposed in rapid succession through different color separation filters. Over twenty-seven hundred contact prints prepared from the "red" separation image are mounted in albums. The photoprints are described in the catalog of the Prints and Photographs Division and most are keyed to the original negatives. English translations of the Russian captions are affixed to each album. Prokudin-Gorskiĭ discussed his color experiments in *Fotograf-Liùbitel'* (1906), a Russian photography journal which he edited.

*Guide,* Vanderbilt, no. 599.

Vanderbilt, Paul, and Alice Lee Parker, "Prints and Photographs," *QJLC,* v. 6, November 1948: 37–38.

# 191

## Pulp Fiction Collection

Popular American fiction magazines, 1920s–1950s

Serial and Government Publications Division
Rare Book and Special Collections Division

Through copyright deposit the Library of Congress has acquired issues of approximately three hundred pulp fiction magazines. Popularly known as "pulps" because of their poor quality wood pulp paper, these magazines specialized in science fiction, adventure, western, detective, war, romance, and sports stories and were important in launching the careers of such writers as Raymond Chandler, Dashiell Hammett, H. P. Lovecraft, and Cornell Woolrich. The 15,000 issues in the collection date from the 1920s to the 1950s and represent the full range of pulp fiction genres. Most items retain their original colored covers. Many series are incomplete, particularly for the early years. The Newspaper and Current Periodical Room of the Serial and Government Publications Division services the majority of the collection and maintains a record of Library holdings by title.

Several famous pulps—*Black Mask, Weird Tales, Amazing Stories*—are kept in the Rare Book and Special Collections Division. A few titles are available on microfilm through the Microform Reading Room.

# 192

## Rachmaninoff Archives

Music manuscripts, papers, and record collection of Sergei
Rachmaninoff

Music Division
Motion Picture, Broadcasting, and Recorded Sound Division

The Rachmaninoff Archives is the largest collection of Sergei
Rachmaninoff holographs, personal papers, and memorabilia outside
of the Soviet Union. Mrs. Sergei Rachmaninoff decided to donate this
extensive family collection to the Library shortly before her death in
1951 and over the years her sister Sophie Satin and daughters, Irina
Wolkonsky and Tatiana Conus, have generously added material. The archives document the composer's career after his emigration from Russia
(1917) with music manuscripts, autograph correspondence, photographs, programs, prizes, clippings, critical studies, biographies, and
lists enumerating his recordings, compositions, performances, and repertory as a pianist, opera conductor, and orchestra director. Many important compositions are represented by autograph sketches and scores,
among them *Prelude in C-sharp Minor, op. 3, no. 2; Piano Concerto
no. 4, op. 40; Russian Songs, op. 41; Corelli Variations, op. 42; Rhapsody on a Theme of Paganini, op. 43; Symphony no. 3, op. 44;* and
*Symphonic Dances,* op. 45. The collection contains correspondence
with Feodor Chaliapin, Nina Koshetz, Serge Koussevitzky, and Leopold
Stokowski. Much of the material in the archives is described in a shelflist compiled by Sophie Satin. The collection measures twenty-four
linear feet.

Rachmaninoff's personal record library is maintained in the Motion Picture, Broadcasting, and Recorded Sound Division. Among the
approximately seven hundred phonodiscs are several unpublished recordings of Rachmaninoff performances, including alternate "takes"
for commercial releases, some with notations by Rachmaninoff on the
record label. The commercial discs comprise by far the greater part of
the collection and are listed in an inventory. Noncommercial recordings are kept as a unit and represented in the division catalog and
reference files.

Waters, Edward N., "Music," *QJLC*, v. 9, November 1951: 39–42.

——, "Music," *QJLC*, v. 20, December 1962: 63–64.

# 193

## Vance Randolph Collection

Vance Randolph's papers, photographs, and field recordings
of Ozark folk music, 1930s–1960s

Archive of Folk Song
Manuscript Division
Music Division

In 1941 the Archive of Folk Song commissioned Vance Randolph
to undertake a recording expedition in southern Missouri and northern
Arkansas. The folklorist recorded many of the songs—in some cases
performed by the same singers—that he had encountered in the late
1920s and 1930s as he researched *Ozark Folksongs* (Columbia, Mo.:
State Historical Society of Missouri, 1946 50. 4 v. M1629.R2309).
Randolph's 200 disc recordings (AFS 5,236–5,425 and 6,897–6,904)
include approximately 170 fiddle tunes and banjo pieces, which he has
identified by title in "The Names of Ozark Fiddle Tunes," in *Midwest
Folklore* (GR109.M5), v. 4, summer 1954, p. 81 86. The collection is
represented on cards and lists filed in the Archive of Folk Song. The
approximately two hundred discs have been copied on tape and are accompanied by field notes and correspondence. Several Library of Congress recordings include selections from the collection.

Mr. Randolph's papers are housed in three locations in the
Library. The largest group is assigned to the Archive of Folk Song and
was presented to the Library by the author in 1972. The material includes research notes, clippings, photographs, and professional correspondence dating from the 1930s through the 1960s. Many of the photographs were taken by Randolph himself and depict Ozark singers and
scenes. The papers occupy six linear feet.

In 1954 the Manuscript Division purchased the original manuscripts, complete with author's marginal notes and publisher's comments, of four published works: *Ozark Superstitions* (1947), *We Always
Lie to Strangers: Tall Tales from the Ozarks* (1951), *Who Blowed Up
the Church House? and Other Ozark Folk Tales* (1952), and *Down in
the Holler: A Gallery of Ozark Folk Speech* (1953).

*Wes Noel of Elk Springs, Missouri, playing a solid wood fiddle (ca. 1930). Vance Randolph Collection, Archive of Folk Song. Courtesy of Vance Randolph. LC–USZ62–67597.*

The Music Division has custody of Randolph's " 'Unprintable Songs' and Other Folklore Materials from the Ozarks"—four boxes of bawdy Ozark music, children's rhymes, riddles, graffiti, and sayings. The folklorist drew upon narratives from this manuscript for his recent book *Pissing in the Snow and Other Ozark Folktales* (Urbana: University of Illinois Press, 1976. xxxiii, 153 p. GR110.M77P57). The Institute of Sex Research at Indiana University has a duplicate set of typescripts and the University of California at Los Angeles has a microfilm copy of the material.

*NUCMC,* 59–7.

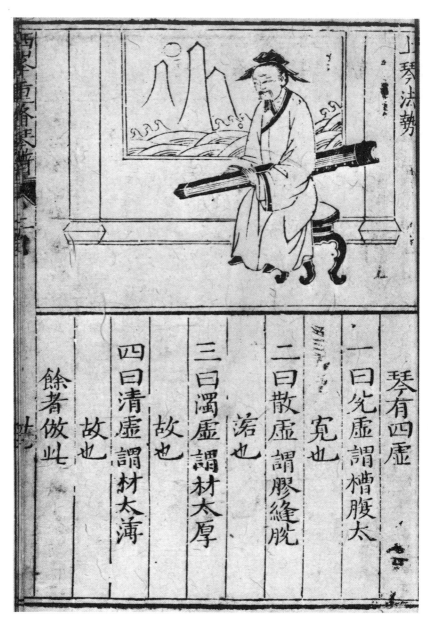

琴有四虛

一曰笑虛謂槽腹太寬也

二曰散虛謂膠縫脫落也

三曰濁虛謂材太厚故也

四曰清虛謂材太薄故也

餘者倣此

*Page from* Ch'in p'u ta ch'üan, *a manual for playing the lute by Yang Piaocheng (1585). This early printed book includes musical scores and fingering illustrations. Rare Chinese Book Collection, Chinese and Korean Section, Asian Division. LC–USZ62–67598.*

# 194

## Rare Chinese Book Collection

Rare Chinese books and manuscripts

Chinese and Korean Section, Asian Division

The Chinese and Korean Section houses the largest collection of rare Chinese books outside of China. Uniting early materials acquired from William W. Rockhill, the John Crerar Library in Chicago, Wang Shu-an of Tientsin, and other sources, the collection consists largely of books and manuscripts produced before the establishment of Manchu rule in 1644. Ming dynasty (1368–1644) imprints account for approximately 85 percent of the 1,777 titles. Among the printed works of the Sung (960–1279) and Yüan (1279–1368) periods are a small Buddhist invocation sutra from Hangchow made in 975; a sixty-eight-foot scroll of *Saddharma Pundarika Sutra* (The Lotus of the Wonderful Law) printed in the mid-eleventh century in Hangchow; the sixty-four-volume *Wei Shu* (1144), probably the oldest and most accurate extant copy of the official history of the Wei dynasty; and a ten-volume herbal printed in Pingyang, Shansi, in 1249, which constitutes one of the finest examples of early Chinese printing. Post-seventeenth-century works in the collection include items annotated by famous scholars or marked with the seal impressions of major libraries, publications banned by the Ch'ing emperors of the eighteenth century, and other books of great bibliographic or historic interest. The collection also encompasses manuscripts of unpublished writings and of texts issued in obscure printed editions. A few of the 140 manuscripts date from as early as the T'ang period (618–906). Titles are listed in a published catalog and in the pre-1958 Chinese Union card catalog kept in the section. Complementing the collection are microfilms of over twenty-eight hundred rare items now in the National Central Library, Taipei.

Hummel, Arthur W., "China," *QJLC*, v. 4, February 1947: 19–21.

U.S., Library of Congress, *Kuo hui t'u shu kuan ts'ang Chung-kuo shan pen shu lu* [A Descriptive Catalog of Rare Chinese Books in the Library of Congress] (Washington: 1957. 2 v. Z881.U5 1957 Orien China; reprint, T'ai-pei: Wen Hai Ch'u Pan She, 1972), compiled by Wang Chung-min, edited by T. L. Yüan.

# 195

## Reformation Collection

Publications relating to the Reformation, sixteenth century

Rare Book and Special Collections Division

In the late nineteenth century 232 works attributed to Martin Luther were transferred to the Library of Congress from the Smithsonian Institution. To these were added approximately fifty volumes selected from the Library's general collections and 142 volumes, donated by Otto Vollbehr in 1938, containing works by Luther, as well as John Calvin, Johann Eck, Hieronymus Emser, Ulrich von Hutten, Philipp Melanchthon, Johann Reuchlin, Johannes Trithemius, and other religious writers of the period. The Reformation Collection consists largely of sixteenth-century editions, some of which contain woodcut border illustrations and contemporary annotations. Items are recorded in card indexes by author, title, or date of publication. The Smithsonian volumes are listed in two handwritten bibliographies—one compiled by the Smithsonian (1867) and the other—with German titles translated—prepared by the Library.

# 196

## Resettlement Administration Collection

Field recordings of American folk music made by the RA, 1936–37

Archive of Folk Song

Probably the first government agency to promulgate folk music as a cohesive force in new farming communities was the Resettlement Administration (RA) established by executive order in April 1935. Between 1936 and 1937 Charles Seeger, technical assistant to the director of the Special Skills Division, sent Sidney Robertson, Margaret Valiant, and others into eastern and midwestern states to make field recordings for use in such government projects as training recreational leaders for rural settlements. The RA team recorded Lithuanian, Finnish, Serbian, Gaelic, Swedish, and American Indian music, and a substantial number of Appalachian and Ozark songs and dance tunes. Shortly after the RA was supplanted by the Farm Security Administration in September 1937, the 159 disc recordings (AFS 3,155–3,313) were transferred to the Library of Congress along with a checklist and brief field notes. The material has been duplicated on tape.

The Archive of Folk Song also maintains a file of the illustrated song sheets issued by the RA for distribution in rural settlements. One original pen-and-ink sketch prepared by Charles Pollock for the series is included in the Seeger Collection (no. 222) in the Music Division. Also serviced through the Music Division are two bound volumes of official RA memos and reports donated to the Library in 1967 by Charles Seeger.

Green, Archie, "A Resettlement Administration Song Sheet," *JEMF Quarterly* (ML1.J55), v. 11, summer 1975: 80–84.

# 197

## Rudolph and Richard Réti Collection

Music manuscripts and papers of composer Rudolph Réti,
papers of chess master Richard Réti

Music Division

It was the wish of Mrs. W. Stanton Forbes, widow of the distinguished composer and critic Rudolph Réti (1885–1957), that the papers of her late husband be donated to the Library of Congress. Rudolph Réti was one of the founders of the International Society for Contemporary Music and a music critic in the 1930s for the Viennese newspaper, *Das Echo*. Coming to America in 1938, he continued to compose choral and instrumental works and became a contributing editor for *The Musical Digest*. The Réti Collection in the Music Division, presented to the Library between 1972 and 1976 by Lucy Forbes Shevenell, Katherine Forbes Lindow, and W. Stanton Forbes, contains music manuscripts, printed music, correspondence, articles, concert programs, news clippings, photographs, and material relating to *The Thematic Process in Music* (New York: Macmillan, 1951. 362 p. MT40.R46; reprints, [1961] 1977), a publication developed from Réti's series of lectures to the American Musicological Society. Correspondents include Olin Downes, Rudolf Klein, Ernst Křenek, Alma Mahler, Yandray Wilson Vance, and Egon Wellesz. A small number of papers produced by the musician's brother Richard Réti (1889–1929), famed chess master and theoretician, are housed with the collection and pertain largely to chess publications. An inventory of nonmusic material is kept on file. The collection occupies approximately twelve linear feet.

*NUCMC*, 77–380.

# 198

## Willard Rhodes Collection

Field recordings of North American Indian music, 1940–1952

Archive of Folk Song

While working for the Bureau of Indian Affairs with equipment supplied in part by the Library of Congress, Willard Rhodes of Columbia University recorded the music of fifty Indian tribes living primarily in the western United States. From the start of the project in 1940, the ethnomusicologist found that Indian music was "not a relic of the dead past but a vital, dynamic force." He documented, in addition to traditional genres, Christian hymns in native languages, songs with English words, and other music of recent composition. The tribes visited by Rhodes during the twelve-year period included the Apache, Bannock, Caddo, Cherokee, Cheyenne, Chinook, Choctaw, Clallam, Comanche, Creek, Delaware, Hopi, Kiowa, Lummi, Navaho, Paiute, Pawnee, Quinault, Shoshone, Sioux, Skagit, Ute, Washo, Wichita, and Zuñi. Through transfer of material from the Bureau of Indian Affairs and the gift of Dr. Rhodes in 1964, the Library has accumulated field recordings from the Rhodes expeditions (AFS 9,519–9,562, 10,090–10,094, 10,453–10,485, 12,097–12,295, and 14,618–14,625). The over 270 original discs and fifty tapes have, for the most part, been duplicated on tape and are listed in a concordance and catalogs supplied by Dr. Rhodes. The Library of Congress has issued ten LP recordings based on the collection through the cooperation of the Bureau of Indian Affairs and the Indian Arts and Crafts Board. Dr. Rhodes has also edited two albums for Folkways Records.

Korson, Rae, and Joseph C. Hickerson, "The Willard Rhodes Collection of American Indian Music in the Archive of Folksong," *Ethnomusicology* (ML1.-E77), v. 13, May 1969: 296–304.

Rhodes, Willard, comp., *Music of the American Indian* (Library of Congress, Division of Music, Recording Laboratory [in cooperation with the Bureau of Indian Affairs and the Indian Arts and Crafts Board, 1954] 20 s. 12 in. 33⅓ rpm. AFS L34–43).

# 199

## Angelo A. Rizzuto Collection

Photographs of New York City, 1950s and 1960s

Prints and Photographs Division

Little is known about Angelo A. Rizzuto (1906–1967) beyond the most basic biographical information. A native of Deadwood, South Dakota, he graduated from Wittenberg College in Ohio in 1931 and spent his later life in New York City. He apparently devoted much of his time to preparing a photographic survey of Manhattan and planned a publication that would document the city's appearance 300 years after it had become an English colony. In 1969, through Rizzuto's bequest, the Library received the working files for his unfinished book. The 60,000 black-and-white negatives and photoprints offer a detailed record of Manhattan from about 1952 to 1966. Emphasized in Rizzuto's work is the vast scale of the Manhattan cityscape and the complex interrelationships between people and their physical environment. Although supplying virtually no caption information, the photographer carefully organized his images by year, month, and date. Chronological files of contact prints dating chiefly from the late 1950s and the few enlargement prints selected by Rizzuto are available to researchers.

Maddox, Jerald, "Photography as Folk Art," in *One Hundred Years of Photographic History: Essays in Honor of Beaumont Newhall* (Albuquerque: University of New Mexico Press, 1975. 180 p. TR15.O53), edited by Van Deren Coke, p. 104–108.

Rizzuto, Angelo, *Angelo Rizzuto's New York: "In Little Old New York, by Anthony Angel"* (Washington: Library of Congress, 1972. [55] p. F128.37.R5).

# 200

## Helen H. Roberts Collection

Field recordings collected by ethnomusicologist
Helen H. Roberts and her papers

Archive of Folk Song

The noted ethnomusicologist Helen H. Roberts participated in recording expeditions in Jamaica, Hawaii, California, and the American Southwest in the 1920s and early 1930s. While affiliated with Yale University in the 1930s, she obtained a Carnegie grant to copy wax cylinder field recordings on aluminum discs. She sent approximately 250 cylinders and seventy disc recordings to the Library of Congress from 1936 to 1937 and later donated an additional 293 discs in 1955. Although predominantly Roberts's own field work, the collection includes cylinders or disc copies of material recorded by Walter McClintock among the Blackfoot Indians in 1898, by Charles Lummis in the American Southwest, by H. E. Crampton in the South Pacific from 1906 to 1907, and by Carl Lumholtz among the Huichol in Mexico in 1898. Also represented is miscellaneous African, Australian, and American Indian music. The discs have been copied on tape. Lists, field and research notes, and musical transcriptions relating primarily to her research on California Indian music are kept in the Archive of Folk Song. Some of the recordings are mentioned in the bibliography of Roberts's publications in *Ethnomusicology* (ML1.E77), v. 11, May 1967, p. 228–233.

# 201

## Rochambeau Collection

Papers and revolutionary war maps of comte de Rochambeau

Manuscript Division
Geography and Map Division

The personal papers of Jean Baptiste Donatien de Vimeur, comte de Rochambeau (1725–1807), commander in chief of the French forces during the American Revolution, were purchased by act of Congress in 1883. Spanning the years 1777 to 1794, the collection consists of one volume of manuscript histories covering some of the revolutionary war years, five volumes of correspondence and papers dating chiefly from the 1780s, and nine letterbooks containing copies of letters sent and received by Rochambeau (1780–84). Of particular note are materials relating to the French branch of the Society of the Cincinnati, which Rochambeau founded in 1784, and correspondence conducted with George Washington chiefly after Rochambeau's return to France in 1783. A partial inventory, received with the 1,800-item collection, complements the finding aid compiled by the Manuscript Division. The Rochambeau papers have been microfilmed.

For his personal use Rochambeau retained maps of fortifications and troop positions prepared by the French army engineers. Forty manuscript and twenty-eight printed maps were acquired with the Rochambeau papers and transferred to the Geography and Map Division along with a manuscript atlas containing plans of fifty-four French encampments during the army's 1782 march from Yorktown to Boston. Selected items are described and reproduced in *The American Campaigns of Rochambeau's Army, 1780, 1781, 1782, 1783* (Princeton: Princeton University Press, 1972. 2 v. E265.R513), translated and edited by Howard C. Rice, Jr., and Anne S. K. Brown. The maps are individually recorded in the Library's computerized map catalog. The atlas is listed in the atlas card file in the division reading room and described as number 1335 in *A List of Geographical Atlases in the Library of Congress* (Washington: Govt. Print Off., 1909. 1208 p. Z6028.U56, v. 1; reprint, Amsterdam: Theatrum Orbis Terrarum, 1971), compiled under the direction of Philip Lee Phillips.

*G&M Div. Guide,* p. 18–19.
*Handbook of MSS. in LC,* p. 352–353.
*NUCMC,* 60–21.

# 202

## William Woodville Rockhill Tibetan Collection

Tibetan religious books and manuscripts

Chinese and Korean Section, Asian Division

Following his graduation from the Ecole spéciale militaire de St. Cyr, France, and his service with the French army in Algeria, William Woodville Rockhill (1854–1914) accepted the position of second secretary of the American legation in Peking. There the American diplomat pursued the Tibetan studies he had begun in Paris and undertook expeditions to Mongolia and Tibet (1888–89 and 1891–92) for the Smithsonian Institution. In 1901, four years before his appointment as American minister to China, Rockhill presented to the Library 6,000 Chinese, Manchu, Mongolian, and Tibetan volumes which he had acquired during his travels. One of the Library's first major acquisitions of Far Eastern materials, the Rockhill gift was dispersed throughout the collections of the Asian Division, with the exception of the Tibetan-language works which were retained as a distinct unit. These items consist largely of Lamaist and Tantric writings which were printed in China, Tibet, and Mongolia, some from woodblocks cut in Tibet. While most of the fifty-seven printed works and eight manuscripts are undated, several items bear seventeenth- and eighteenth-century imprints. The donor's handwritten catalog provides provenance information and serves as the finding aid.

*ARLC,* 1901, p. 14–15.

# 203

## Richard Rodgers Collection

### Music manuscripts of Richard Rodgers

Music Division

During the 1950s and 1960s American composer Richard Rodgers (1902–1979) presented to the Library music manuscripts from all periods of his career. Rodgers's early years are represented by autograph piano-vocal scores for many popular musical comedies written with Lorenz Hart, Rodgers's lyricist for eighteen years—*The Garrick Gaieties* (1925), *Evergreen* (1930), *Jumbo* (1935), *Babes in Arms* (1937), *The Boys from Syracuse* (1938), *Pal Joey* (1940), and *By Jupiter* (1942). Manuscript scores produced during Rodgers's long association with Oscar Hammerstein II (Oscar Hammerstein II Collection, no. 106) include *Oklahoma* (1943), *Carousel* (1945), *Allegro* (1947), *South Pacific* (1948), *The King and I* (1951), *Me and Juliet* (1953), *Pipe Dream* (1955), *Flower Drum Song* (1958), and *The Sound of Music* (1959). There are also manuscripts for later musicals, the films *Love Me Tonight* and *State Fair*, the television series *Victory at Sea*, and the folk ballet *Ghost Town,* as well as incomplete scores for many other works. The collection measures three linear feet and is recorded in the Music Division catalog. The orchestrations prepared by Robert Russell Bennett for eight Rodgers and Hammerstein musicals were donated by Dorothy Hammerstein and Richard Rodgers in 1966 and are kept with other arrangements and original compositions by Bennett.

Waters, Edward N., "Music," *QJLC*, v. 13, November 1955: 24–25.

——, "Harvest of the Year: Selected Acquisitions of the Music Division," *QJLC*, v. 24, January 1967: 60–61.

# 204

## Bruce Rogers Collection

Books designed by Bruce Rogers and his personal papers

Rare Book and Special Collections Division

In 1959 bookdealer S. R. Shapiro presented to the Library a collection of trade books that had been designed under the supervision of Bruce Rogers (1870–1957) during his years at the Riverside Press in Cambridge, Massachusetts (1895–1912). In 1973 Mr. Shapiro added to the collection letters, proofcuts, financial papers, and ephemera relating to the work of this important American book designer. The papers (790 manuscript items) include transcripts of Rogers's letters to his friend Harry Watson Kent, secretary of the Metropolitan Museum of Art; a collection entitled "E-pistoleary Letter's to My Co-respondents Written on my tipewriter by Gess Whoo?" which Rogers had intended for publication; material pertaining to the preparation and distribution of his anthology, *Pi* (1953); and Mr. Shapiro's personal correspondence with Rogers. The 226 volumes in the collection are represented in chronological and shelflist files in the Rare Book and Special Collections Division.

Matheson, William, "Recent Acquisitions of the Rare Book Division," *QJLC*, v. 31, July 1974: 180.

# 205

## Roman Law Collection

Publications and manuscripts on Roman law

Law Library

The single most important contribution to the Roman Law Collection came in 1930 with the purchase of the personal library and manuscripts of Paul Krüger (1840–1926), the German legal scholar who edited *Corpus Juris Civilis* with Theodor Mommsen. While the Library of Congress had been acquiring Roman law materials since the early nineteenth century, this purchase prompted the systematic development of the collection. The present 15,000-volume collection in the Law Library contains extensive holdings of every type of Roman law source and embraces works of recent scholarship as well as late medieval manuscripts and incunabula. Among the 1,600 rare volumes in the collection are the earliest edition of Du Rivail's *Civilis Historiae Juris* (1515)—the first printed work to include the Twelve Tables, the foundation of Roman jurisprudence; Denis Godefroy's *Corpus Juris Civilis in IIII Partes Distinctum* (1583), which introduced the designation "Corpus Juris Civilis" to the body of civil law codified under the Roman emperor Justinian; Peter Schöffer's edition of the *Institutes* (1468); two fourteenth-century manuscript copies of the *Institutes,* one illuminated and in French translation; and numerous sixteenth-century editions of the interpretive writings of Guillaume Budé and Jacques Cujas. Titles are noted in the Law Library catalog and shelflist. A typewritten inventory of the Krüger purchase is also available.

*Law Library,* p. 24–29.

# 206

## Sigmund Romberg Collection

Music manuscripts and recordings of composer Sigmund Romberg

Music Division
Motion Picture, Broadcasting, and Recorded Sound Division

Sigmund Romberg (1887–1951), composer of over seventy operettas and two thousand songs, was one of the most prolific writers of popular music in the twentieth century. Romberg came to America in 1909 and soon enjoyed success as the producer-composer of his own Broadway shows. He branched into motion pictures in 1929, broadcast on radio, organized "pop" concert tours, and worked for the Songwriters Protective Association and ASCAP. Many of Romberg's most popular works, including *Blossom Time* (1921), *The Student Prince* (1924), *The Desert Song* (1926), and *The New Moon* (1928), are represented in the forty-one-volume set of original manuscripts presented to the Library by his widow, Lillian H. Romberg, in the late 1950s and 1960s. The manuscripts contain sketches for instrumental works from as early as 1918 and piano-vocal and orchestral scores for his operettas. In 1967 Mrs. Romberg's sister, Mae H. Rhodes, donated autograph music manuscripts, copyists' manuscripts, printed music, librettos, and film scripts to supplement the Romberg Collection. The Rhodes gift measures six linear feet. Most material received from Mrs. Romberg is listed in the Music Division catalog.

The Motion Picture, Broadcasting, and Recorded Sound Division houses Romberg's personal collection of 543 phonodiscs. The noncommercial recordings, which account for approximately half of the collection, include transcriptions of radio shows featuring Romberg as a conductor and of Romberg's Swift programs from the 1934 to 1935 season. Some of the discs preserve performances and informal conversations of Romberg and his friends Jerome Kern, Deems Taylor, and Alexander Woollcott. The noncommercial discs have been copied on tape, represented in the division catalog, and fully described in an inventory. The published records are listed by label in an inventory.

Waters, Edward N., "Music," *QJLC*, v. 15, November 1957: 22–23.

———, "Paean to a Year of Plenty: Recent Acquisitions of the Music Division," *QJLC*, v. 26, January 1969: 43, 45.

# 207

## Theodore Roosevelt Association Collection

News films of Theodore Roosevelt

Motion Picture, Broadcasting, and Recorded Sound Division

In 1967 the National Park Service transferred to the Library of Congress 375 early news films documenting the career of Pres. Theodore Roosevelt (1858–1919). Collected in the 1920s and 1930s by the Theodore Roosevelt Association, the films were housed in the association's library at the Roosevelt birthplace in New York City and turned over to the National Park Service when the building was designated a national historic site in 1962. The collection covers the president's activities from his Rough Rider days through his later life, with the emphasis on the period from 1909 to 1919. Roosevelt, a favorite subject for newsmen, is shown at major political events of the day as well as in the company of family members, friends, and internationally famous celebrities. Also in the collection are films of Roosevelt's funeral and several posthumous tributes. The films are individually described in the published title catalog and indexed by subject, date, place, and name. Reference prints are available for most films.

Gillespie, Veronica M., "T. R. on Film," *QJLC*, v. 34, January 1977: 39–51.

Theodore Roosevelt Association, "The Theodore Roosevelt Association and the T.R.A. Motion Picture Collection," *Theodore Roosevelt Association Journal* (E757.2.T47a), v. 2, winter/spring 1976: 14–15.

[Film catalog in preparation]

# 208

## Theodore Roosevelt Hunting Library

Publications on hunting, natural history, and exploration

Rare Book and Special Collections Division

Theodore Roosevelt (1858–1919) took great personal interest in his "big-game library" and bequeathed this portion of his book collection to his youngest son Kermit, who in turn left it to his son and namesake. In 1963 and 1964 Kermit Roosevelt presented his grandfather's hunting collection to the Library of Congress. Although composed primarily of late nineteenth- and early twentieth-century publications on hunting, natural history, exploration, ornithology, and sport, the collection includes a number of significant early editions such as Jean de Clamorgan's *La Chasse dv lovp* (Paris: 1566); Robert de Salnove's *La Venerie royale* (Paris: 1655); *L'Histoire naturelle* (Paris: 1767), a work by John Ray that was translated into French by François Salerne; and *The Historie of Fovre-Footed Beastes* (London: 1607) and *The Historie of Serpents* (London: 1608) by Edward Topsell. Most of the 254 volumes bear Roosevelt's bookplate. Items are recorded in the collection author/title and shelflist files and in the division dictionary catalog.

Goff, Frederick R., "T. R.'s Big-Game Library," *QJLC*, v. 21, July 1964: 166 [i.e., iv]–171.

# 209

## Jim Rosellini Collection

Field recordings of the folklore of the Republic of Upper Volta, 1969–75

Archive of Folk Song

Jim Rosellini began documenting the music and oral traditions of the Republic of Upper Volta in 1969 while working as a Peace Corps volunteer. Thanks to the interest of several American institutions, including the Library of Congress, he extended the scope of his project to sixty ethnic groups of the region and established a sound archive in the Centre Voltaïque de la Recherche Scientifique to preserve recordings, films, photographs, and field notes. Between 1970 and 1976 the Library of Congress duplicated field recordings made by Jim Rosellini and Kathleen Johnson, his coworker in later years. The collection (AFS 14,251–14,252, 15,078–15,083, 18,754–18,761, 18,800–18,801, and 18,807–18,848) contains folktales, proverbs, historical narratives, and traditional music, and features performances on the various types of drums, fiddles, flutes, harps, horns, idiophones, rattles, and xylophones favored by local musicians. The sixty reels of tape are accompanied by field notes, correspondence, a concordance, and over fifty photographs. The Indiana University Archives of Traditional Music and the University of Washington Archives of Ethnic Music and Dance have also received project material.

*Michael Yougma, Mossi musician of the court of the chief of Koupéla, Upper Volta, playing a gourd drum at a harvest feast (1970). Jim Rosellini Collection, Archive of Folk Song. Courtesy of Jim Rosellini and the Centre Voltaïque de la Recherche Scientifique. LC–USZ62–67599.*

# 210

## Harry Rosenthal Collection

Music manuscripts and papers of composer Franz Liszt

Music Division

In 1965 Harry Rosenthal, a New York businessman and collector, presented to the Library of Congress an important group of manuscripts by the Hungarian composer and piano virtuoso Franz Liszt (1811–1886). Over a thirty-year period, Mr. Rosenthal uncovered a number of Liszt's autograph letters and several music manuscripts that were thought to have been lost. The twenty music manuscripts date chiefly from Liszt's later years and include *Csárdás* (1884), a *Salve Regina* for organ (1877), the piano duet *Festpolonaise* (1876), a sketch for his unfinished oratorio *St. Stanislaus,* and piano transcriptions of works by Mendelssohn, as well as Hans von Bülow, César Cui, Josef Dessauer, and Eduard Lassen. Most of the 121 autograph letters in the collection (1829–86) are three or more pages in length. The forty-eight letters addressed to the music critic Richard Pohl and his wife are discussed in Edward N. Waters's article, "Franz Liszt to Richard Pohl," published in *Studies in Romanticism* (PN751.S8), v. 6, summer 1967, p. 193–202. The remainder were written by Liszt to his publisher C. F. Kahnt, Franz von Schober, the Grand Duke Karl Alexander, Carl Gille, Pierre Erard, and others. Also donated by Mr. Rosenthal are books on Liszt, a few photographs, and an essay attributed to Liszt and written in the hand of Hans von Bülow. The collection measures five linear feet.

Waters, Edward N., "Harvest of the Year. Selected Acquisitions of the Music Division," *QJLC,* v. 24, January 1967: 51–54, 64.

*Woodcut from William Caxton's first illustrated edition of Jacobus de Cessolis's* De Ludo Scachorum *(On the Game of Chess) (ca. 1482), one of sixteen books in the Rosenwald Collection from the press of England's first printer. Lessing J. Rosenwald Collection, Rare Book and Special Collections Division.*

# 211

## Lessing J. Rosenwald Collection

The illustrated book, fifteenth through twentieth centuries

Rare Book and Special Collections Division

The Lessing J. Rosenwald Collection stands out among the distinguished resources of the Rare Book and Special Collections Division. Taking the illustrated book as its central theme and containing books from the last six centuries and manuscripts from the three preceding, the collection's greatest strengths are in fifteenth-century woodcut books, early sixteenth-century illustrated books, William Blake, and twentieth-century *livres des peintres.* Within this grand design the late Mr. Rosenwald sought books produced by the earliest printers and outstanding presses of later periods, and books on the following subjects: science, calligraphy, botany, and chess. The catalog describing the collection published in 1978 contains 2,653 entries, many for books represented by more than one copy.

Among the characteristics which make this collection such a rich potential resource for study are the presence of an amazing number of unique books and books of such great rarity that only a handful of copies is known. Virtually every book in the collection is in superb condition and many contain such special features as original drawings, artists' proofs, trial states, and laid-in letters. Mr. Rosenwald's assemblage of books, plates, drawings, and engravings by William Blake is one of the finest ever brought together. Of the twenty illuminated books described in Geoffrey Keynes's Blake bibliography, the collection contains fourteen, as well as duplicates and extra plates. Finding that the Blake materials received more use than any other section of the collection, Mr. Rosenwald made copies of many of the illuminated books available to the Trianon Press for a series of facsimiles.

Outstanding rarities include a volume containing four complete books printed by William Caxton, England's finest printer; eleven block books; the magnificent fifteenth-century manuscript known as the Giant Bible of Mainz, kept on permanent exhibit in the Library's Great Hall; and one of two known copies of the 1495 edition of *Epistolae et Evangelia,* called by some the finest illustrated book of the fifteenth century. Rarities are, however, but one aspect of the collection. Its particular importance arises from the quantity and the unity of the material, much of it still awaiting scholarly investigation. Before being purchased by Mr. Rosenwald, the 160 fifteenth- and sixteenth-century Dutch and Flemish books from the library of the Dukes of Arenberg had been inaccessible to generations of scholars and bibliographers.

The collection catalog describes Mr. Rosenwald's gifts to the Library of Congress in the years 1943 to 1975. Accounts of subsequent additions can be found in the division's acquisitions reports in the *Quarterly Journal.*

During Mr. Rosenwald's lifetime the collection was housed in his private gallery, the Alverthorpe Gallery in Jenkintown, Pennsylvania. Not long after his death on June 24, 1979, the collection was brought to Washington and is available for consultation in the Rare Book and Special Collections Division. The division houses a card catalag containing author entries for the books and manuscripts in the collection.

Goff, Frederick R., "The Gift of Lessing J. Rosenwald to the Library of Congress: A Bibliographer's Survey of the Collection, from the 15th through the 18th Century," *QJLC,* v. 22, July 1965: 170–193.

Lehrer, Ruth Fine, "A Checklist of Blake Material in The Lessing J. Rosenwald Collection, Alverthorpe Gallery, Jenkintown, Pennsylvania," *Blake Newsletter* (PR4147.B47), v. 9, winter 1975/76: 60–85.

Matheson, William, "Lessing J. Rosenwald: 'A Splendidly Generous Man,' " *QJLC,* v. 37, winter 1980: 3–24.

Rosenwald, Lessing J., "The Formation of the Rosenwald Collection," *QJLC,* v. 3, October 1945: 53–62.

U.S., Library of Congress, *The Lessing J. Rosenwald Collection: A Catalog of the Gifts of Lessing J. Rosenwald to the Library of Congress, 1943 to 1975* (Washington: Library of Congress, 1977. xxi, 517 p. Z881.U5 1977).

U.S., Library of Congress, *Treasures from the Lessing J. Rosenwald Collection: An Exhibit Honoring Mr. Rosenwald's Eighty-Second Birthday* (Washington: 1973. [57] p. Z1029.U55).

Zigrosser, Carl, "So Wide a Net: A Curator's View of the Lessing J. Rosenwald Collection, 17th to the 20th Century," *QJLC,* v. 22, July 1965: 194–205.

# 212

## Ruth Rubin Collection

Field recordings of Jewish folklore, 1940s–1960s

Archive of Folk Song

The Rubin Collection, purchased by the Library of Congress in the late 1960s and 1970s, consists of field recordings made by Ruth Rubin in the late 1940s, 1950s, and 1960s in Jewish communities in Canada, the eastern United States, Britain, and Israel. Mrs. Rubin, author of *Voices of a People: The Story of Yiddish Folksong,* 2d ed. (New York: McGraw Hill [1973] 558 p. PJ5122.R8 1973), recorded songs of eastern European origin and interviews illuminating the history of the music and the performers' personal background. To a lesser degree, the New York folklorist documented Yiddish art songs, songs reflecting the lives of immigrants, and songs created by Soviet Jews in the 1920s and 1930s. The 126 tapes (AFS 13,504–13,553, 14,516–14,555, 14,665–14,695, and 19,253–19,256) are listed in a concordance. Portions of the Rubin Collection have been duplicated for the New York Public Library, the Wayne State University Archive, the National Museum of Canada, and the Haifa Music Museum. Selections recorded in the United States and Canada are included on the commercial release, *Jewish Life, the Old Country (Folkways Records* [1963] 2 s. 12 in. 33⅓ rpm. FG 3801).

# 213

## Albert Ruger Collection

Panoramic maps of U.S. cities, late nineteenth century

Geography and Map Division

In the decades following the Civil War, Albert Ruger (1829–1899), one of the best represented panoramic mapmakers in the Geography and Map Division's collections, produced "bird's-eye" views of settlements in twenty states from New Hampshire to Alabama. His works were published under the name of Ruger and Ruger & Stoner. Most of the 198 panoramic maps forming the Ruger Collection can be traced to the artist's personal collection which the Library purchased from John Ramsey of Canton, Ohio, in 1941. The majority date from the 1860s and 1870s and portray midwestern cities. The maps are described in the Library's computerized map catalog and listed by town in John Hébert's checklist of 1,117 panoramic maps in the division. Panoramic maps by Thaddeus M. Fowler are described in entry number 85. A number of panoramic maps are kept in the Prints and Photographs Division.

Hébert, John R., "Panoramic Maps of American Cities," *Special Libraries* (Z671.S72), v. 63, December 1972: 554–562.

U.S., Library of Congress, Geography and Map Division, *Panoramic Maps of Anglo-American Cities: A Checklist of Maps in the Collections of the Library of Congress, Geography and Map Division* (Washington: Library of Congress, 1974. 118 p. Z6027.U5U54 1974), compiled by John R. Hébert.

# 214

## Russian Imperial Collection

Books from the libraries of the Russian imperial family

Rare Book and Special Collections Division

In the early 1930s, 2,600 volumes from the book collections of the Romanov family were purchased by the Library of Congress through a New York book dealer. Variously called the Winter Palace Collection, the Tsar's Library, and (more accurately) the Russian Imperial Collection, these elaborately bound volumes have been assigned, for the most part, to the Rare Book and Special Collections Division. The collection includes eighteenth- and nineteenth-century documents, biographies, works of literature, and military, social, and administrative histories, and reflects the reading interests of the imperial family and the types of publications they received as gifts. Books in English, French, and German are well represented, although the majority of the publications are in Russian. The volumes carry the bookplates of Alexander III, his wife Maria Fedorovna, Nicholas II, his wife Alexandra Fedorovna, their son Alekseĭ Nikolaevich, and other family members.

Two other divisions maintain significant portions of the original purchase. The music from the collection—largely nineteenth-century Russian scores—has been integrated into the rare book collection of the Music Division and includes a presentation copy of the first edition of the full score of Glinka's *Ruslan i Liudmila* (1878), prepared as two volumes and bound with an added dedicatory leaf, and the 1894 edition of Rimsky-Korsakov's first opera *Pskovitĭanka*. The 1931 *Annual Report of the Librarian of Congress* highlights the most important music items.

The Law Library received copies of military laws, laws regarding the abolition of serfdom, revisions of civil and criminal laws, and various texts on special legal subjects. The legal titles are listed in the 1931 *Annual Report of the Librarian of Congress* and are now part of the holdings of Russian legal sources and literature in the European Law Division.

ARLC, 1931, p. 38–42, 137–142, 223–225; 1932, p. 29, 111–115.

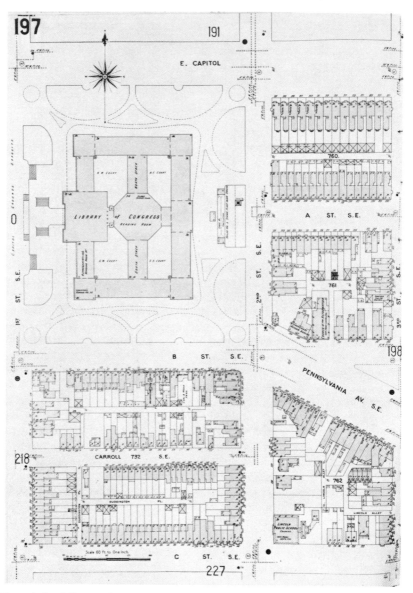

*Plan of the Library of Congress and adjacent structures from the second volume of* Insurance Maps of Washington, D.C. *(1904). The James Madison Memorial building, the Thomas Jefferson building and the Folger Shakespeare Library now occupy the blocks directly south and east of the original Library of Congress building. Sanborn Fire Insurance Map Collection, Geography and Map Division. Negative in division.*

# 215

## Sanborn Fire Insurance Map Collection

Insurance maps of U.S. cities, late nineteenth and twentieth centuries

Geography and Map Division

The fire insurance map is probably the single most important record of urban growth and development in the United States during the past one hundred years. It contains data used in estimating the potential risk for urban structures and includes such information as their construction material, height, and function as well as the location of lot lines. The Sanborn Map Company has been the dominant American publisher of fire insurance maps and atlases for over seventy years. Founded by D. A. Sanborn in 1867, the firm has issued and periodically updated detailed plans of 12,000 American cities and towns. In 1967, shortly after the Sanborn Company discontinued its large-scale map series, the Census Bureau transferred to the Library of Congress 1,840 volumes of Sanborn maps. Together with material acquired through copyright deposit, the Sanborn Fire Insurance Map Collection numbers approximately seven hundred thousand sheets in bound and unbound volumes. While the earliest atlas dates from 1867, most fall within the period 1876 to 1961. Some areas are represented by as many as seven or eight different editions. A small number of atlases are described in *A List of Geographical Atlases in the Library of Congress* (Washington: Library of Congress, 1973. lxxii, 681 p. Z6028.U56, v. 7). A checklist for the collection is in publication.

Ristow, Walter W., "United States Fire Insurance and Underwriters Maps, 1852–1968," *QJLC,* v. 25, July 1968: 194–218.

U.S., Library of Congress, Geography and Map Division, *Fire Insurance Maps in the Library of Congress: Plans of North American Cities and Towns Produced by the Sanborn Map Company* (Washington: Library of Congress, 1980).

# 216

## Francis Maria Scala Collection

Music, music manuscripts, and papers of band leader Francis Maria Scala

Music Division

Francis Maria Scala (1819?–1903) was the first musician to be designated Leader of the Marine Band. He joined the Fife and Drum Corps of the U.S. Marines in 1842 and was promoted to the important position of fife-major the following year. During his tenure as leader from 1855 to 1871, the Marine Band grew to over thirty musicians and became well known through its public outdoor concerts. In 1952 Norman P. Scala presented to the Library of Congress his father's collection of manuscript and printed music, photographs, clippings, programs, and correspondence. The collection, measuring approximately twelve linear feet, consists primarily of music arranged or composed by Scala for band concerts, military formations, and White House functions. The music (608 titles) is listed in an inventory included in David M. Ingalls's thesis. Most of the collection has been microfilmed. Through the bequest of Norman P. Scala, a trust fund has been established at the Library for the study and promotion of the music of Francis Scala and his period.

Ingalls, David M., "Francis Scala: Leader of the Marine Band from 1855 to 1871" (1957. Thesis (M.A.), Catholic University of America), leaves 2–5, 32–133.

# 217

## Albert Schatz Collection

Early opera librettos and research files assembled by Albert Schatz

Music Division

German businessman Albert Schatz (1839–1910) assembled over twelve thousand printed librettos in preparation for a projected work on the history of opera. The Schatz Collection in the Music Division, purchased by the Library in 1908, brings together an outstanding selection of German and Italian texts, particularly from the seventeenth and eighteenth centuries, and is the major source for Oscar George Theodore Sonneck's *Catalogue of Opera Librettos Printed Before 1800*. As an adjunct to the libretto collection, the Library acquired Schatz's research files two years later. The material consists chiefly of a chronological list of opera performances from 1541 to 1901. Sixty card files contain information (title, composer, librettist, genre, number of acts, and date, city, and theater of the premiere performance) for as many productions as Schatz could document. Schatz also compiled in ledgers detailed chronological lists, complete with dates of first and subsequent performances, of operas by fourteen eighteenth-century composers. In addition to the above-mentioned "Operngeschichte Statistik," the collection includes notes, correspondence, playbills, manuscripts for articles, and clippings pertaining to the history of opera in Europe and the United States. The manuscripts measure thirty linear feet. The librettos and manuscripts have been microfilmed.

*ARLC,* 1911, p. 45–48.

*NUCMC,* 67 656.

U.S., Library of Congress, Music Division, *Catalogue of Opera Librettos Printed Before 1800* (Washington: Govt. Print. Off., 1914. 2 v. ML136.-U55C45; reprints, New York: B. Franklin [1967] and New York: Johnson Reprint Corp., 1968), prepared by Oscar George Theodore Sonneck.

CONCILIO DI D. M. NI CONTRO. S. ORSOLA
ATTO PRIMO

Alfonso Parigi I

*Illustration from the libretto for* La Regina Sant' Orsola, *text by Andrea Salvadori, music by Marco da Gagliano, published for a 1625 performance at the Pitti Palace in Florence. Many librettos in the Schatz Collection include set designs, portraits, or illustrations of dramatic scenes. Albert Schatz Collection, Music Division. LC–USZ62–67600.*

# 218

## Arthur P. Schmidt Company Archive

Business papers and music manuscripts of the Schmidt Company

Music Division

In 1876 Arthur Paul Schmidt (1846–1921) founded a music store in Boston which was to become one of the largest music publishing and importing firms in the United States. The firm was especially sympathetic to American composers and over a forty-year period absorbed the costs of publishing major chamber and orchestral works, often with full scores and parts, by Arthur Bird, Edward MacDowell, and other New England musicians. The Schmidt Company's massive archive of music manuscripts, correspondence, and business and financial records was donated to the Library in 1959 by the Summy-Birchard Company of Evanston, Illinois, shortly after Summy-Birchard purchased the Boston firm. The holographs include numerous works by Mrs. H. H. A. Beach, George W. Chadwick, Henry Clough-Leighter, Charles Dennée, Arthur Foote, Henry K. Hadley, and Horatio Parker and occupy approximately sixty-three linear feet. Most of the correspondence with composers, printers, and foreign publishers (forty-two linear feet) postdates 1907. In addition there are over three hundred letters written to the company in the late nineteenth and early twentieth centuries that had been acquired before the 1959 gift. The letters are currently arranged by year and will be reorganized by correspondent. The business records (twelve linear feet) consist of royalty statements, catalogs, cashbooks, ledgers, and miscellaneous printed material. A portion of the music manuscripts and letters are recorded on lists.

Krummel, Donald W., "Arthur P. Schmidt Company Archive," *LCIB*, v. 18, August 3, 1959: 475.

Waters, Edward N., "Music," *QJLC*, v. 15, November 1957: 27.

# 219

## Arnold Schoenberg Collection

Papers and recordings of composer Arnold Schoenberg

Music Division
Motion Picture, Broadcasting, and Recorded Sound Division

Substantial portions of the correspondence of Arnold Schoenberg (1874–1951) were given to the Library by the composer's family between 1952 and 1972. While the collection encompasses material from all periods of Schoenberg's life, the majority of the letters were written after Schoenberg emigrated to the United States in 1933. Schoenberg's two famous pupils, Alban Berg and Anton von Webern, are represented by a long series of letters dating respectively from 1911 to 1934 and 1907 to 1936 and containing significant information on their creative work and personal lives. An important Wassily Kandinsky letter—Schoenberg exhibited his paintings with the Blue Rider group in 1912—deals with the artist's aesthetic philosophy. Other major correspondents include Rudolf Kolisch, Ernst Křenek, Gustav Mahler, Thomas Mann, Egon Wellesz, and Alexander Zemlinsky. Drafts and carbons of business letters, concert programs, and clippings documenting Schoenberg's early career are also preserved in the collection. The letters are organized by correspondent and, together with the other papers, measure four linear feet. Researchers desiring to use the collection must obtain permission from the Schoenberg estate; however, preliminary inquiries should be addressed to the Music Division. Through other sources, the Library has acquired a significant number of Schoenberg's music holographs and a few letters. The music manuscripts include all five of his string quartets, *Verklärte Nacht* (1899), *Pierrot Lunaire* (1912), *Die glückliche Hand* (1913), *Serenade,* op. 24 (1923), and *A Survivor from Warsaw* (1947).

Wire and disc recordings from the Schoenberg Collection preserve drafts for letters, a few lectures, a radio talk delivered in 1949, and a 1931 performance of *Variations for Orchestra,* op. 31. The material has been reproduced on three tapes and is listed in the Motion Picture, Broadcasting, and Recorded Sound Division catalog.

Hill, Richard S., "Music," *QJLC,* v. 10, November 1952: 43–44.

——, "Music," *QJLC,* v. 11, November 1953: 20–23.

Waters, Edward N., "Music," *QJLC,* v. 16, November 1958: 16–17.

# 220

## Wilhelm Schreiber Collection

European book illustrations, fifteenth to eighteenth centuries

Prints and Photographs Division

Wilhelm Schreiber (1855–1932), German scholar and author of the major reference work *Manuel de l'amateur de la gravure sur bois et sur metal au XV$^e$ siècle* (1891–1911), organized a personal study collection of over twenty thousand book illustrations produced during the fifteenth through the eighteenth centuries. Through the generosity of Dr. and Mrs. Otto Vollbehr, the Library acquired this collection in 1929 along with Schreiber's handwritten inventory. The collection is rich in sixteenth-century prints and includes title pages, borders, portraits, and illustrations from books produced throughout Europe. Among the many artists represented are Jost Amman, Hans Sebald Beham, Urs Graf, and Hans Baldung Grien. For the most part, illustrations from a single published work are filed together in folders and listed by subject in a card index. While imprint information is not noted on most folders, sources can often be determined by consulting the original inventory. The collection is being processed and is closed to researchers at the present time. Plans are underway to preserve the material on microfilm.

*ARLC,* 1929, 200–202.

*Guide,* Vanderbilt, no. 645.

Schreiber, Wilhelm Ludwig, *Catalogue of the . . . Collection of Prof. W. L. Schreiber . . . Which Will Be Sold by Auction* ([Vienna: Druck von W. Fischer, 1909] 89 p., 40 plates. NE59.S35).

Vollbehr, Otto H. F., *Introduction to a Collection of Book-illustrations in the Possession of Dr. Otto Vollbehr* ([n.p.] 1928. 14 p. NE1247.V6).

# 221

## John Secrist Collection

### Early operatic and vocal recordings

Motion Picture, Broadcasting, and Recorded Sound Division

The outstanding collection of early operatic and vocal recordings assembled by John Secrist (1918–1958) was presented to the Library of Congress by his parents in 1962. Mr. Secrist, a mathematician by profession, was well known among collectors for the excellent condition and preservation of his record library. He assembled virtually complete sets of the commercial releases of Enrico Caruso and Rosa Ponselle, two artists for whom he compiled discographies published in *The Record Collector* (ML156.9.R35), v. 6, November/December 1951, p. 245–280 and v. 5, May 1950, p. 104–117. Caruso is represented by 259 recorded performances, and Rosa Ponselle by transcriptions of radio broadcasts, published phonograph discs, and private recordings made at the soprano's estate near Baltimore. At the time of his death, Mr. Secrist was working on a John McCormack discography and had acquired a large number of his Victor and HMV recordings. The collection also contains rare acoustic discs featuring Suzanne Adams, Edouard de Reszke, Ernestine Schumann-Heink, Giovanni Zenatello, and other leading singers. The 1,700 discs have been transcribed on tape alphabetically by artist. (The sequence follows that used by Mr. Secrist in his personal catalog.) Individual recordings can be located by using this catalog and notes filed in the Motion Picture, Broadcasting, and Recorded Sound Division. One thousand early record manufacturers' catalogs, books, photographs, selected correspondence, and research notes donated by Mr. and Mrs. J. B. Secrist are also available for reference.

Favia-Artsay, Aida, "The John Secrist Collection at the Library of Congress," *Hobbies* (AM201.H6), v. 69, June 1963: 30–32; and July: 30–31.

Lowens, Irving, "Music," *QJLC*, v. 21, January 1964: 15–19.

Waters, Edward N., "In All Forms & For All Mediums: Music Division Acquisitions," *QJLC*, v. 30, January 1973: 80–81.

*Record label (ca. 1902). The Secrist Collection includes all seven of the rare recordings Enrico Caruso made in Milan for the International Zonophone Company when he was still a relatively unknown tenor. John Secrist Collection, Motion Picture, Broadcasting, and Recorded Sound Division. LC–USP6–6389A.*

# 222

## Charles Louis Seeger Collection

Music and other material relating to the Workers Music League, 1930s

Music Division

In 1940 musicologist Charles Louis Seeger (1886–1979) donated to the Library a small collection of material relating chiefly to the activities of the Workers Music League (WML), an affiliate of the International Music Bureau which was established in New York City in 1931. Under the slogan "Music for the Masses," the WML guided the musical aspects of the revolutionary workers movement and undertook the publication of protest songs and marches. Music and important theoretical statements were written for the WML by the Composers' Collective of New York City and issued, in some cases, under the pseudonyms "Carl Sands" and "L. E. Swift." The Seeger gift includes WML songbooks and sheet music from England, the United States, and the U.S.S.R. that may have been distributed through the organization, and related concert programs, periodicals, news clippings, and notes. The collection occupies two linear feet and is, at present, unorganized.

# 223

## Gisella Selden-Goth Collection

### Rare music manuscripts

Music Division

During the 1960s and 1970s Hungarian musicologist and composer Gisella Selden-Goth (1884–1975) presented to the Library of Congress an outstanding collection of music manuscripts. The collection contains twenty-two holographs by leading eighteenth-, nineteenth-, and twentieth-century European composers: Béla Bartók, Ludwig van Beethoven, Hector Berlioz, Johannes Brahms, Anton Bruckner, Ferruccio Busoni, César Franck, Charles Gounod, Michael Haydn, Franz Liszt, Gustav Mahler, Nicolò Paganini, Nicola Antonio Porpora, Friedrich Wilhelm Rust, Arnold Schoenberg, Franz Schubert, Robert Schumann, Johann Strauss the younger, Richard Strauss, Giuseppe Verdi, Richard Wagner, and Hugo Wolf. Some of the manuscripts are unpublished. The holographs are listed in an inventory and described in the donor's catalog.

Waters, Edward N., "The Realm of Tone—Music," *QJLC*, v. 22, January 1965: 30–33.

# William Tecumseh Sherman Collection

Papers and Civil War maps of General Sherman

Manuscript Division
Geography and Map Division

The papers of Gen. William Tecumseh Sherman (1820–1891), assembled by the Library over the past seventy-five years through purchase and gift, chiefly cover the years 1818 to 1891 and include correspondence, military documents, printed matter, photographs, memorabilia, manuscripts of Sherman's *Memoirs,* and a journal kept during the Mexican War. Over half of the collection deals with Sherman's post-Civil War career, particularly his service as commanding general of the army (1869–83). The greater part of the correspondence from this period concerns military expeditions against the western Indian tribes, the maintenance of Indian reservations, and the affairs of the military territorial government. Approximately one-tenth of the 18,000-item collection relates to Sherman's early army commissions (1840–53) and his civilian experience in business, banking, law, and education (1853–61), and another tenth pertains to his Civil War service (1861–65). The Sherman papers have been microfilmed and described in a published register.

Three atlases and 202 maps which belonged to General Sherman are kept in the Geography and Map Division. Unlike the papers, the cartographic material focuses on Sherman's Civil War campaigns in the Carolinas, Mississippi, Tennessee, and Georgia. Included are numerous reconnaissance and battle plans in manuscript and a series of tracings from Robert Mills's *Atlas of the State of South Carolina* ([Columbia? S.C.] 1825) that were apparently used as reference maps. One of the three atlases, Henry Schenck Tanner's *A New Universal Atlas* (Philadelphia: Carey & Hart, 1844), bears Sherman's signature and bookplate and contains annotations and sketches. The collection is described in the division card catalog of rare materials. Richard Stephenson's *Civil War Maps: An Annotated List of Maps and Atlases in the Map Collections of the Library of Congress* (Washington: 1961. 138 p. Z6027.U5U55) lists maps with military information and will be expanded in the next edition to cover all the Sherman material.

*NUCMC,* 59–42.

U.S., Library of Congress, Manuscript Division, *William T. Sherman: A Register of His Papers in the Library of Congress,* rev. ed. (Washington: 1977. 10 p. Z6616.S55U54 1977).

# 225

## Nicolas Slonimsky Collection

Papers and music manuscripts of musical lexicographer
Nicolas Slonimsky

Music Division

Nicolas Slonimsky, prominent musical lexicographer, conductor,
and pianist, came to the United States in 1923. As director of the
Chamber Orchestra of Boston (1927–34), he introduced American
audiences to significant new compositions and established himself as an
advocate for contemporary music. During the past forty years, Slonimsky has compiled numerous reference books, including *Music Since
1900* ([1937]; 4th ed., New York: C. Scribner's Sons [1971] xvii,
1595 p. ML197.S634 1971), the revised sixth edition of Theodore
Baker's *Biographical Dictionary of Musicians*, first issued in 1958, and
revised editions of Oscar Thompson's *The International Cyclopedia
of Music and Musicians*. In 1969 Mr. Slonimsky presented his papers
and research files to the Library of Congress. Among the 1,840 letters
in the collection are long exchanges with Eric Blom, Aleksandr Grechaninov, Roy Harris, Charles Ives, and Edgard Varèse, and biographies
and theoretical explanations supplied by many of the leading musicians
of the twentieth century. The collection also contains programs, documentary material used in preparing his publications, and drafts for
talks, reviews, articles, and books, including an unpublished biography
of Roy Harris. Also in the Music Division are over twenty holograph
compositions by Slonimsky, among them the piano work *Studies in
Black and White*. The letters are filed by correspondent and many are
represented in an inventory. The collection measures twenty-one linear
feet.

*NUCMC*, 70–2026.

# 226

## Erwin E. Smith Collection

Photographs of American cowboys, 1905–15

Prints and Photographs Division

Erwin Evans Smith (1886–1947) photographed everyday scenes of ranch life while working as a cowboy between 1905 and 1915. He visited large ranches in Texas, New Mexico, and Arizona, including the SMS, JA, Matador, LS, Three Circles, and R2. Some of his best work stemmed from his association with George Pattullo, a former *Boston Herald* reporter whose western stories were illustrated by Smith. His photographs received national attention in 1912 when the Eastman Kodak Company used them to demonstrate the technical excellence that could be achieved with a simple box camera. In 1949 the photographer's sister, Mrs. L. McCullough Pettis, presented to the Library 1,776 original glass and nitrate film negatives. The photographs show cowboys roping, branding, and herding cattle, riding, doing chores, gathering around the chuckwagon, and performing in rodeos. Included are many group and individual portraits. Most images have been reproduced as reference prints and furnished with captions and dates. The collection file is arranged by subject and kept in the reading room of the Prints and Photographs Division. Many of Smith's photographs are reproduced and described by J. Evetts Haley in *Life on the Texas Range* (Austin: University of Texas Press, 1952. 112 p. SF85.S57). Permission is required to reproduce material from this collection.

*Guide,* Vanderbilt, no. 661.

McKeen, Ona Lee, "Erwin Evans Smith, Cowboy Photographer," *QJLC,* v. 9, May 1952: 133–138; reprinted in *A Century of Photographs, 1846–1946, Selected from the Collections of the Library of Congress* (Washington: Library of Congress, 1980. TR6.U62.D572), compiled by Renata V. Shaw.

# 227

## Smithsonian-Densmore Collection

North American Indian music recordings made by Smithsonian ethnologists, 1900s–1930s; papers and photographs of Frances Densmore

Archive of Folk Song

In 1907 and 1908 the Bureau of American Ethnology of the Smithsonian Institution provided Frances Densmore (1867–1957) with a portable cylinder machine to further her study of Chippewa (Ojibway) Indian songs. Over the next twenty-five years Frances Densmore became the Bureau's official collector of North American Indian music, obtaining 2,500 recordings of thirty-five tribal groups. She disseminated the results of her regional studies largely through articles and monographic issues of the *Bureau of American Ethnology Bulletin*. In 1940 the Bureau sent the bulk of her recordings along with about one thousand additional cylinders and a few discs to the National Archives. Eight years later the 3,591 wax cylinders were transferred to the Library of Congress with a generous grant from Eleanor Reese to copy the Densmore material on discs and issue representative recordings to the public. The Smithsonian/Densmore Collection includes the work of at least fifteen other researchers, many of whom were affiliated with the Bureau between 1900 and 1930: Jesse Walter Fewkes, Alice Cunningham Fletcher, Leo Joachim Frachtenberg, John Peabody Harrington, Melville Jacobs, Herbert W. Krieger, Francis La Flesche, Thurlow Lieurance, Washington Matthews, Truman Michelson, James Mooney, James R. Murie, Frans M. Olbrechts, Maurice G. Smith, and John Reed Swanton. Many of the cylinders are listed in a catalog prepared by the National Archives. Recordings by Densmore (AFS 10,515–10,744), Frachtenberg, Lieurance, Olbrechts, and Smith have been duplicated on tape. Dr. Densmore completed a handbook for the recordings in 1943—a copy of the manuscript is kept in the Archive of Folk Song—and selected songs for seven Library of Congress releases. Two Folkways albums are also based on recordings in the collection.

Beginning in 1944, Dr. Densmore donated portions of her personal papers to the Library of Congress. In addition to lecture programs and articles, the collection contains nine annotated scrapbooks documenting

*Frances Densmore using a wax cylinder phonograph to record Mountain Chief, a Blackfoot Indian (1916). Smithsonian-Densmore Collection, Archive of Folk Song. LC–USZ62–67601.*

her activities from 1889 to 1957, drafts for lectures and reviews, a chronology of her career prepared from her diaries, lantern slides, a few letters, and papers pertaining to an analysis of her early field recordings done by the physicist Dayton C. Miller. The collection measures seven linear feet and is briefly described in lists on file in the Archive of Folk Song.

Densmore, Frances, comp., *Songs of the Chippewa* (Library of Congress, Division of Music, Recording Laboratory [1950] 2 s. 12 in. 33⅓ rpm. AFS L22).

——, comp., *Songs of the Menominee, Mandan, and Hidatsa* (Library of Congress, Division of Music, Recording Laboratory [1952] 2 s. 12 in. 33⅓ rpm. AFS L33).

——, comp., *Songs of the Nootka and Quileute* (Library of Congress, Division of Music, Recording Laboratory [1952] 2 s. 12 in. 33⅓ rpm. AFS L32).

——, comp., *Songs of the Papago* (Library of Congress, Division of Music, Recording Laboratory [1952] 2 s. 12 in. 33⅓ rpm. AFS L31).

——, comp., *Songs of the Pawnee: Songs of the Northern Ute* (Library of Congress, Division of Music, Recording Laboratory, 1951. 2 s. 12 in. 33⅓ rpm. AFS L 25).

——, comp., *Songs of the Sioux* (Library of Congress, Division of Music, Recording Laboratory, 1951. 2 s. 12 in. 33⅓ rpm. AFS L23).

——, comp., *Songs of the Yuma, Cocopa, and Yaqui* (Library of Congress, Division of Music, Recording Laboratory, 1951. 2 s. 12 in. 33⅓ rpm. AFS L24).

——, "The Study of Indian Music," in *Annual Report of the Board of Regents of the Smithsonian Institution* (Q11.S66), 1941: 527–550.

# 228

## Oscar George Theodore Sonneck Collection

Papers and music manuscripts of musicologist Oscar George Theodore Sonneck

Music Division

As the first chief of the Music Division, Oscar George Theodore Sonneck (1873–1928) transformed the Library's scattered holdings of copyrighted music into one of the world's largest archives for music research. He devised the music classification scheme which, with updating and various modifications, is still used today at the Library; arranged for the first government publication of music bibliographies; and systematically developed an international collection of printed music, holographs, and music literature. An eminent musicologist, Sonneck was the founding editor of one of America's leading music journals *The Musical Quarterly*. Soon after resigning from the Library, he became vice president of the New York music publishing firm, G. Schirmer, Inc.

The Sonneck Collection contains material from all periods of his career. In 1920 Sonneck himself presented to the Library research notes which he described in a letter of 1922 as covering "90 per cent of what any scholar will be able to find in the contemporary historical sources of secular musical life in America up to 1800." The manuscripts include notes for published and unpublished works and have been microfilmed. In 1929 Julia Sonneck, the musicologist's mother, donated the manuscript of Sonneck's *Early Concert-Life in America (1731–1800)* (Leipzig: Breitkopf & Härtel, 1907. 338 p. ML200.3.S6; reprints, 1949, 1969, 1978) and approximately forty personal letters. The majority of Sonneck's papers, however, consist of his correspondence as editor of *The Musical Quarterly* and personal correspondence with musical and literary figures. The over thirty-one hundred letters (1914–28) were the gift of G. Schirmer, Inc., in 1946 and Nathan Broder in 1965. An inventory is kept on file. Also in the collection are Sonneck music manuscripts donated by G. Schirmer, Inc. Irving Lowens indicates in his bibliography which Sonneck manuscripts are available in the Music Division. The collection measures about seven linear feet.

Lowens, Irving, "Oscar George Theodore Sonneck: His Writings and Musical Compositions," in H. Wiley Hitchcock's *After 100* [*!*] *Years: The Editorial Side of Sonneck* (Washington: Library of Congress, 1975. 39 p. ML423.S7H6), p. 20–38.

*NUCMC,* 67–662.

# 229

## South Central Georgia Folklife Project Collection

Recordings, photographs, and related documentation from the 1977 field study of south Georgia folklife

American Folklife Center

During the summer of 1977, the American Folklife Center conducted a six-week field survey of the folk culture of south Georgia's "wiregrass" region. The research team studied patterns of traditional life and work in the eight counties served by the Arts Experiment Station at Abraham Baldwin Agricultural College in Tifton, Georgia. Rich documentation was gathered on vernacular architecture, food customs, storytelling, and gospel singing traditions in local white and black communities. The center has assembled an extensive collection of the project material—field notes, research papers, 5,000 color transparencies, black-and-white contact prints from 320 rolls of film, 320 sound recordings, and eight videotapes—as well as songbooks, hymnals, and ephemera accumulated in the course of research. The Folklife Center is indexing the collection and plans to transfer material to the appropriate custodial units. A photographic essay was published in conjunction with the Library's exhibit on south Georgia folklife.

American Folklife Center, "Traditional Life and Work in Georgia's 'Wiregrass' Region," in its *Folklife Center News* (GR105.A63a), v. 1, January 1978: 1, 4.

*Sketches of South Georgia Folklife* (Washington: Library of Congress, 1977. 32 p. GR110.G4S57), edited by Carl Fleischhauer and Howard W. Marshall.

# 230

## Spanish Play Collection

**Spanish plays published in the late nineteenth and early twentieth centuries**

Collections Management Division

In 1938, shortly before the establishment of a center for Hispanic studies at the Library of Congress, the Hispanic Society of America donated to the Library an extensive drama collection. The 8,000 plays in the collection were published principally in Madrid and Barcelona after 1850 and include many works by lesser-known Spanish authors and regional pieces written in the Catalan and Galician dialects. Drama, comedy, and *zarzuela* (a Spanish genre similar to operetta or vaudeville) are well represented. In some cases, the items are inscribed by the author or contain handwritten stage directions and textual changes. The three-volume inventory which accompanied the original gift can be consulted in the Hispanic Society Room of the Hispanic Division. Arranged by playwright, the inventory provides a shelf identification number for each item. The plays can be requested by number through the Collections Management Division. Microfilms of the collection will be completed in 1980 and made available in the Microform Reading Room.

# 231

## Ephraim George Squier Collection

### Ephraim George Squier's papers and maps of Central America

Manuscript Division
Geography and Map Division

The papers of Ephraim George Squier (1821–1888)—author of *Aboriginal Monuments of the State of New-York* (1850), *Nicaragua* (1852), *Notes on Central America* (1855), *Honduras* (1870), and *Peru* (1877)—pertain chiefly to his anthropological research and diplomatic and business affairs in Central America. Acquired from Frank Squier (1905), William Gates (1941), and Richard S. Wormser (1948), the papers include correspondence, business records, manuscripts for publications, and related material from the period 1841 to 1888. Correspondents include Henry Bowen Anthony, Charles Eliot Norton, and Josiah Clark Nott. The published checklist prepared by Jerry E. Patterson and William R. Stanton provides a complete list of correspondents. The 2,500-item collection has been microfilmed and described in an unpublished finding aid.

Thirty-eight maps of Central America and Peru drawn or annotated by Squier were acquired by the Library in 1909. The greatest number are detailed, unfinished manuscript maps, prepared from field notes, of locations in Honduras, El Salvador, and Nicaragua. While the maps were compiled mostly for Squier's canal and railway ventures in Central America, they are also of interest as background information for the study of U.S.-British rivalry in Central America in the mid-nineteenth century. The collection is described in the Geography and Map Division card catalog of rare materials and listed in John R. Hébert's *Quarterly Journal* article.

Hébert, John R., "Maps by Ephraim George Squier: Journalist, Scholar, Diplomat," *QJLC,* v. 29, January 1972: 14–31.

*NUCMC,* 64–1580.

Patterson, Jerry E., and William R. Stanton, "The Ephraim George Squier Manuscripts in the Library of Congress: A Checklist," *Papers of the Bibliographical Society of America* (Z1008.B51P), v. 53, 4th quarter 1959: 309–326.

# 232

## Benedict Stambler Archive of Recorded Jewish Music

Commercial recordings of Jewish music

Motion Picture, Broadcasting, and Recorded Sound Division

Nearly fourteen hundred commercial phonograph discs from the Jewish music collection of New York lawyer and musicologist Benedict Stambler (d. 1967) were presented to the Library in 1970 by his widow, Helen Stambler Latner. The gift includes recordings of the leading American and European cantors of the first four decades of the twentieth century as well as a sampling of performances by Yiddish comedians, folksingers, and popular musicians. Mr. Stambler drew upon his extensive collection in preparing a series of historic reissues of early Jewish recordings. When cataloging is completed, material will be represented by performer, title, and collector in the catalog of the Motion Picture, Broadcasting, and Recorded Sound Division. Items are listed by label in an inventory. The greater portion of Mr. Stambler's record collection was donated to the New York Public Library.

I have stated upon former occasions, and I may as well state again, what I understand to be the real issue in this controversy between Judge Douglas and myself. On the point of my wanting to make war between the free and the slave States, there has been no issue between us. So, too, when he assumes that I am in favor of introducing a perfect social and political equality between the white and black races. These are false issues, upon which Judge Douglas has tried to force the controversy. There is no foundation in truth for the charge that I maintain either of these propositions. The real issue in this controversy — the one pressing upon every mind — is the sentiment on the part of one class that looks upon the institution of slavery *as a wrong*, and of another class that *does not* look upon it as a wrong. The sentiment that contemplates the institution of slavery in this country as a wrong is the sentiment of the Republican party. It is the sentiment around which all their actions — all their arguments circle — from which all their propositions radiate. They look upon it as being a moral, social and political wrong; and while they contemplate it as such, they nevertheless have due regard for its actual existence among us, and the difficulties of getting rid of it in any satisfactory way and to all the constitutional obligations thrown about it. Yet having a due regard for these, they desire a policy in regard to it that looks to its not creating any more danger. They insist that it should as far as may be, *be treated* as a wrong, and one of the methods of treating it as a wrong is to *make provision that it shall grow no larger*. [Loud applause.] They also desire a policy that looks to a peaceful end of slavery at sometime, as being wrong. These are the views they entertain in regard to it as I understand them; and all their sentiments — all their arguments and propositions are brought within this range. I have said

*Excerpt (Lincoln's speech, final debate with Stephen A. Douglas) from Abraham Lincoln's scrapbook of the Illinois political campaign of 1858. The printer set the type for the first edition of the Lincoln-Douglas debates from this compilation of newspaper accounts edited by Lincoln. Alfred Whital Stern Collection of Lincolniana, Rare Book and Special Collections Division. LC–USZ62–67602.*

340

# 233

## Alfred Whital Stern Collection of Lincolniana

Publications, manuscripts, prints, and other material relating to Abraham Lincoln

Rare Book and Special Collections Division

Alfred Whital Stern (1881–1960) of Chicago presented his outstanding collection of Lincolniana to the Library in 1953. Begun by Mr. Stern in the 1920s, the collection documents the life of Abraham Lincoln (1809–1865) through writings by and about Lincoln, contemporary newspapers, sheet music, broadsides, prints, stamps, coins, autograph letters, and a large body of publications concerned with slavery, the Civil War, Reconstruction, and related topics. The collection includes copies of the three speeches deliverd by Lincoln during his term as congressman from Illinois (1847–49), Lincoln's own scrapbook of the 1858 political campaign against Stephen A. Douglas, a rare copy of the first edition of the Lincoln-Douglas debates that was printed from this scrapbook (Columbus, 1860), numerous campaign biographies prepared for the 1860 presidential election, printed materials relating to the assassination and funeral, and a Lincoln life mask cast in bronze by Leonard Volk. Probably the single most famous Lincoln manuscript in the collection is the letter to Maj. Gen. Joseph Hooker dated January 26, 1863, placing him in command of the Army of the Potomac. Since Mr. Stern's death, the collection has continued to grow through the provisions of an endowment established by his family and it now numbers over 11,100 pieces. Items are represented in the author/title and shelflist card files and, to a limited extent, in format and subject indexes. The published catalog describes the collection as of September 1958. Subsequent additions are described in *Quarterly Journal* articles.

Eaton, Vincent L., "Some Highlights of the Alfred Whital Stern Collection,' *QJLC*, v. 9, February 1952: 65–73.

Edelstein, J. M., "Lincoln Papers in the Stern Bequest," *QJLC*, v. 19, December 1961: 7–14.

Mearns, David C., "Alfred Whital Stern and the Hoof Prints," *QJLC*, v. 9, February 1952: 57–64.

U.S., Library of Congress, *A Catalog of the Alfred Whital Stern Collection of Lincolniana* (Washington: 1960. 498 p. Z8505.U47).

# 234

## Willard D. Straight Collection

### French graphic art relating to World War I

Prints and Photographs Division

Maj. Willard D. Straight (1880–1918), American financier and diplomat, collected graphic art related to World War I while serving as a liaison officer in France. His collection of 5,000 drawings, watercolors, prints, and posters was deposited in the Prints and Photographs Division in 1950 and donated to the Library by the Straight family in 1978. The Straight Collection encompasses works by 125 French draftsmen, printmakers, and cartoonists, and includes several hundred drawings by Blois, Georges Domergue, Lucien Léandre, and Leka, and print series by Lucien-Hector Jonas, d'Ostoya, and Louis Raemaekers. By and large, the works portray French political and military figures, veterans, the impact of war on civilian life, and the aftermath of battle rather than actual combat scenes. An inventory and a partial card file arranged by artist are kept with the collection and serve as finding aids. Accompanying the French material are several volumes of American posters issued by the armed forces and patriotic organizations involved with the war effort.

*Guide,* Vanderbilt, no. 686.

# 235

## Caroline and Erwin Swann Collection

Caricature and cartoon drawings

Prints and Photographs Division

Erwin Swann, New York advertising executive, established a foundation to collect original cartoon drawings of artistic and humorous interest. At the time of Mr. Swann's death in 1973, the collection numbered more than three thousand items and was considered one of the finest of its kind in America. The executors of the Swann estate deposited the cartoons at the Library of Congress in 1974 and established a special fund to support the exhibition, maintenance, and development of the collection. Although containing original drawings from as early as the late eighteenth century, the Swann Collection is strongest in the work of contemporary cartoonists. Among the 400 artists represented are Peter Arno, Bil Canfield, Al Capp, Miguel Covarrubias, Louis Dalrymple, Whitney Darrow, Rube Goldberg, Thomas Nast, José Guadalupe Posada, Edward Sorel, and John Tenniel. The drawings are arranged by artist and accompanied by a name roster which indicates other collections in the Prints and Photographs Division containing each cartoonist's works. A sampling of the Swann cartoons was displayed at the Library in 1977 and listed in *They Made Them Laugh and Wince and Worry and . . . : Drawings for Six American Magazines, an Exhibition in the Great Hall of the Library of Congress, March 13 through June 12, 1977* (Washington: Library of Congress, 1977. [32] p.). The book issued on the occasion of the exhibition, *Posada's Mexico* (Washington: Library of Congress, 1979. 315 p. NE546.P6A4 1979), edited by Ron Tyler, is the first major publication made possible through the Caroline and Erwin Swann Fund.

# 236

## Raymond Swing Collection

Papers and broadcast recordings of news commentator
Raymond Swing

Manuscript Division
Motion Picture, Broadcasting, and Recorded Sound Division

During the years 1944 to 1964 the radio news commentator Raymond Swing (1887–1968) presented his papers and broadcast recordings to the Library of Congress. Raymond Swing achieved enormous popularity in the late 1930s and early 1940s through his news analysis broadcasts for the Mutual Broadcasting System and the British Broadcasting Corporation. In 1942 he began working for the NBC-blue Network (later the American Broadcasting Company) and in later years broadcast political commentaries on the Liberty Network and Voice of America (VOA). The Swing papers in the Manuscript Division consist mostly of radio scripts from the 1930s through the 1960s. Also included are articles prepared for the *London Sunday Express* (1941–43), lectures, literary writings, and selected correspondence with Albert Einstein, Edward R. Murrow, and others. An unpublished finding aid has been prepared for the 5,600-item collection.

Instantaneous recordings of Raymond Swing's broadcasts are preserved in the Motion Picture, Broadcasting, and Recorded Sound Division. These include several hundred broadcasts carried by the Mutual and NBC-blue Networks in the 1940s, and VOA programs (1951–53) that were transferred from the Department of State. The broadcasts have been copied on tape and listed by date in the collection inventory.

Broderick, John C., "New Gift of Raymond Swing Papers," *LCIB,* v. 23, December 28, 1964: 697.

*NUCMC,* 70–977.

# 237

## Technical Report Collection

Scientific and technical reports, 1940s to present

Science and Technology Division

Probably the largest collection of scientific and technical reports in the United States is serviced through the Library's Science and Technology Division. The division has gathered over 1.6 million studies generated by U.S. government agencies or by government-sponsored research projects and receives an estimated 110,000 new items yearly in printed copy or microform. While containing technical reports in many areas of interest dating from the early 1940s to the present, the collection is particularly strong in studies conducted under the auspices of the Department of Energy, the Department of Defense, the National Aeronautics and Space Administration, the Office of Education, and their predecessors. The collection includes a virtually complete set of war-related studies prepared for the Office of Scientific Research and Development from 1941 to 1946. In addition, the Division services 250,000 reports released by the Office of the Publication Board and its successor, the Office of Technical Services. The "PB" series includes captured German scientific documents such as unpublished patent applications deposited with the German Patent Office from 1940 to 1945. Requests for photocopies of the PB reports should be sent directly to the Library's Photoduplication Service and should indicate the number of the desired report and the type of reproduction required. The Science and Technology Division provides reference assistance for the Technical Report Collection and has prepared finding aids to several series. Access tools compiled by abstracting and indexing services are kept in the Science Reading Room. The early history of the collection is discussed in John Sherrod's article, "The Technical Report in the Library of Congress," in *QJLC*, v. 16, February 1959, p. 47–50.

# 238

## John Boyd Thacher Collection

Incunabula, early Americana, material pertaining to the French Revolution, autographs

Rare Book and Special Collections Division

The book and manuscript collection of John Boyd Thacher (1847–1909), a manufacturer and politician from Albany, New York, was deposited at the Library in the 1910s and 1920s and donated through his widow's bequest. The 5,193-item collection is composed of four distinct bodies of material—incunabula, early Americana, material pertaining to the French Revolution, and autographs. The early printed books include works produced by more than five hundred fifteenth-century presses and such outstanding items as a vellum copy of *Rationale Divinorum Officiorum* by Gulielmus Durantis (Mainz: Johann Fust and Peter Schöffer, 1459) and the only known American copies of *Breviarium Moguntinum* (Marienthal: Fratres Vitae Communis, 1474) and *Vocabularius ex Quo* (Eltvil: Nicolaus Bechtermüntze, 1476). Mr. Thacher drew upon his extensive collection of Americana for his publications, *The Continent of America* (1896) and *Christopher Columbus* (1903–4). This segment of the Thacher collection is highlighted by copies of thirty-four early editions of Ptolemy's *Geographia,* three editions of Martin Waldseemüller's *Cosmographiae Introductio* printed before 1510, and the famous Trevisan manuscript, written in Venice about 1503, concerning Spanish explorations in America during the period 1492 to 1500 and Portuguese voyages to India from 1497 to 1502. Mr. Thacher also assembled books, contemporary newspaper accounts, pamphlets, and manuscripts as source material for a projected work on the French Revolution. Virtually every figure important to the revolutionary movement is represented by autographs, including Danton, Lavoisier, Marat, and Robespierre. The autograph collection focuses on the European royal families and contains items dating from as early as the fourteenth century. The Library has published a three-volume catalog of the collection.

*ARLC,* 1927, p. 25–29.

*Rare Bk. Div. Guide,* p. 14–16.

U.S., Library of Congress, John Boyd Thacher Collection, *The Collection of John Boyd Thacher in the Library of Congress* (Washington: Govt. Print. Off., 1931. 3 v. Z881.U5 1931).

# 239

## Third Reich Collection

Publications and photographs from the libraries of Nazi leaders

Rare Book and Special Collections Division
Prints and Photographs Division

The Third Reich Collection, a miscellany of books, albums, and printed materials from the Reichskanzlei Library in Berlin and the private book collections of several high-ranking Nazi Party officials, was discovered in a salt mine near Berchtesgaden among Nazi property that had been removed from Berlin during the last stages of World War II. The so-called Hitler Library was screened by the U.S. Army Document Center in Munich and shipped to the Library of Congress in 1946. A large number of the 1,019 volumes transferred to the Rare Book and Special Collections Division are official presentation copies which bear dedications, notes of transmittal, or in some cases Hitler's eagle bookplate. Several books were acquired by Hitler before 1930. The Third Reich Collection also includes a set of *Die Alte Garde spricht,* a series of typed autobiographies of Nazi Party members; a Braille edition of *Mein Kampf;* and materials from the libraries of Hermann Göring, Heinrich Himmler, Franz Xaver Schwarz, and other Nazi leaders. Books are briefly listed in an author/title card file. A provenance file is being created as the collection is being fully cataloged.

The over seventy photo albums from the Third Reich Collection have been transferred to the Prints and Photographs Division. Most of the albums were prepared as gifts for party leaders and contain photographs of German cities, official construction projects, scenic points of interest, art works, and Nazi activities. Some albums include German captions. The items are listed in the division catalog as the Hitler Collection.

*Guide,* Vanderbilt, no. 347.

Jacobius, Arnold J., "The Private Library of Adolf Hitler," *LCIB,* v. 12, April 27, 1953: 14–15.

Phelps, Reginald H., "Die Hitler-Bibliothek," *Deutsche Rundschau* (AP30.D4), v. 80, September 1954: 923–931.

# 240

## Tissandier Collection

Manuscripts, pictorial material, and publications relating to
the history of aeronautics

Manuscript Division
Prints and Photographs Division

The Tissandier Collection, purchased by the Library in 1930, was
described in the *Annual Report of the Librarian of Congress* for that
year as containing "approximately all the worth-while aeronautic
literature published in France up to 1900." The brothers Albert (1836–
1906) and Gaston Tissandier (1843–1899), balloonists, dirigible build-
ers, and aeronautical historians, assembled a research library that included numerous sixteenth- and seventeenth-century publications.
Gaston Tissandier used this collection to compile his *Bibliographie
aéronautique: catalogue de livres d'histoire, de science, de voyages et de
fantaisie, traitant de la navigation aérienne ou des aérostats* (Paris: H.
Launette, 1887. 62 p. Z5063.T61). His son Paul made further additions before its acquisition by a London bookdealer.

Six thousand items from the Tissandier Collection, spanning the
years 1776 to 1914, are housed in the Manuscript Division. The manuscript material, clippings, and memorabilia pertain largely to the work
of French aeronauts and, to a lesser degree, the efforts of their English,
Spanish, German, and Italian counterparts. Most of the material is in
French. Among the early aeronauts represented by letters, notebooks,
reports, and autographs are François Arban, Pierre Blanchard, Octave
Chanute, Jacques A. C. Charles, François Lhoste, Vincenzo Lunardi,
and the Montgolfier brothers. The biographical files compiled by Jules
François Dupuis-Delcourt, an airship designer whose library was purchased by the Tissandiers, are retained as a unit, except for the items
annotated by the Tissandiers. The Tissandiers' own correspondence,
scrapbooks, and manuscripts for speeches, articles, and books form a
significant portion of the collection. The division has prepared an unpublished finding aid for the material.

The Tissandier brothers were keenly interested in pictorial documentation of lighter-than-air travel. Albert Tissandier illustrated several

EXPERIENCE DU GLOBE AEROSTATIQUE DE MM CHARLES ET ROBERT au Jardin des Thuileries
le 1er Decembre 1783

*Engraving of the balloon ascent by Jacques Alexandre César Charles and M. N. Robert from the gardens of the Tuileries, Paris, on December 1, 1783. Charles landed the hydrogen-filled balloon near Nesle after two hours of flight, discharged his companion, and completed the journey by himself. Tissandier Collection, Prints and Photographs Division. LC–USZ61–1722.*

of his brother's writings, and Gaston translated an early handbook on photography. Seven hundred watercolors, photographs, and prints from their picture files, including some items that were reproduced in their publications, have been transferred to the Prints and Photographs Division. The images date from the late eighteenth and nineteenth centuries and are mostly European in origin. A checklist for the collection is currently being prepared.

Many rare aeronautical publications in the general classified collections of the Rare Book and Special Collections Division can be traced to the Tissandier library, including early works of aeronautical fiction, pamphlet accounts of balloon voyages, and such important scientific and technical books as Joseph Galien's *L'Art de naviger dans les airs* (1757). The remaining publications have been integrated with the Library's general collections. The inventory listing the 1,800 volumes in the original 1930 purchase is kept in the division.

*ARLC,* 1930, p. 249–255.

*Guide,* Vanderbilt, no. 703.

*NUCMC,* 62–4888.

# 241

## Tobacco Label Collection

### Packaging for American tobacco products, 1840s–1880s

Prints and Photographs Division

The nineteenth-century tobacco labels in the Prints and Photographs Division were largely acquired by the Library through copyright deposit. The elaborate packaging of luxury items such as tobacco and wine became possible during the nineteenth century with the increase in the number of retail shops and the advent of machine-produced paper and color lithography. Labels were developed to attract the attention of the consumer and increase sales. The examples in the collection range from simple, black-and-white engravings from the 1840s to eye-catching chromolithographs of the 1860s, 1870s, and 1880s that incorporate brand names with depictions of celebrities, sporting events, mermaids, Indians, and other subjects intended to interest the tobacco user. The approximately one thousand tobacco labels are arranged by subject and recorded as a collection in the catalog of the Prints and Photographs Division.

Shaw, Renata V., "19th-Century Tobacco Label Art," *QJLC*, v. 28, April 1971: 76–102; reprinted in *Graphic Sampler* (Washington: Library of Congress, 1979. NE400.G7), compiled by Renata V. Shaw.

# 242

## Charles Todd and Robert Sonkin Collection

Field recordings made in California migratory labor camps, 1940–41

Archive of Folk Song

In 1940 and 1941 Charles Todd and Robert Sonkin of the College of the City of New York took disc recording equipment supplied by the Archive of Folk Song to migratory labor camps in California. Working chiefly with migrants from Oklahoma, Arkansas, Missouri, and the Texas panhandle who had settled in Farm Security Administration camps in Fresno, Tulare, and Kern counties, the pair recorded dance tunes, songs of the American Southwest, traditional ballads, songs describing the dust bowl and life in California, camp council meetings, interviews, conversations, and readings of original poems. Todd and Sonkin subsequently edited their "Okie" field recordings for radio programs broadcast by New York City station WNYC (AFS 6,314–6,316). The 119 discs (AFS 4,088–4,158 and 5,099–5,146) have been duplicated on tape and are accompanied by field notes, song texts, and concordances in the Archive of Folk Song files. The journal of the 1940 trip has been microfilmed.

Todd, Charles, and Robert Sonkin, "Ballads of the Okies," *New York Times Magazine* (AP2.N6575), November 17, 1940: 6–7, 18; reprinted in *American Folk Music Occasional*, v. 1, 1964: 87–91.

# 243

## Raymond Toinet Collection

*Early editions of French literary works*

In 1929 the Library of Congress purchased the French literature collection formed by Raymond Toinet (b. 1843) of Tulle, France. While containing representative works of the late sixteenth, eighteenth, and nineteenth centuries, the 2,500-volume collection was strongest in early editions of seventeenth-century writers. Rare volumes such as early editions of Jean de La Bruyère's *Les Caractères de Théophraste* and a group of 150 *mazarinades* (verses attacking Cardinal Mazarin) have been incorporated into the classified collections of the Rare Book and Special Collections Division. The remaining material has been assigned to the Library's general collections. A typed inventory of the 1929 purchase is kept in the division.

*ARLC,* 1929, p. 38–39.

# 244

## John Toland Collection

Interviews recorded in the 1970s and research files relating to Nazi Germany

Motion Picture, Broadcasting, and Recorded Sound Division
Manuscript Division

When researching his biography *Adolf Hitler* (Garden City, N.Y.: Doubleday, 1976. xx, 1035 p. DD247.H5T56), John Toland interviewed intimates of Hitler and witnesses to key events of the Nazi period. In 1972 Mr. Toland deposited approximately 150 of his cassette tapes at the Library of Congress. Reference copies of many items, including interviews with Adm. Karl Donitz and Albert Speer, are available to researchers in the Motion Picture, Broadcasting, and Recorded Sound Division. The tapes are being indexed by speaker and date.

Correspondence, research files, photographs, maps, drafts, and galleys relating to many of Mr. Toland's earlier publications are maintained in the Manuscript Division. In 1967 and 1968 the author gave the Library papers which include over twelve hundred transcribed interviews with Americans, Germans, Russians, Englishmen, and Frenchmen involved in the destruction of Nazi Germany and the fall of Berlin. Mr. Toland conducted these interviews as source material for *The Last 100 Days* (New York: Random House [1966] 622 p. D755.7.T6). The contents of the 8,150-item collection are outlined in an unpublished finding aid.

*NUCMC,* 68–2079.

U.S., Library of Congress, Manuscript Division, "Recent Acquisitions of the Manuscript Division," *QJLC,* v. 25, October 1968: 342.

# 245

## Joseph Meredith Toner Collection

Publications and papers relating to the history of American medicine, eighteenth and nineteenth centuries; early American imprints

Rare Book and Special Collections Division
Manuscript Division

In 1882 Joseph Meredith Toner (1825–1896), Washington physician and medical historian, presented his research collection to the Library of Congress. Counting the many volumes added to the collection in later installments, Dr. Toner donated nearly fifty thousand books, pamphlets, scrapbooks, and issues of periodicals as well as maps, manuscripts, and innumerable files of newspaper clippings. Aside from the research value of this material, the Toner Collection is historically significant to the Library of Congress as it marks, in the words of the Senate Report of May 16, 1882, "the first instance in the history of this government of the free gift of a large and valuable library to the nation." Dr. Toner described his library in a letter included in the same report:

They are chiefly medical works and general and local American histories; publications relating to our climate and diseases; biographies of medical men . . . and works on the history of medicine in America from the settlement of the country to the end of the first half century of our national existence. . . . My collection is . . . measurably rich in the early literature of small-pox, yellow fever, cholera, and the other epidemics, general and local, which have appeared in our country. My special collection of the early contributions to the literature of medicine in America and early American imprints is scarcely second to any in the country.

Aside from the legal works that have been assigned to the Law Library, the printed material from the Toner Collection is kept in the Rare Book and Special Collections Division. The 30,851 volumes and 7,739 pamphlets include extensive runs of nineteenth-century medical journals. Cataloged items are represented in the Toner Collection shelflist and the general dictionary catalog of the division.

For the most part, Toner's personal papers, a massive collection of 75,000 items in the Manuscript Division, were accumulated after his move to Washington, D.C., in 1855. Included are medical papers, diaries, personal and professional correspondence, notes, biographical files on American physicians (1732–1896), papers and autographs collected by Toner, and other material. Toner devoted much of his later life to research on George Washington and compiled transcripts and printed copies of pertinent journals, diaries, letters, and documents. The division has prepared an unpublished finding aid for the papers. Some material has been microfilmed.

*ARLC,* 1897, p. 37–38.

*Handbook of MSS. in LC,* p. 413–421.

*NUCMC,* 67–634.

U.S., Congress, Joint Committee on the Library, *Report to Accompany S. Res. 66* (Washington: 1882. 3 p. 47th Congress, 1st session. Senate. Report no. 578. Z733.U63T6).

*Poster for* Gold Diggers of 1933 *(1933). Directed by Mervyn Leroy, this Warner Brothers film in the United Artists Collection featured three lavish production numbers by Busby Berkeley. Poster Collection, Prints and Photographs Division. LC–USZ62–66567.*

# 246

## United Artists Collection

American films, 1913–1948

Motion Picture, Broadcasting, and Recorded Sound Division

In 1969 the United Artists Corporation presented to the Library the earliest surviving preprint material for approximately three thousand motion pictures from the pre-1949 film library of Warner Brothers pictures. The collection contains fifty silent features (1913–30), 750 sound features (1927 48), 1,800 sound shorts (1926–48), and 400 cartoons, among them Looney Tunes and Merrie Melodies. While consisting largely of Warner Brothers releases, the collection includes nearly two hundred sound features released by Monogram Pictures Corporation and a number of Popeye cartoons produced by Fleischer Studios. Most motion pictures exist in the original black-and-white or Technicolor camera negatives. The Library is converting the nitrate film to acetate safety stock and has obtained reference prints for seventy of the better known Warner Brothers features, such as *Gold Diggers of 1935* (1935), *High Sierra* (1941), *I Am a Fugitive from a Chain Gang* (1932), *The Jazz Singer* (1927), and *Little Caesar* (1930). All titles are recorded in the collection shelflist in the Motion Picture, Broadcasting, and Recorded Sound Division and in a catalog published by the American Film Institute. United Artists has donated 16mm reference prints of most Monogram and Warner Brothers films to the Wisconsin Center for Film and Theater Research in Madison.

American Film Institute, *Catalog of Holdings, the American Film Institute Collection and the United Artists Collection at the Library' of Congress* (Washington: American Film Institute, 1978. 214 p. PN1998.A575 1978).

# 247

## United Nations Recordings Collection

Recordings of UN proceedings, 1946–63

Motion Picture, Broadcasting, and Recorded Sound Division

During the 1970s the official sound recordings of the meetings of the United Nations General Assembly and its major committees and commissions were transferred to the Library of Congress. Produced by the UN Sound Recording Unit largely between 1946 and 1963, these sixteen-inch acetate discs constitute the full, unedited transcription of UN proceedings in the original languages of the speakers and include special addresses by foreign dignitaries and rare voice recordings of contemporary African and Asian leaders. The UN Sound Recording Unit has compiled finding aids for the many thousands of discs produced under its direction as well as a partial list of the material transferred to the Library. The discs are arranged by date. The recordings supplement the Library's extensive holdings of UN documents and official records.

United Nations, Secretariat, *Catalogue of Sound Recordings of United Nations Meetings Transferred to the Library of Congress of the United States* ([New York?] 1974. 5 p. ST/OGS/SER.F/5).

# 248

## United States Congressional Publications Collection

Law Library

The Law Library's collection of U.S. congressional publications is probably surpassed only by those maintained by the House of Representatives and the Senate libraries. Housed in the gallery above the Main Reading Room, these 30,000 volumes encompass House and Senate bills and resolutions in their various versions, beginning with the 6th Congress, 2d session; reports and documents dating back to the 15th Congress, 1st session; *Calendars of the United States House of Representatives and History of Legislation* from the 75th Congress to the present; and printed debates and proceedings of the two houses appearing in the *Journals of the Continental Congress,* the *Annals of Congress,* the *Register of Debates,* the *Congressional Globe,* and the *Congressional Record.* Much of the material is also available on microfilm. Of related interest is the extensive collection of the public documents of the first fourteen Congresses housed in the Rare Book and Special Collections Division (no. 63).

*Law Library,* p. 20.

# 249

## University of Arkansas Collection

Recordings of Arkansas folk music, late 1940s–late 1960s

Archive of Folk Song

While research assistant in folklore at the University of Arkansas in 1949, Merlin Mitchell began recording regional folk music and oral traditions for preservation in the University of Arkansas Folklore Archives. This project was continued from 1951 to 1952 by Irene Carlisle with the assistance of the Library of Congress and subsequently directed by Mary Celestia Parler, a professor who encouraged her students to make field recordings for the university collection. Through the cooperation of the University of Arkansas Library, the Library of Congress has duplicated recordings collected for the archives between the late 1940s and the late 1960s. The collection offers a cross section of the ballads, work songs, hymns, spirituals, camp and prison songs, hobo songs, and traditional instrumental music of Arkansas and neighboring states, and includes performances by such well-known local singers as Booth Campbell of Cane Hill, Doney Hammondtree of Farmington, Fred High of High, May Kennedy McCord of Springfield, Missouri, Gerald Pipes of Reeds Spring, Missouri, B. J. Whittington of Springdale, and Fred Woodruff of Lincoln. The checklist and supplement published in 1954 and 1957 cover a total of 855 songs and 1,062 variant texts in the collection. Catalogs and concordances provide access to the ninety-six tapes.

"A Checklist of Arkansas Songs: Supplement I," *Arkansas Folklore* (GR108.-A73), v. 7, March 1957: 1–10.

"A Checklist of Tape-recorded Songs in the University of Arkansas Folklore Archives," *Arkansas Folklore* (GR108.A73), v. 4, January 1, 1954: 1–15.

# 250

## University of Wisconsin Collection

Field recordings of Wisconsin folk music, 1940–46

Archive of Folk Song

Between 1940 and 1946 the Library of Congress and the University of Wisconsin cosponsored a field survey of Wisconsin folk music. Initiated by Prof. Leland Coon, the project sent Helene Stratman Thomas Blotz and other collectors into the field to study the ethnic diversity of the state's musical traditions. The recordings include songs in many languages and performances on such characteristic folk instruments as the Norwegian *psalmodicon* and the Croatian *tamburica*. The collection is especially rich in the music of French-Canadian, Norwegian, Swedish, Dutch, and German immigrants. In addition, the collection contains the music of Native American groups; occupational songs by lumberjacks, sailors, miners, railroadmen, and cranberry pickers; and Appalachian music performed by Kentuckians who settled in northern Wisconsin. The 224 instantaneous disc recordings (AFS 4,159–4,193, 4,948–5,025, and 8,362–8,473) have been duplicated on tape and are listed in the catalog of the Archive of Folk Song, a concordance, and field notes. Mrs. Blotz selected dance tunes and English-language songs from the collection for a Library of Congress album. Song texts and selections from Mrs. Blotz's photographs and field journals are included in *Folk Songs Out of Wisconsin*.

*Folk Songs Out of Wisconsin* (Madison: State Historical Society of Wisconsin, 1977. 311 p. M1629.F687), edited by Harry B. Peters, p. 8, 23–41.

Stratman-Thomas, Helene, ed., *Folk Music from Wisconsin* (Library of Congress, Music Division, Recording Laboratory [1960] 2 s. 12 in. 33⅓ rpm. AFS L55).

# 251

## William Treat Upton Collection

Music and research files relating to the American art song

Music Division

William Treat Upton (1870–1961), professor of piano at Oberlin College from 1893 to 1936 and an expert on eighteenth- and nineteenth-century secular music of the United States, is best known as the author of *Art-Song in America* (Boston: O. Ditson Co. [1930] 279 p. ML2811.U7) and its *Supplement* ([Boston] O. Ditson Co. [1938] 41 p.). In studying the development of the song during the period 1750 to 1938, he examined thousands of published vocal compositions and acquired important examples for his personal collection. In addition, he gathered biographical information on many composers and retained his correspondence in alphabetically arranged files. In 1949 Professor Upton presented his research collection of letters and songs to the Library of Congress along with his extensive card indexes. The 2,965 songs are alphabetically organized by composer. The collection measures twelve linear feet.

# 252

## Vellum Chart Collection

### Rare nautical charts

Geography and Map Division

The collection of nautical charts on vellum in the Geography and Map Division contains representative works of several major schools of chart making. With specimens ranging from an anonymous fourteenth-century chart of the eastern Mediterranean and Black Sea areas to the eighteenth- and early nineteenth-century works from the Naval School of Cadiz, Spain, the collection provides examples for the study of the development of navigation charts over more than four centuries. Of exceptional interest are the manuscript chart of the Mediterranean, Atlantic, and North Sea coastlines drawn by Mateo Prunes in 1559 and Arnaldo Domenech's 1484 guide to weights and measures for European and Mediterranean cities. The Library of Congress has built the collection during the last seventy years. The six atlases and twenty-seven charts are described in a published catalog.

U.S., Library of Congress, *Nautical Charts on Vellum in the Library of Congress* (Washington: 1977. 30 p. Z6026.H9U66 1977), compiled by Walter W. Ristow and R. A. Skelton.

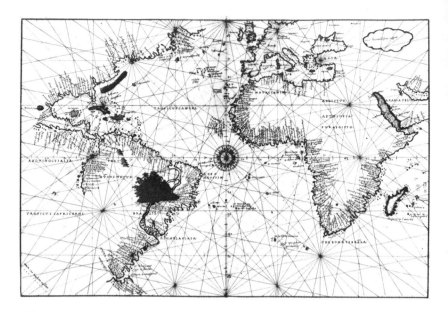

*Chart of the Atlantic Ocean from an illuminated portolan atlas on vellum (ca. 1544) by Battista Agnese, a Genoese mapmaker credited with producing over seventy atlases for wealthy Venetian merchants and government officials. Vellum Chart Collection, Geography and Map Division. Negative in division.*

# 253

## Jules Verne Collection

Early editions of Jules Verne's writings

Rare Book and Special Collections Division

The Jules Verne Collection in the Rare Book and Special Collections Division was presented to the Library in 1961 by Rilma Hurd. Assembled by her father, Willis E. Hurd of Arlington, Virginia, the collection consists largely of late nineteenth- and early twentieth-century editions of the science fiction writer's works which were issued in translation in England and the United States. The books have distinctive illustrations and decorated covers. The 146 volumes are represented in the division dictionary catalog and listed by title in an inventory on file.

# 254

## Voice of America Collection

Broadcast recordings of VOA music programs

Motion Picture, Broadcasting, and Recorded Sound Division
Archive of Folk Song

Voice of America (VOA), the broadcasting service of the International Communication Agency of the United States, began transferring transcriptions of its music programs to the Library of Congress in the mid-1960s. Totaling approximately sixty-five thousand recordings, the VOA Collection includes important performances—dating from as early as 1945—by major symphony orchestras, jazz instrumental ensembles, and soloists. The radio broadcasts feature performances at the Newport Jazz Festival; concerts of the Louisville Philharmonic, the New York Philharmonic, the Oklahoma Symphony Orchestra, and the Philadelphia Orchestra; and recitals by Jascha Heifetz, James Melton, Ezio Pinza, and Maggie Teyte. One VOA series entitled *U.S. Composers* contains performances of lesser known works by George W. Chadwick, Paul Creston, Roy Harris, Walter Piston, William Grant Still, Randall Thompson, and other notable American composers. The pressed discs are shelved by the series title and program number, and the instantaneous discs have been copied on tape. Separate finding aids for both sets are on file in the Motion Picture, Broadcasting, and Recorded Sound Division. VOA broadcasts originally recorded on tape are being processed.

The VOA recordings also include Asian, African, and American folk music and performances from the National Folk Festival and similar events. Many of these folk recordings have been taped and are represented in the Archive of Folk Song catalog.

# 255

## Otto Vollbehr Collection

Incunabula

Rare Book and Special Collections Division

The Vollbehr Collection, stated George Parker Winship of the Harvard Library shortly before its purchase by act of Congress in 1930, "is representative, to an amazing degree, of every sort of publication which came from the fifteenth century presses." The collection contains incunabula produced at 635 different printing establishments and a rich selection of books in vernacular languages. This acquisition quadrupled the number of fifteenth-century books held by the Library of Congress and established the Library as a leading center for the study of early printing.

The treasure of the Vollbehr Collection is the copy of the Bible produced by Johann Gutenberg at Mainz about 1456—the first book printed with movable type in the western world. The Library's Gutenberg Bible is one of the three surviving perfect copies on vellum. The work had been in the possession of the Benedictine Order for nearly five centuries before it was acquired by Dr. Otto Vollbehr from the Abbey of Saint Paul in eastern Carinthia, Austria. Bound as three volumes, the Bible retains the bookplate of the monastery of Saint Blasius (the owner of the work until the late eighteenth century) as well as its late sixteenth-century white pigskin binding. The 3,114 volumes from the collection are kept in the Rare Book and Special Collections Division and arranged according to the systems established by various incunabula bibliographies. Vollbehr's notes on the collection are available to researchers.

Decretals, papal bulls, canon law commentaries, and other legal works from the Vollbehr purchase have been integrated with the rare book collections of the Law Library.

*ARLC,* 1930, p. 12–15, 51–52, 126–131.

*Rare Bk. Div. Guide,* p. 7–10.

U.S., Congress, House, Committee on the Library, *Vollbehr Collection of Incunabula; Hearing . . . on H.R. 6147* (Washington: Govt. Print. Off., 1930. 66 p. Z240.V92.U5).

U.S., Library of Congress, *Exhibit of Books Printed During the XVth Century and Known as Incunabula, Selected from the Vollbehr Collection Purchased by Act of Congress, 1930: List of Books* (Washington: Govt. Print. Off., 1930. 78 p. Z881.U5 1930).

———, *The Vollbehr Collection of Incunabula and the Gutenberg Bible* ([Washington: Govt. Print. Off., 1939] [4] p. Z733.U63V8 1939).

# 256

## Waggaman and Ray Collection

Drawings by the Washington, D.C., architectural firm, Waggaman and Ray, early twentieth century

Prints and Photographs Division

The Waggaman and Ray Collection, given by Peter and Judith Ray Van Dyke in 1976 and supplemented by Mrs. William Frederick Holtzman in 1979, documents the work of an accomplished, though relatively unknown, architectural firm active in Washington, D.C., during the first three decades of the twentieth century. The company formed by Clarke Waggaman (1872–1919) and George N. Ray (1887–1959) specialized in residential buildings and small-scale commercial structures and frequently worked in the Georgian revival style. The office participated in the development of the Connecticut Avenue and Kalorama Circle areas of Washington, D.C., and designed buildings throughout the metropolitan area. The Waggaman and Ray Collection contains presentation drawings, working sketches, renderings of structural and mechanical details, blueprints, and a small number of photographs and letters pertaining to 400 different projects. The 16,000-item collection constitutes a comprehensive record of the architects' commissions and documents the working procedures developed by the firm. Waggaman and Ray's card index, alphabetically organized by client, lists and dates items prepared for most projects. A separate roster is organized by address. A few designs in the collection were apparently made by the architects before they began their partnership. Plans are underway to make the Waggaman and Ray materials available to researchers.

# 257

## William C. Wakefield Collection

English legal documents, thirteenth through twentieth centuries

Manuscript Division

The Wakefield Collection, acquired in 1939 from William C. Wakefield of Chicago, consists largely of deeds and related legal documents pertaining to estates and property holdings in England. While the majority of the 1,900 manuscripts date from the seventeenth and eighteenth centuries, the collection includes over 180 items from the thirteenth through fifteenth centuries, 200 from the sixteenth century, and a sampling of nineteenth- and twentieth-century material. Most of the documents from after the mid-sixteenth century are in English. Items are arranged chronologically by reign. A few documents of special interest have been transcribed.

# 258

## Frank and Anne Warner Collection

American folk music recordings collected by Frank and Anne Warner, mid-twentieth century

Archive of Folk Song

In 1972 Frank and Anne Warner, collectors of American folk music since 1938, donated their field recordings to the Library of Congress. Working principally in North Carolina, New York, and New Hampshire during the 1940s, the Warners recorded performances of such outstanding traditional singers as Frank Proffitt of North Carolina, the Tillett family of the Outer Banks, Lena Bourne Fish of East Jaffrey, New Hampshire, and Yankee John Galusha of upstate New York. Frank Warner (1903–1978), a YMCA executive for many years, performed music from the collection in lecture-recitals across the country. His Lamar lecture at Wesleyan College, Georgia, has been published as *Folk Songs and Ballads of the Eastern Seaboard: From a Collector's Notebook* (Macon, Ga.: Southern Press [1963] 75 p. ML3551.W37). The 105 discs (AFS 15,261–15,384) have been copied on tape and, together with the nineteen tapes (AFS 15,385–15,400, 15,564–15,565, and 17,769) received from the Warners, are listed in a concordance on file. Also available in the Archive of Folk Song are concert recordings of Frank Warner.

U.S., Library of Congress, Music Division, "Recent Acquisitions of the Music Division," *QJLC*, v. 31, January 1974: 52.

*Anne Warner recording Frank Proffitt in Watauga County, North Carolina (1941). Proffitt introduced the Warners to "Tom Dula," a ballad that was later made famous as "Tom Dooley" by the Kingston Trio. Frank and Anne Warner Collection, Archive of Folk Song. Photograph by Frank Warner, courtesy of Anne Warner. LC–USZ62–67603.*

# 259

## Langdon Warner Collection

### Rare maps of China and Korea

Geography and Map Division

In 1929 the Library of Congress purchased ten maps and atlases of China and Korea from archaeologist Langdon Warner (1881–1955), director of the first and second China expeditions of the Fogg Museum of Harvard University. While one manuscript atlas—a set of maps depicting the thirteen Chinese provinces and the metropolitan areas of Nanking and Peking—was executed during the Ming period (1368–1644), the remainder were produced in the eighteenth and nineteenth centuries. Most pertain to the administrative circuits of Korea. The maps are described in the Library's computerized map catalog, and the atlases are listed in the division atlas catalog and reported without collection designation in *A List of Geographical Atlases in the Library of Congress* (Washington: Library of Congress, 1963. lxxii, 681 p. Z6028.U56, v. 6), compiled by Clara Egli LeGear.

*ARLC,* 1929, p. 149–150.

# 260

## Washington Press-Photo Bureau Collection

Portrait photographs of prominent figures of Washington, D.C., late 1930s and early 1940s

Prints and Photographs Division

Nine thousand sets of portrait negatives prepared by the Washington Press-Photo Bureau in the late 1930s and early 1940s were purchased by the Library in 1952. Assembled as a picture resource file for newspapers and information agencies, the collection contains commercial portraits of virtually all the prominent residents of Washington, D.C., during this period. Represented are members of the seventy-sixth Congress, government officials, diplomats, military personnel, businessmen, social and religious leaders, lawyers, educators, entertainers, and doctors. The agency's alphabetical card index of sitters, also in the Prints and Photographs Division, frequently records the portraits' dates and the clients' occupations. Photographs of congressmen have been integrated with the division's central portrait file.

*Guide,* Vanderbilt, no. 752.

Milhollen, Hirst D., "Saved from the Silver Mines," *LCIB,* v. 11, June 23, 1952: 2.

# 261

## Walt Whitman Collection

Early editions of Walt Whitman's writings

Rare Book and Special Collections Division

The outstanding Whitman collection formed by Carolyn Wells Houghton (d. 1942), American mystery writer and anthologist, was received by bequest in 1942. Miss Wells secured copies of every publication cited in *A Concise Bibliography of the Works of Walt Whitman, With a Supplement of Fifty Books About Whitman* (New York and Boston: Houghton Mifflin Co., 1922. 106 p. Z8971.5.W45; reprint, New York: B. Franklin [1968]), which she compiled with Alfred F. Goldsmith. The collection contains nearly one hundred copies of *Leaves of Grass,* including both issues of the first edition published in Brooklyn in 1855; an autographed copy of the exceedingly rare *Memoranda During the War* (Camden, N.J.: 1875–76); and one of the five known copies (the Library received a second copy through copyright deposit) of *Letters Written by Walt Whitman to his Mother from 1866 to 1872* (New York and London: G. P. Putnam's Sons, 1902), a work which was edited by Thomas B. Harned, Whitman's close friend and an executor of his literary estate. The Wells bequest is shelved in the Rare Book and Special Collections Division with other Whitman publications (some copyright deposit copies) selected from the Library's general collections. Many of the 480 volumes in the Whitman Collection are listed in *Walt Whitman: A Catalog Based Upon the Collections of the Library of Congress* (Washington: Library of Congress, 1955. 147 p. Z8971.5.U62; reprints), with notes on Whitman collections and collectors by Charles E. Feinberg. The Feinberg-Whitman Collection in the Manuscript Division, probably the finest collection of Whitman materials ever assembled, is discussed in entry number 79.

*Autograph manuscript (last movement, first page) of Beethoven's* Piano Sonata no. 30 in E Major, *op. 109. Gertrude Clarke Whittall Foundation Collection, Music Division. Negative in division.*

# Gertrude Clarke Whittall Foundation Collection

Rare music manuscripts and letters; papers and research materials relating to Nicolò Paganini and Felix Mendelssohn

Music Division

Mrs. Gertrude Clarke Whittall (1867–1965) was one of the Library of Congress's great patrons of music and literature. Soon after moving to Washington in 1934, she presented to the Library five Stradivari instruments and established a foundation to support chamber music concerts at which these instruments would be played by the Library's "quartet in residence." In 1941 with the purchase of portions of the collection assembled by Jerome Stonborough of Vienna, Mrs. Whittall expanded the foundation's activities to include the acquisition of original eighteenth-, nineteenth-, and twentieth-century manuscripts by European composers. The Gertrude Clarke Whittall Collection contains important manuscript sketches and scores of Bach, Beethoven, Berg, Brahms, Haydn, Mendelssohn, Meyerbeer, Mozart, Reger, Schoenberg, Schubert, Wagner, and Weber, as well as correspondence between Brahms and conductor Hermann Levi (1864–78) and letters of Beethoven, Mozart, and Weber. The Brahms material constitutes the largest group of Brahms manuscripts outside Vienna. Several holographs have been published in facsimile by the Library.

Through the years funds provided by the foundation have enabled the Library to acquire, in addition to individual holographs, two complete manuscript collections. The archive assembled by Maia Bang Hohn for a projected biography of violinist Nicolò Paganini (1782–1840) was purchased in 1944. Kept as a distinct unit within the Whittall Collection, the Paganini material includes correspondence, notebooks, music manuscripts, and personal documents, as well as clippings, early biographies, posters, and prints. Many items were originally owned by the Paganini family. The items are listed in a handwritten catalog and discussed by Harold Spivacke in "Paganiniana," in *QJLC*, v. 2, February 1945, p. 49–67. A second unit within the Whittall Collection is devoted to the composer Felix Mendelssohn (1809–1847). Acquired in 1947, this material includes over three hundred autograph letters (1825–47) and lists of original source material and printed music compiled by collector W. T. Freemantle.

The music manuscripts in the Whittall Collection are described in a catalog published in 1953 and reported in the *Quarterly Journal's* acquisition summaries. Most of the collection, including the Paganiniana, has been microfilmed. The manuscripts measure approximately twenty linear feet.

*ARLC,* 1936, p. 131–132; 1937, p. 139–140; 1941, p. 120–121.

*NUCMC,* 67–646 and 67–654.

Orcutt, William Dana, *The Stradivari Memorial at Washington, the National Capital* ([Washington, D.C.] Library of Congress, Gertrude Clarke Whittall Foundation [1938] 49 p. ML462.L55O7; reprint, 1977).

U.S., Library of Congress, Gertrude Clarke Whittall Foundation Collection, *Autograph Musical Scores and Autograph Letters in the Whittall Foundation Collection* (Washington: 1951. 17 p. ML30.8v.W32; rev., 1953), prepared by Edward N. Waters.

Waters, Edward N., "The Gertrude Clarke Whittall Foundation in the Library of Congress," *D.C. Libraries* (Z673.D61), v. 32, January 1961: 5–7.

# 263

## Woodrow Wilson Library

Books and personal mementos of Woodrow Wilson

Rare Book and Special Collections Division

The personal library of Woodrow Wilson (1856–1924) was presented to the Library of Congress by Edith Bolling Galt Wilson in 1946 and installed in the Woodrow Wilson Room adjacent to the Rare Book and Special Collections Division. Containing books associated with every period of Wilson's life, the collection includes volumes read as a child; texts used at preparatory school, college, and law school; works in the fields of economics, political science, history, and literature which Wilson acquired during his years as an educator; and hundreds of inscribed volumes that were presented to him during and after his presidency. Also preserved in the Wilson Room are over one hundred diplomas, medals, and personal mementos. Publications are listed by author and title in a two-volume catalog. The Wilson Library contains 6,792 volumes and 1,122 pamphlets and complements the presidential papers donated to the Library by Mrs. Wilson beginning in 1939.

Eaton, Vincent L., "Books and Memorabilia of Woodrow Wilson," *QJLC*, v. 4, November 1946: 2–6.

Goff, Frederick R., "The Library of Woodrow Wilson," *Virginia Librarian* (Z732.V8V84), v. 3, October 1956: 37–38.

# 264

## Work Projects Administration Folklore Collection

WPA research files, recordings, and publications relating to American folklore

Archive of Folk Song

Nine branches of the Work Projects Administration (WPA) were involved in the collection of American folklore, according to Benjamin A. Botkin in "WPA and Folklore Research: 'Bread and Song,' " in *Southern Folklore Quarterly* (GR1.S65), v. 3, March 1939, p. 7–14. The Federal Writers' Project (FWP) began collecting folklore in 1936 as an adjunct to the preparation of the state guides. The program was expanded later that year under the direction of John A. Lomax and restructured in 1938 by Botkin to place greater emphasis on oral history and urban and ethnic studies. Following the reorganization of the WPA in 1939, miscellaneous folklore publications, sound recordings, and research files were transferred to the Library of Congress.

The WPA material available through the Archive of Folk Song derives from the FWP and to a lesser degree from the Federal Music Project (FMP) and Federal Theatre Project (FTP). Research files contain interviews, correspondence, papers, clippings, and photographs and retain their original organization by state and FWP genre. "Living Lore" materials consist principally of personal chronicles and occupational lore gathered in New York and New England. "Folklore" files contain information on folk beliefs, customs, tales, proverbs, place names, songs, rhymes, and related topics. "Social-ethnic Studies" include surveys of foreign-language-speaking communities ("Pockets in America") ; "Negro Studies" treat such topics as black education and business in various states. "The Lexicon of Trade Jargon" is represented by correspondence, data files, and a three-volume typescript of work-related phrases arranged by occupation. "Ex-slave Narratives" are described in entry number 72. The files fill more than forty-five drawers. Botkin discusses aspects of the FWP folklore program in "We Called It 'Living Lore,' " in *New York Folklore Quarterly* (GR1.N473), v. 14, fall 1958, p. 189–201.

The Archive of Folk Song supported the limited sound-recording activities of the WPA Folklore programs by providing equipment and assuming custody of completed discs. More than half of these discs were produced in 1939 by a special recording project conducted in the southern states that was sponsored by the WPA's Joint Committee on Folk Arts under the direction of Herbert Halpert of the FTP. The 419 discs (AFS 2,735–3,153) are listed in field notes and the catalog of the archive. The remaining recordings were made primarily in Florida, California, and New York City through the cooperation of the local FWP, FTP, and FMP units. The extensive California field studies conducted by Sidney Robertson, largely in ethnic and migrant communities from 1938 to 1940, are documented by photographs, field notes, and 237 discs (AFS 3,342–3,377, 3,809–3,880, and 4,194–4,325). The WPA folk recordings have been copied on tape.

Mimeographed collections of folk song texts, melodies, and articles published by the FTP and other branches of the WPA are also housed in the archive. Herbert Halpert describes the folklore publications of the FTP in "Federal Theatre and Folksong," *Southern Folklore Quarterly* (GR1.S65), v. 2, June 1938, p. 81–85. The Archive of Folk Song has prepared a bibliography entitled "Folklore and the W.P.A.," which is available on request.

# 265

## Work Projects Administration Poster Collection

Prints and Photographs Division

Seven hundred and fifty silk-screened posters produced in the 1930s by various branches of the Work Projects Administration (WPA) are kept in the Prints and Photographs Division. Transferred to the Library in the 1940s along with other WPA materials, these posters were used to publicize exhibits, community activities, theatrical productions, and health and educational programs in twenty states. Projects in Illinois, New York, Ohio, and Pennsylvania are particularly well represented. The posters are mounted and filed alphabetically by state. On some items the name of the artist and the date are included. The collection has been reproduced on microfilm. The Library's major collection of WPA theater posters is discussed in entry number 78.

Of related interest are the 220 prints produced by WPA artists that have been integrated into the division's fine print collection. Individual items are listed by artist in the fine prints card index and in the publication *American Prints in the Library of Congress: A Catalog of the Collection* (Baltimore: Published for the Library of Congress by the Johns Hopkins Press [1970] xxi, 568 p. NE505.A47), compiled by Karen F. Beall and others.

*Guide,* Vanderbilt, no. 787.

# 266

## Wilbur and Orville Wright Collection

Papers and photographs of the Wright brothers

Manuscript Division
Prints and Photographs Division

The papers of Wilbur Wright (1867–1912) and Orville Wright (1871–1948) were given to the Library in 1949 by the executors of the latter's estate and have been supplemented over the years by additional acquisitions. Totaling over thirty thousand items, the collection includes diaries, notebooks, family papers, general correspondence, scrapbooks of clippings and memorabilia, legal and business papers, and related materials. Among the most historically significant items are diaries and notebooks describing the first successful flight in a motor-powered airplane at Kitty Hawk (1903), later flights at College Park, Maryland (1909), and Montgomery, Alabama (1910), and trips abroad (1907, 1908, and 1913); and the series of letters received from the American engineer and aeronautical pioneer Octave Chanute. Chanute's papers, also in the Manuscript Division, contain the Wright brothers' replies. Portions of the papers have been published in book form, and the entire collection is described in a published register. Some material has been microfilmed.

Three hundred original glass plate negatives showing the Wright family, the family home in Dayton, Ohio, and the brothers' early flight experiments are housed in the Prints and Photographs Division. The Wright brothers regarded photography as a scientific tool and recorded for each photograph the time of exposure, stop setting, date, place, glide, type of plate, and subject. The photographs, reproduced as captioned reference prints, have been itemized in a shelflist. Some images were used to illustrate *The Papers of Wilbur and Orville Wright*. The entire collection, complete with catalog, has been published as a microfiche set.

*Guide,* Vanderbilt, no. 789.

McFarland, Marvin W., and Arthur G. Renstrom, "The Papers of Wilbur and Orville Wright," *QJLC,* v. 7, August 1950: 22–34.

*NUCMC,* 60–588.

U.S., Library of Congress, Manuscript Division, *Wilbur and Orville Wright: A Register of Their Papers in the Library of Congress* (Washington: Library of Congress, 1976. 22 p. Z8986.33.U54 1976).

Wright, Wilbur, and Orville Wright, *The Papers of Wilbur and Orville Wright, including the Chanute-Wright Letters and Other Papers of Octave Chanute* (New York: McGraw-Hill [1953] 2 v. TL540.W7A4; reprint, [New York] Arno Press [1972]), edited by Marvin W. McFarland.

——, *Photographs by the Wright Brothers* (Washington: Library of Congress, 1978. 20 p., includes microfiche (5 sheets). Microfiche TL521).

# 267

## Gary Yanker Collection

### Political propaganda posters, late 1960s to present

Prints and Photographs Division

The Yanker Collection of contemporary political posters, given to the Library between 1975 and 1978, is one of the largest of its kind in the United States. Since the late 1960s Gary Yanker has actively collected propaganda posters ("prop art") produced by organizations as diverse as the National Association for Irish Freedom, Parti Communist Français, and the League of Women Voters. Although strongest in posters from the United States, the collection also contains material from nearly fifty Asian, African, European, and Latin American nations and includes examples produced in China, the U.S.S.R., and Cuba. Mr. Yanker has also added to the collection buttons, patches, bumper stickers, banners, and other printed items he considers to be "poster substitutes." For the most part, the 4,500 items are arranged geographically. Gary Yanker based his book *Prop Art: Over 1000 Contemporary Political Posters* (New York: Darien House; distributed by New York Graphic Society, Greenwich, Conn. [1972] 256 p. D445.Y36 1972b) on material in the collection. Additions to the collection are anticipated.

Американскія правительства, при-
няли свободу печатанія, между первѣй-
шими законоположеніями, вольность
гражданскую утверждающими. Пенси-
льванская область въ основательномъ
своемъ законоположеніи, въ главѣ I, въ
предложительномъ объявленіи правъ
жителей Пенсильванскихъ, въ 12 ста-
тьѣ говоритъ: „народъ имѣетъ право
говорить, писать и обнародовать
свои мнѣнія; слѣдовательно свобода
печатанія, никогда недолженствуетъ
быть затрудняема.,, Въ главѣ 2, о
образѣ правленія, въ отдѣленіи 35: „пе-
чатаніе да будетъ свободно для всѣхъ,
кто хощетъ изслѣдовать, положенія
законодательнаго собранія, или другой
отрасли правленія. „Въ проектѣ о
образѣ правленія въ Пенсильванскомъ
государствѣ, напечатанномъ дабы жи-
тели онаго могли сообщать свои при-
мѣчанія въ 1776 году въ Іюлѣ. Отдѣ-
леніе 35. „Свобода печатанія, отверста
да будетъ всѣмъ желающимъ изслѣ-

*In this passage from* Puteshestvie iz Peterburga v Moskvu (*A Journey from St. Petersburg to Moscow*) (1790), *which was suppressed by the Russian govern-ment, A. N. Radishchev cites excerpts from the Pennsylvanian constitution of 1776 which guarantee freedom of the press. The Library's copy of this rare publication was acquired through the purchase of the Yudin Collection. Rare Book and Special Collections Division. LC–USZ62–67604.*

# Yudin Collection

Publications relating to Russian history, bibliography, and literature, eighteenth and nineteenth centuries; pictorial material; papers of the Russian American Company

Rare Book and Special Collections Division
Prints and Photographs Division
Manuscript Division

Gennadiĭ Vasil'evich Yudin (1840–1912), a wealthy Siberian distiller and amateur bibliographer, developed one of the finest personal libraries in the Russian Empire. Collecting extensively in the fields of Russian bibliography, history, and literature, Yudin accumulated significant holdings of provincial gazettes, early editions of eighteenth- and nineteenth-century literary works, early Russian-language imprints, and Russian literary and historical magazines. From his home near Krasnoyarsk, Siberia, he was able to procure local publications that had escaped the attention of the major Russian libraries and so amassed an unparalleled collection on his native region. Many contemporaries were impressed by the scope of the Yudin library, among them Lenin, who used the collection while exiled in Siberia from 1897 to 1898. The Yudin Collection was purchased by the Library of Congress in 1906 and forms the cornerstone of the Library's present Russian-language resources. Although the 80,000 volumes have been absorbed into the general collections, the original handwritten inventory can be consulted in the Rare Book and Special Collections Division and is also available on microfilm. Sergius Yakobson's article, "An Autobiography of Gennadiĭ Vasil'evich Yudin," in *QJLC*, v. 3, February 1946, p. 13–15, includes a biographical statement by Yudin and information on his library.

Scores of rare imprints from the Yudin library are housed in the Rare Book and Special Collections Division and form the greater part of the division's eighteenth-century Russian-language holdings. Alexis Babine's account of the Yudin library highlights such valuable items as the first edition of A. N. Radishchev's critique of serfdom *Puteshestvie iz Peterburga v Moskvu* (A Journey from St. Petersburg to Moscow) (1790); *Irtysh* (1789), the first magazine published in Siberia; a Slavonic ABC book issued in Rome in 1753; and the first Russian geometry book (1725). These are listed, without indication of prove-nance, in *Eighteenth Century Russian Publications in the Library of Congress: A Catalog* (Washington: 1961. xvi, 157 p. Z2502.U5), pre-pared by Tatiana Fessenko. Rare nineteenth-century books include the earliest edition of Dostoevskiĭ's first published novel *Biednye liudi* (Poor People) (1847) and one of the few copies of the first edition of the medieval poem *Slovo o polku Igoreve* (Song of Igor's Campaign) (1800) to escape the burning of Moscow in 1812.

The Prints and Photographs Division maintains photographs, en-gravings, lithographs, and drawings collected by Yudin. Among the most interesting are 333 original drawings of Chinese subjects—cos-tumes, architecture, furniture, people, animals—that were executed about 1860. Occasional annotations in Russian and Chinese do not indicate who executed these sketches. Pictorial material from the Yudin Collection is represented in the division catalog. Photostatic reproduc-tions of the drawings are available for reference.

Also acquired through the Yudin purchase were the business papers of the Russian American Company (1786–1830). These 150 items in the Manuscript Division pertain chiefly to the company's foreign trade and its activities in Siberia and Alaska. English transla-tions of the papers appear in the third volume of the unpublished compilation "Documents Relative to the History of Alaska," prepared by the Alaska History Research Project of the University of Alaska. This work is available for use in the division reading room and on microfilm.

Russian provincial gazettes assembled by Yudin have been micro-filmed.

*ARLC,* 1907, p. 20–24.

Babine, Alexis V., *The Yudin Library, Krasnoiarsk (Eastern Siberia)* (Washing-ton: [Press of Judd and Detweiler] 1905. 40 p. Z997.Y85B).

*NUCMC,* 63–410.

U.S., Library of Congress, Prints and Photographs Division, "Library Exhibits 19th-Century Drawings of China," *LCIB,* v. 37, March 24, 1978: 185–186.

# 269

## Henrietta Yurchenco Collection

Field recordings of Mexican and Guatemalan Indian music, 1944–46

Archive of Folk Song

Following her 1942 recording expedition among the Tarascan Indians of Mexico, Henrietta Yurchenco was engaged by the Library of Congress, the Inter-American Indian Institute, and the Department of Education of Mexico to document the music of some of the most isolated Indian communities of Mexico and Guatemala. From 1944 to 1946 the ethnomusicologist made field recordings among the Seri and Yaqui of the state of Sonora, the Tarahumara of Chihuahua, the Cora of Nayarit, the Huichol of Jalisco, the Tzotzil and Tzeltal of Chiapas, and the Quiché, Kekchi, and Ixil of Guatemala. Aside from the hunting, love, and war songs of the Seri, the resulting 151-disc collection (AFS 7,612 7,650, 8,106–8,202 and 8,912–8,926) consists primarily of vocal and instrumental music from religious festivals and rituals. The collection includes performances on both indigenous and Hispanic instruments. The recordings have been copied on tape and described in lists on file. Excerpts from the collection have been published on a Library recording and a Folkways release.

*Indian Music of Mexico* (Folkways Records [1952]   2 s.   12 in.   33⅓ rpm. FE 4413 (P 413)), recorded by Henrietta Yurchenco.

Yurchenco, Henrietta, comp., *Folk Music of Mexico* (Library of Congress, Division of Music, Recording Laboratory [1960]   2 s.   12 in.   33⅓ rpm. AFS L19).

—, "Grabación de música indígena," *Nuestra música* (ML5.N85), v. 1, May 1946: 65–78.

# The
# Special Collections by Division
## An Appendix

This appendix is alphabetically arranged by division name and consists of brief descriptions of the collections and services of the divisions mentioned in this guide. Each description is followed by references to selected publications about the division and by a list of those of its special collections which are described in this volume. For collections known in a division by a name different from that used here, the alternative form is provided in parentheses. Pertinent dispersed collections are noted.

## African and Middle Eastern Division

The three sections of the African and Middle Eastern Division—African, Hebraic, and Near East—provide reference assistance and guide the development of the Library's collections in their areas of specialty.

The African Section is the focal point of the Library's reference and bibliographic service on Africa south of the Sahara, which includes all African countries and dependencies except Algeria, Egypt, Libya, Morocco, and Tunisia. Reference aids, including published bibliographies, yearbooks, pamphlets, selected current periodicals, and card indexes to monographs and periodical articles, may be consulted in the section. Other Library resources relating to sub-Saharan Africa are available through the general reading rooms and the various specialized reading facilities. As part of its continuing bibliographic program, the section prepares for publication bibliographic studies ranging in scope from general guides on sub-Saharan Africa to bibliographies of official publications of a single country or region and lists covering more narrowly defined topics.

The Hebraic Section has custody of manuscripts, newspapers, periodicals, books, and microforms in Hebrew, Yiddish, Aramaic, Amharic, and cognate languages. The collection covers all phases of the history and cultures of the ancient Near East and of Judaism and Jewish life. It includes extensive resources for the study of the rabbinical literature, the Bible and its various editions beginning with the sixteenth century, and the politico-historical, economic, sociological, and cultural development of the state of Israel. Holdings are estimated at 114,000 volumes. The section maintains the Hebraic Union Catalog containing reports from the major collections in the United States and Canada, and is assisting in the preparation of the Union Catalog of Yiddica.

The collection of the Near East Section contains over 110,000 volumes in Arabic, Turkish, Persian, and other languages (excluding those within the scope of the Hebraic Section) of the region extending from Afghanistan in the east to Morocco in the west and from Central Asia in the north to Sudan in the south. The collection encompasses calligraphy specimens dating from as early as the tenth century, manuscripts, newspapers, periodicals, government publications, monographs, and microforms. It provides extensive coverage, particularly in Arabic-language materials, in the fields of literature, language and linguistics, religious studies, history, and politics. The section has prepared finding aids to its holdings and is developing a Near East National Union List, a computerized catalog in the Roman alphabet for Arabic-, Persian-, and Turkish-language publications held by American libraries.

Material in Hebraic and Near Eastern languages is made available to readers in the division reading room. Publications in Western languages pertaining to Judaic studies and the Middle East are assigned to the Library's general collections. For more information, see "The Hebraic Collection in the Library of Congress" by Lawrence Marwick, in *Jewish Book Annual* (PN6067.J4), v. 36, 1978/79, p. 60–66; "Africana in the Library of Congress: The Role of the African Section" by Julian W. Witherell, in *QJLC*, v. 27, July 1970, p. 184–196; and brochures and descriptions prepared by the division.

Special collections in the African and Middle Eastern Division described in this volume:

155.   Sheikh Maḥmūd al-Imām al-Manṣūrī Collection

160.   Kirkor Minassian Collection

# American Folklife Center

The American Folklife Center, established in 1976 by act of Congress, coordinates folklife activities within the federal government, assists local organizations and government agencies in documenting the folk cultures of their regions, and conducts projects in the field. The results of studies initiated or directed by the center are made available to the public through publications, exhibits, demonstrations, and interpretive programs. Documentary materials collected in the course of research—photographs, field notes, sound recordings, and videotapes—are assigned to the appropriate custodial units within the Library.

## The Archive of Folk Song

The Archive of Folk Song is administratively linked to the American Folklife Center. The archive guides the development of the Library's resources for the study of folk music, folklore, folklife, and oral history and, since its establishment in 1928, has been instrumental in adding over thirty thousand recordings and 225,000 sheets of field notes, correspondence, and related manuscript materials to the Library's holdings. Although focused on the music and lore of English-speaking communities in the United States, particularly in Appalachia, the Deep South, the Ozarks, Texas, California, Wisconsin, Michigan, Ohio, New York, Vermont, and Maine, the collection also documents the traditions of Native American groups and ethnic communities (approximately 20 percent of the total collection). Another 20 percent of the collection was recorded outside the United States largely by American ethnomusicologists. Original field recordings are in the custody of the Motion Picture, Broadcasting, and Recorded Sound Division and are listed, as are manuscripts and microfilms, in card catalogs compiled by the archive. The archive maintains copies of many original recordings and a reference collection of books, periodicals, and ephemera. Available on request are more than 150 bibliographies and study guides prepared by the archive.

For additional information, see the archive's descriptive brochure and "The Archive of Folksong: Library of Congress" by Joseph C. Hickerson, in *The Folk Music Source Book* (New York: Knopf; distributed by Random House, 1976. 260 p. ML19.S26), by Larry Sandberg and Dick Weissman, p. 249–251.

Special collections assembled by the American Folklife Center and described in this volume:

45. Chicago Ethnic Arts Project Collection
229. South Central Georgia Folklife Project Collection

Special collections * available through the Archive of Folk Song and described in this volume:

32. Laura Boulton Collection
33. Paul Bowles Collection
36. Frank C. Brown Collection
41. James Madison Carpenter Collection
42. Tom Carter and Blanton Owen Collection
57. Arthur Kyle Davis Collection
72. Ex-slave Narrative Collection
81. Austin E. Fife Collection
98. Robert Winslow Gordon Collection
101. Percy Grainger Collection
104. Woody Guthrie Collection
105. Joseph S. Hall Collection
137. George Korson Collection
149. Bascom Lamar Lunsford Collection
164. Ferdinand ("Jelly Roll") Morton Collection
177. Office of War Information Collection
181. Peabody Museum Collection
193. Vance Randolph Collection
196. Resettlement Administration Collection
198. Willard Rhodes Collection
200. Helen H. Roberts Collection
209. Jim Rosellini Collection
212. Ruth Rubin Collection
227. Smithsonian-Densmore Collection
242. Charles Todd and Robert Sonkin Collection
249. University of Arkansas Collection
250. University of Wisconsin Collection
254. Voice of America Collection
258. Frank and Anne Warner Collection
264. Work Projects Administration Folklore Collection
269. Henrietta Yurchenco Collection

---

* Generally, taped copies of noncommercial recordings in these collections are available for listening.

# Asian Division

The Asian Division has custody of books, periodicals, newspapers, manuscripts, and microforms in the languages of East Asia, Southeast Asia, and the South Asian subcontinent, with the exception of legal materials housed in the Law Library. The three sections of the division —Chinese and Korean, Japanese, and Southern Asia—prepare bibliographies and provide reference assistance for both material in their custody and related publications in Western languages in the Library's general collections. Asian-language material is available to readers in the division reading room.

Containing over 430,000 volumes in Chinese and several thousand volumes in Manchu, Mongolian, Tibetan, and Moso (Nashi), the Chinese collection of the Chinese and Korean Section is the largest in the West. Areas of emphasis are Chinese local history, agriculture, botany, medicine, and the collected writings of individual authors. The 61,000 volumes comprising the Korean-language collection consist chiefly of publications from the Republic of Korea. The section maintains catalogs of its holdings and union catalogs of the Chinese and Korean materials available in American libraries.

The holdings of the Japanese Section (approximately 591,000 volumes) form the largest collection of Japanese-language materials outside Japan. It is strongest in the humanities and social sciences, scientific and technical serials, statistical information, and Japanese government publications at both the national and prefectural level. The section has separate catalogs for books and serials and maintains the Japanese Union Catalog and the Union Card File of Japanese Serials.

The collection of the Southern Asia Section contains over 144,000 volumes in the classical and vernacular languages of Pakistan, India, Sri Lanka, Bangladesh, Nepal, Bhutan, Burma, Thailand, Laos, Cambodia, Vietnam, Singapore, Malaysia, Brunei, Indonesia, and the Philippines. The section has a subject catalog to current Western- and Asian-language publications relating to Southeast Asia and a union catalog of Burmese titles.

For additional information, see "The Growth of the Orientalia Collections" by Arthur W. Hummel, in *QJLC*, v. 11, February 1954, p. 69–87; "A History of the Japanese Collection in the Library of Congress, 1874–1941" by Andrew Y. Kuroda, in *Senda Masao Kyoju koki kinen toshokan shiryo ronshu* (Tenri: Senda Masao Kyoju Koki

Kinenkai, 1970. 327, 139 p. Z665.S394 Orien Japan), p. 281–327 (separate reprint of article, Washington: 1970. Z733.U63O74 1970); and U.S., Library of Congress, *Chinese Collections in the Library of Congress: Excerpts from the Annual Report(s) of the Librarian of Congress, 1898–1971* (Washington: Center for Chinese Research Materials, Association of Research Libraries, 1974. 3 v. Z733.U63O688), compiled by Ping-kuen Yu.

Special collections in the Asian Division described in this volume:

176. Crosby Stuart Noyes Collection
194. Rare Chinese Book Collection
202. William Woodville Rockhill Tibetan Collection

## Collections Management Division

The Collections Management Division maintains and services the Library's general classified book collections and telephone and city directories. Totaling approximately ten million serial and monographic volumes, the general book collections encompass materials in all languages employing the Roman, Cyrillic, or Greek alphabets and in all LC subject classifications except class K (law) and class M (music). The general book collections are recorded in the Library's principal card catalog and made available to researchers in the Main Reading Room, the Thomas Jefferson Reading Room, and the Science Reading Room. Recent acquisitions in Roman-alphabet languages are also accessible by computer terminal.

Special collections available through the Collections Management Division and described in this volume:

62. Luis Dobles Segreda Collection
230. Spanish Play Collection

## European Division

The European Division provides reference service and prepares bibliographies of scholarly interest relating to all regions of Europe except the British Isles and the Iberian peninsula. The division assists in the development of the Library's collections of Slavic and other European materials. It has custody of unbound periodicals in Slavic and Baltic languages, 8,000 Russian pamphlets from the period 1880–1940, approximately twenty-five thousand late nineteenth- and early twentieth-century journals and books listed in the Cyrillic Union Catalog, and a 9,000-volume reference collection, all of which are available to researchers through the division's European Reading Room.

The overwhelming majority of the Library's Slavic and European collections are maintained and serviced by other divisions and are available in the Main Reading Room, the Thomas Jefferson Reading Room, the Microform Reading Room, the Newspaper and Current Periodical Room, and the various specialized reading facilities.

For additional information, see Steven A. Grant's *Scholars' Guide to Washington, D.C. for Russian/Soviet Studies* (Washington: Smithsonian Institution Press, 1977. 403 p. Z2491.G67), p. 34–55; "The Slavic and East European Resources and Facilities of the Library of Congress" by Paul L. Horecky, in *Slavic Review* (D377.A1A5), v. 22, June 1964, p. 309–327; "The Slavic and Central European Division and the Slavic Collections of the Library of Congress" by David H. Kraus, in *The Federal Linguist* (P1.F4), v. 7, 1976, p. 4–11; and *East Central and Southeast Europe: A Handbook of Library and Archival Resources in North America* (Santa Barbara, Ca.: CLIO Press [1976] 467 p. Z2483.E2), edited by Paul L. Horecky and David H. Kraus, p. 213–280.

# General Reading Rooms Division

The General Reading Rooms Division provides bibliographic and reference services in fields outside the scope of the Library's specialized language, subject, and format divisions. The division assigns study facilities to readers; provides reference service in the Main Reading Room, the Thomas Jefferson Reading Room, the Local History and Genealogy Room, and the Microform Reading Room; assists researchers by mail and telephone; and prepares bibliographic studies and publications.

The Main Reading Room reference collection contains approximately forty-five thousand volumes (15,000 individual titles) chiefly in the humanities, social sciences, and bibliography. Sets of some national bibliographies are kept in the collection, as well as numerous biographical reference works, Library of Congress publications, congressional hearings (1944 to the present), current U.S. telephone and city directories, and current foreign telephone books. Subject areas covered by the Library's specialized reading rooms, such as science and music, are represented but not emphasized. Finding aids include card catalogs by call number and author/title, a printed computer-produced subject catalog, and a printed shelflist with an author/title index.

The Thomas Jefferson Reading Room houses a general reference collection of 12,000 volumes. Items are recorded in author/title and shelflist card catalogs. Material in the Library's general book collections may be requested by readers and consulted in the Main Reading Room and Thomas Jefferson Reading Room.

The Local History and Genealogy Room maintains a 5,000-volume reference collection covering such topics as colonial families, census and military service records, local history, immigration and naturalization records, passenger lists, land grants, birth, marriage, and death records, tax lists, patriotic societies, peerage, heraldry, European lineages, and origins of names. A local history shelflist, an author index to the Library's holdings in genealogy and local history, and card indexes to family names, individuals, and coats of arms may be consulted in this room.

The Microform Reading Room Section of the Division has custody of the Library's major collection of microfilms, microfiche, and other microformat materials—over 1.675 million pieces, including microformat publications, commercially issued sets, and microfilms produced by special projects such as the Mount Athos microfilming expedition in the early 1950s. The division also maintains a small sample collection of filmstrips. Holdings are described in the card catalog of the Microform Reading Room and in finding aids prepared by the section. The African and Middle Eastern, Asian, Geography and Map, Manuscript, Music, Prints and Photographs, Science and Technology, and Serial and Government Publications Divisions and the Law Library maintain microformat materials in their areas of specialty.

Brochures describing the division's collections and services are available on request.

# Geography and Map Division

The Geography and Map Division maintains the largest and most comprehensive cartographic collection in the world—over 3.6 million maps, forty thousand atlases, and eight thousand reference works. About 55 percent of the maps are individual sheets of large- and medium-scale set maps and charts published in the nineteenth and twentieth centuries. Maps of the Americas, particularly the United

States and its political subdivisions, predominate, although official topographic, geologic, soil, mineral, and resource maps and nautical and aeronautic charts are available for most countries in the world. The division also has custody of approximately two hundred globes, three-dimensional plastic relief models, and cartographic material in other formats. While there is no single catalog of the division's total holdings, book and card catalogs located in the division reading room provide access to specialized segments of the collection. Since 1968 current single-sheet maps and selected retrospective material have been recorded in the Library's computerized map cataloging system, MARC Map.

For a detailed description of the division's holdings, see the revised edition of U.S., Library of Congress, Geography and Map Division, *The Geography and Map Division: A Guide to its Collections and Services* (Washington: Library of Congress, 1975. 42 p. Z733.-U63G46 1975). Brochures describing the division's collections and services are available on request.

Special collections in the Geography and Map Division described in this volume:

11.   American Map Collection
68.   Melville Eastham Collection
74.   William Faden Collection
75.   Ethel M. Fair Collection
82.   Millard Fillmore Collection
84.   Peter Force Library
85.   Thaddeus M. Fowler Collection
108   Henry Harrisse Collection
109.  Hauslab-Liechtenstein Collection
115.  John Hills Collection
116.  John L. Hines Collection
121.  Jedediah Hotchkiss Collection
123.  Richard Howe Collection
125.  Arthur W. Hummel Collection
127.  Andrew Jackson Collection (Blair Collection)
136.  Johann Georg Kohl Collection
143.  Lewis and Clark Collection
148.  Woodbury Lowery Collection
179.  Pierre Ozanne Collection
201.  Rochambeau Collection
213.  Albert Ruger Collection
215.  Sanborn Fire Insurance Map Collection

# Hispanic Division

The Hispanic Division is the Library's center for the pursuit of studies in the cultures of Latin America, the Iberian peninsula, and related areas. The division guides the development of the Library's Hispanic collections; assists scholars, government officials, and the general public in the use of these materials; and describes and interprets Hispanic library resources through the preparation of guides, bibliographies (including the annual *Handbook of Latin American Studies*), and other publications of scholarly interest. With the exception of the reference collection, pamphlets, and the Archive of Hispanic Literature on Tape recordings assembled for use in the division's Hispanic Society Room, the Library's vast Hispanic collections are maintained and serviced by other divisions and are available in the Main Reading Room, the Thomas Jefferson Reading Room, the Microform Reading Room, the Newspaper and Current Periodical Room, and the various specialized reading facilities.

For information on the Library's resources for the study of Hispanic culture, see "The Hispanic Collections of the Library of Congress" by John R. Hébert, in *The Federal Linguist* (P1.F4), v. 7, 1976, p. 12–17; and Michael Grow's *Scholar's Guide to Washington, D.C., for Latin American and Caribbean Studies* (Washington: Smithsonian Institution Press, 1979. 346 p. Z1601.G867). Brochures describing the division's services are available on request.

Special collections in the Hispanic Division described in this volume:

18. Archive of Hispanic Literature on Tape

# Law Library

The holdings of the Law Library, established by act of Congress in 1832, contain materials relating to the legal history and current legal systems of 155 nations and their subordinate jurisdictions and constitute the largest legal collection in the world. Although roughly one-third of the material pertains to the United States and its political subdivisions, holdings are extensive for Great Britain, East and West Germany, Japan, India, France, Italy, imperial Russia, the U.S.S.R., Canada, China and Taiwan, Australia, the Middle East, Spain, Brazil, Argentina, and Mexico. The collection also includes legal works on the history, philosophy, and theory of law, jurisprudence, international law, comparative law, Roman law, canon law, and various other specialized fields of legal study. Containing in 1979 over 1.5 million volumes, 18,100 reels of microfilm, and 350,000 microfiche cards, the collection encompasses the full range of legal resources from incunabula and early manuscripts to over forty-three hundred American and foreign legal periodicals.

The Law Library has five divisions—American-British Law, European Law, Far Eastern Law, Hispanic Law, and Near Eastern and African Law—which are responsible for reference service and the development and maintenance of the collections for specific jurisdictions and language areas. Open to researchers are facilities for microforms and Anglo-American reference material, a congressional documents reading area, and three reading rooms for foreign-language publications and rare books. Materials are organized by jurisdiction and recorded in the card catalogs of the Law Library. Legal works receive Library of Congress classification numbers as the new classification scheme for law is developed.

In addition to bibliographies and related publications of scholarly interest, the division has prepared a guide to its resources, *The Law Library of Congress: Its History, Collections, and Services* (Washington: Library of Congress, 1978. 47 p. Z733.U63L224), compiled by Kimberly W. Dobbs and Kathryn A. Haun. Brochures describing the Law Library's collections and services are available on request.

Special collections in the Law Library described in this volume:

# Manuscript Division

The Manuscript Division has custody of manuscripts, personal papers, and organizational records, chiefly American, numbering more than thirty-five million items and organized in some ten thousand collections. Focused on the history of the United States, the division's collections include personal papers of colonial officials; twenty-three U.S. presidents; cabinet officers; members of Congress; Supreme Court and other federal judges; army, navy, and air force officers; and U.S. diplomatic and consular officers as well as the papers of leading American architects, artists, businessmen, clergymen, educators, journalists, literary figures, physicians, reformers, and scientists. In addition the division houses the papers of a number of prominent American families, the records of private organizations and societies, microfilm of some of its own collections as well as collections in other repositories, and extensive transcriptions and microforms of documents in foreign archives which relate to American history.

Available for use in the division's reading room is the master record of manuscript collections, a guide which provides a current listing by title of all collections held by the division. There are also separate finding aids (some published) for most large collections and annual reports in the Library's *Quarterly Journal* identifying acquisitions of the previous year. An important guide to manuscript collections acquired in the nineteenth and early twentieth centuries is U.S., Library of Congress, Manuscript Division, *Handbook of Manuscripts in the Library of Congress* (Washington: Govt. Print. Off., 1918. xvi, 750 p. Z6621.U55). Many of the Library's manuscript collections are described in *The National Union Catalog of Manuscript Collections* (Washington: Library of Congress, 1959/61+ Z6620.U5N3). Collections on microfilm available for purchase or interlibrary loan are listed in *Manuscripts on Microfilm: A Checklist of the Holdings in the Manuscript Division* (Washington: Library of Congress, 1975. 82 p. Z6621.U572 1975), compiled by Richard B. Bickel. For an overview of the division's holdings, see U.S., National Historical Publications Commission, *A Guide to Archives and Manuscripts in the United States* (New Haven: Yale University Press, 1961. xxiii, 775 p. CD3022.A45), edited by Philip M. Hamer, p. 85–121. Brochures describing the division's facilities and services are available on request. Only a small fraction of the division's holdings are listed below.

Special collections in the Manuscript Division described in this volume:

# Motion Picture, Broadcasting, and Recorded Sound Division

The Motion Picture, Broadcasting, and Recorded Sound Division has custody of the largest and most varied collection of sound recordings, motion picture and television films, and videotapes in the United States. The division's film and television holdings—over two hundred and fifty thousand reels (seventy-five thousand titles) of motion picture film negatives, master positives, work prints, videotapes, and viewing copies—include American features, shorts and nontheatrical films (1894 to the present), and a selection of German, Italian, and Japanese releases from the 1930s and early 1940s as well as approximately twelve thousand American television programs produced chiefly during the last fifteen years for prime-time telecast on commercial networks. The division also houses a small collection of reference books, film stills, and descriptive material for motion pictures registered for copyright after 1912. The principal access tool is the alphabetical title catalog in the Motion Picture and Television Reading Room; specialized finding aids have been prepared for portions of the collection.

The division's 1.2 million music and speech recordings (6.25 million titles as of 1979) date from the earliest years of the recording industry to the present. Noncommercial material comprises approximately 60 percent of the collection—American radio broadcasts (late 1920s to the present), original field recordings of ethnographic interest, recordings of the Library's music and literary programs, material transferred from government agencies, and unpublished voice transcriptions and popular, folk, and classical music performances acquired from private collectors. Although international in scope, the collection of commercial sound recordings is predominantly American and includes an outstanding selection of pre-1900 releases and extensive twentieth-century holdings, particularly of material published since 1972. The collections contain sound recordings in such forms as wax cylinder, instantaneous disc, pressed disc, magnetic wire, and tape. Several specialized inventories, indexes, and catalogs have been prepared for portions of the collection. Orders for the duplication of sound recordings must be accompanied by the written authorization of those holding copyright and proprietary rights.

Viewing and listening facilities may be used free of charge by serious researchers. Appointments should be made in advance.

For additional information, see "Opportunities for Film Study at the Library of Congress" by John B. Kuiper, in *Film Library Quarterly* (Z692.M9F5), v. 1, winter 1967/68, p. 30–32; "Scholar and Screen: Notes on the Motion Picture Collection of the Library of Congress" by Kemp R. Niver, in *QJLC*, v. 21, October 1964, p. 265–269; and "Recorded Sound in the Library of Congress" by Donald L. Leavitt, in *Library Trends* (Z671.L6173), v. 21, July 1972, p. 53–59. An issue of the Library's *Quarterly Journal* devoted to the history, collections, and services of the division is planned for mid-1980. Brochures describing the division's collections and services are available on request.

Special collections in the Motion Picture, Broadcasting, and Recorded Sound Division described in this volume:

## Films and videotapes

5. *Amateur Hour* Collection
8. American Film Institute Collection
69. Edison Laboratory Collection
93. German Collection
126. Italian Collection
129. Japanese Collection
135. George Kleine Collection
158. *Meet the Press* Collection
180. Paper Print Collection
185. Mary Pickford Collection
207. Theodore Roosevelt Association Collection
246. United Artists Collection

## Sound recordings *

5. *Amateur Hour* Collection
9. American Forces Radio and Television Service Collection
15. George Antheil Collection
19. Archive of Recorded Poetry and Literature
21. *Arthur Godfrey Time* Collection
30. Ernest Bloch Collection
56. Damrosch Family Collection
64. Jessica Dragonette Collection
77. Geraldine Farrar Collection
83. Irving Fine Collection
86. John Ross Frampton Collection (dispersed)
91. General Foods Corporation Collection
94. German Speech and Monitored Broadcast Collection
95. George and Ira Gershwin Collection
103. H. Vose Greenough Collection
106. Oscar Hammerstein II Collection
111. Wally Heider Collection

---

* In most cases commercial recordings from these collections have been integrated with the division's general holdings. Usually taped copies of noncommercial recordings are available for listening.

# Music Division

The holdings of the Music Division constitute one of the largest and most comprehensive music libraries in the world—300,000 books, countless programs, pamphlets, microforms, periodicals, music manuscripts, personal papers of leading musicians, as well as a collection of rare flutes and stringed instruments and over four million pieces of music ranging from early printed editions of classical works to contemporary rock. The division has assembled literature on virtually every aspect of the history and performance of Western music from earliest times to the present. Its greatest strengths are collections relating to the music of the United States, opera, the work of the so-called second Viennese school, and early music printing. Manuscript resources, consisting chiefly of autograph scores, letters, and scrapbooks of composers and performers from the late eighteenth through the twentieth centuries, are exceptionally rich for the modern period. Among the many twentieth-century figures represented by collections of music manuscripts are Leonard Bernstein, Elliott Carter, Mario Castelnuovo-Tedesco, Aaron Copland, Henry Cowell, Roy Harris, Alan Hovhaness, Cole Porter, David Raksin, Harold Rome, William Schuman, John Philip Sousa, and Igor Stravinsky. Major collections of correspondence are included in many of the special collections listed below. Card catalogs in the Music Reading Room are the principal access tools and are supplemented by various indexes, catalogs, inventories, and finding aids prepared by the division.

For additional information, see Charles A. Goodrum's *The Library of Congress* (New York: Praeger [1974] 292 p. Z733.U6G66), p. 152–158, 160–163; "The Music Division of the Library of Congress" by Harold Spivacke, in *Library Trends* (Z671.L6173), v. 8, April 1960, p. 566–573; and U.S., Library of Congress, *The Music Division: A Guide to Its Collections and Services* (Washington: 1972. 22 p. ML136.U5M9 1972). Brochures describing the division's collections and services are available on request.

Special collections in the Music Division described in this volume:

# Prints and Photographs Division

Although international in scope, the collections of the Prints and Photographs Division (over ten million items) are the richest in material relating to the history and culture of the United States. Roughly 90 percent of the collections consist of photographic prints and negatives of documentary interest such as news photos, portraits, scenic views, and stereographs. The division's architectural resources, totaling 100,000 items and encompassing photographs, measured survey drawings, historical data, and original sketches, form the most comprehensive archive of its kind in the United States. The division also has custody of about seventy thousand posters, one hundred and ten thousand woodcuts, engravings, etchings, lithographs, and works in related print media by significant artists of the last five hundred years, forty thousand examples of popular and applied graphic art ranging from original cartoon drawings to printed advertisements, and a select collection of master photographs by contemporary artists and photographers important to the development of the medium. While many images are arranged in self-indexing files, the greater portion of the division's pictorial material is accessible through specialized card catalogs and indexes in the division reading room.

The general holdings of the Prints and Photographs Division are discussed in U.S., Library of Congress, Prints and Photographs Division, *Viewpoints: A Selection from the Pictorial Collections of the Library of Congress* (Washington: Library of Congress, 1975. 223 p. E178.5.U54 1974; reprint, New York: Arno Press [1976]), by Alan Fern, Milton Kaplan, and the staff of the Prints and Photographs Division; and "Picture Research at the Library of Congress" by Edgar Breitenbach, in *Special Libraries* (Z671.S72), v. 51, July/August 1960, p. 281–287. Pictorial resources throughout the Library are enumerated in U.S., Library of Congress, Reference Department, *Guide to the Special Collections of Prints & Photographs in the Library of Congress* (Washington: 1955. 200 p. NE53.W3A52), compiled by Paul Vander-

411

bilt. Brochures describing the division's collections and services are available on request.

Special collections in the Prints and Photographs Division described in this volume:

412

413

# Rare Book and Special Collections Division

The collections of the Rare Book and Special Collections Division contain rare and historically significant publications in non-Oriental languages representing most fields in which the Library of Congress acquires books as well as various special collection materials. Two outstanding strengths are early printing—the division holds the majority of the Library's incunabula, the largest assemblage of fifteenth-century books in the Western Hemisphere—and Americana, particularly pre-1801 American imprints and nineteenth-century pamphlets. In addition, the division has extensive resources for the study of fine printing and the book as a physical object. The collections total more than three hundred thousand volumes and two hundred thousand broadsides, pamphlets, theater playbills, title pages, prints, manuscripts, posters, and photographs. Over one-third of the volumes are arranged in a continuous sequence by Library of Congress classification number, and the remaining material is organized in special collections, most of which are listed below. The division maintains custody of nonprint items when they are integral components of its special collections. Access to the collections is through the central card catalog in the division reading room, special card files, and printed bibliographies and finding aids.

For a discussion of the division's historic development and major collections, see "The Oldest Library in Washington: The Rare Book Division of the Library of Congress" by Frederick R. Goff, in *Records* of the Columbia Historical Society of Washington, D.C. (F191.C72), v. 69/70, p. 332–345, and the revised edition of U.S., Library of Congress, Rare Book Division, *The Rare Book Division: A Guide to its Collections and Services* (Washington: Reference Department, Library of Congress, 1965. 51 p. Z733.U63R23 1965). Brochures describing the division's collections and services are available on request.

Special collections in the Rare Book and Special Collections Division described in this volume:

# Science and Technology Division

The Library of Congress maintains extensive collections in all fields of science and technology except technical agriculture and clinical medicine, the subject domains of the National Agricultural Library and the National Library of Medicine. The Science and Technology Division provides reference and bibliographic services and participates in the development of these collections. Its bibliographic publications range from the *LC Science Tracer Bullet* series (informal reference guides for the general reader) to the *Antarctic Bibliography,* compiled under the sponsorship of the National Science Foundation. In addition to assisting researchers in the use of science resources in all languages and formats held by the Library of Congress, the division houses the National Referral Center, a service which directs researchers to more than twelve thousand organizations capable of supplying specialized information on the physical, biological, social, and engineering sciences. A computer-based inventory of such organizations is maintained by the center.

Most of the Library's technical reports and a reference collection of abstracting and indexing journals, bibliographies, technical dictionaries, encyclopedias, and related works are available for use in the Science Reading Room. Aside from these reference works and technical reports, the Library's vast collections of scientific material from the Library's general book collections may be requested by readers and consulted in the Main Reading Room, the Thomas Jefferson Reading Room, and the Science Reading Room.

For more information on the division's services and publications, see "Science, Technology, and the Library of Congress" by Dwight E. Gray, in *Physics Today* (QC1.P658), v. 18, June 1965, p. 44–48; "The Role of the National Library in Science and Technology, with special reference to the United States Library of Congress" by L. Quincy Mumford, in *UNESCO Bulletin for Libraries* (Z671.U5), v. 18, July/August 1964, p. 172–177, 192; and brochures prepared by the division.

Special collections in the Science and Technology Division described in this volume:

237. Technical Report Collection

# Serial and Government Publications Division

The Serial and Government Publications Division maintains the largest collection of newspapers, unbound periodicals, and serially issued government publications in the United States. The division currently receives over sixteen hundred domestic and foreign newspapers and has extensive eighteenth-, nineteenth-, and twentieth-century holdings in bound volumes, on microfilm, and on microprint cards. With the exception of music (class M) and legal (class K) serials, the division has custody of the Library's unbound periodicals and serial publications of local, state, federal, and foreign governments that are published in languages using the Roman alphabet—a total of approximately seventy-five thousand titles or 2.6 million pieces. Newspapers and periodicals in Oriental languages are in the custody of the Asian and the African and Middle Eastern Divisions and current serials in Slavic and Baltic languages are available through the European Reading Room. Periodicals held in the division are listed by title in the catalog of the Newspaper and Current Periodical Room. The division has assembled a 6,500-volume reference collection for use in its reading room and has prepared various brochures, bibliographies, and finding aids describing its collections, among them the sixth edition of *Newspapers Received Currently in the Library of Congress* (Washington: Library of Congress, 1978. 47 p. Z6945.U5N42 1978).

Special collections in the Serial and Government Publications Division described in this volume:

# Acknowledgments

While this guide could not have been completed without the co-operation of dozens of Library staff members, it could not even have been undertaken without the support and encouragement of John Finzi, director of the Collections Development Office, and Alan Fern, director for special collections. William Sittig, technical officer in the Collections Development Office, under whose general supervision this volume was prepared, patiently guided and reviewed my work and shaped the development of the guide. Many thanks are due to Ruth S. Freitag, assistant chief bibliographer, for devising the bibliographic style used in this volume and for carefully checking the bibliographic citations, and to John Y. Cole, executive director of the Center for the Book, for assembling the research files that provided the starting point. I would also like to thank the staff of the Gift Section, particularly Mary B. Smith and Charles V. Stanhope, and Shirley B. Lebo, principal evaluations officer, for clarifying the acquisitions history of many collections.

Many subject specialists provided information for this guide, read portions of the manuscript, and offered valuable comments. I would like to thank the following staff members for their generous assistance with the collection descriptions: George N. Atiyeh, African and Middle Eastern Division; Alan Jabbour, American Folklife Center, Joseph C. Hickerson and Gerald E. Parsons, Archive of Folk Song; Richard C. Howard, Asian Division; Margaret N. Coughlan and Virginia Haviland, Children's Literature Center; Marybeth Peters, Copyright Office; Robert V. Allen and David H. Kraus, European Division; Robert V. Gross, General Reading Rooms Division; Walter W. Ristow, Richard W. Stephenson, and John A. Wolter, Geography and Map Division; Georgette M. Dorn, John R. Hébert, and Mary Ellis Kahler, Hispanic Division; Kimberly W. Dobbs, Law Library; John C. Broderick and Carroll Shurney, Manuscript Division; Samuel Brylawski, Gerald D. Gibson, Patrick J. Sheehan, and James R. Smart, Motion Picture, Broadcasting, and Recorded Sound Division; Elizabeth H. Auman, Rembert Herbert, Jon W. Newsom, William C. Parsons, and Wayne D. Shirley, Music Division; Karen F. Beall, Elisabeth W. Betz, Dale Haworth, George S. Hobart, Mary M. Ison, Jerry L. Kearns, Jerald C.

419

Maddox, Elena G. Millie, C. Ford Peatross, Bernard Reilly, and Renata V. Shaw, Prints and Photographs Division; Leonard N. Beck, Thomas D. Burney, and William Matheson, Rare Book and Special Collections Division; Karl R. Green, Science and Technology Division; and Bernard A. Bernier and Jean C. Sansobrino, Serial and Government Publications Division. I would also like to thank Barbara G. Davis and Patricia Anne White for typing the index and the many staff members who provided reference assistance, helped locate materials, and facilitated the preparation of the introduction and appendix.

# How to Order Reproductions

In the absence of copyright and other restrictions, photoprints may be obtained of all illustrations belonging to the Library of Congress. Orders should be addressed to the Library of Congress, Photoduplication Service, Washington, D.C., 20540. Each request should include a brief description of the picture, its page and position in this book, the location of the original item (such as American National Red Cross Collection, Prints and Photographs Division), and the photographic negative number or location of the negative as cited in the caption (for example, LC-USZ62-34120 or negative in Music Division). All orders must be prepaid; prices are available from the Photoduplication Service.

# Index

Numbers refer to collection descriptions, except when they are preceded by the abbreviation "p." Page references direct the reader to the introduction, appendix, and illustrations. The index is alphabetized word by word.

Index terms refer chiefly to important corporate, geographic, and personal names and to subjects represented by significant holdings in the special collections discussed in this volume. The subject terms do not constitute a complete analysis of topics covered in these collections but refer only to those subjects specifically mentioned in the descriptions.

Materials in book form carry no special reference; however, there are references to most pertinent nonbook materials. These format terms ("Posters," for example) are used as main entries and as subentries under subjects (such as "Propaganda" and "World War I"). Groups of drawings, music manuscripts, and correspondence are indexed by author. The subentry "MS. material" is applied to personal and family papers, organizational records, and other collections of handwritten or typewritten texts. Music holographs are referred to by the subentry "autograph music MSS."

The administrative units and reading rooms of the Library are only indexed when described in the appendix. The reader should consult the appendix for a listing of special collections discussed in this guide arranged by custodial division. Items used as examples and individual book, motion picture, music, and serial titles are not represented in the index unless they are exceptionally rare. Similarly, authors cited in bibliographic references are not included; the reader is directed to the Library's public catalogs and to auxiliary finding aids prepared by the custodial divisions for specific author/title information and for extensive research guidance.

# A

424

426

# B

Chanler, Theodore, correspondence, 163

Chanute, Octave, MS. material, 240, 266

Charles, Jacques A. C.
balloon ascent, *illus.,* p. 350
MS. material, 240

Charpentier, Gustave, correspondence, 77

Charts. *See* Aeronautical charts *and* Nautical charts

Chávez, Carlos, autograph music MS. and correspondence, 52

Cherokee Indians
laws and constitution, 65
recordings, 198

Chess
rare books, 211
Réti, R., MS. material, 197

Cheyenne Indians, recordings, 198

Chicago Ethnic Arts Project Collection, 45; *illus.,* p. 62

Chicanos in Chicago, folklife study, 45

Chickasaw Indians, laws and constitution, 65

Child labor, MS. material and photos, 169

Children's Book Collection, 46; *illus.,* p. 64

Children's literature, 24, 46
by Andersen, H. C., 114
drawings for book illustrations, 37
*see also* Big Little Book Collection, Comic Book Collection, Schoolbooks, *and* Verne, Jules

China
drawings (19th cent.) of, 268
law, p. 403
maps (pre-1900), 125, 259
photos (1919–24), 162

Chinese and Korean Section, p. 397

Chinese in the U.S.
folklife study (Chicago), 45
photos, 92, 100

Chinese-language material, p. 397
rare, 194

Chinese literature, p. 397

Chinook Indians, recordings, 198

Chippewa Indians, recordings, 227

Choctaw Indians
laws and constitution, 65
recordings, 198

Christian, Mrs. R. E., gift, 121

Cincinnati, Society of the. *See* Society of the Cincinnati

Cinema. *See* Films

Cines, early films, 135

Cities and towns
maps, 11, 82, 84, 85, 109, 213, 215, 259
*see also* Urban life

*Cities Service Concerts,* broadcast recordings, 64

City directories, pp. 398, 399

Civil engineering, landmarks and sites, 118

Civil War, U.S., 233
Confederate operations, Va. and W. Va., 121
drawings, 47
Lowe, T. (balloonist), 10
MS. material, 10, 121, 224, 233
maps, 82, 121, 224
photos, 34, 48
Sherman, W., 224
*see also* Confederate States of America

Civil War Drawing Collection, 47

Civil War Photograph Collection, 48; *illus.,* p. 68

Civil Works Administration. *See* Federal Civil Works Administration

Clallam Indians, recordings, 198

Clark, William, maps used by, 143

Cleveland, Grover, MS. material, 189

Clinton, Sir Henry, maps of campaigns, 74, 115

Clough-Leighter, Henry, autograph music MSS., 218

Coal miners
folk music recordings, 137
photos, 131
*see also* Miners and mining

Coast and Geodetic Survey, 136

Cobb, Ty, *illus.,* p. 32

Cocopa Indians, recordings, 227

Coggeshall, Howard, correspondence, 99

Collections Management Division, p. 398

Colonization
of Liberia, 7
*see also under* names of mother countries, e.g., Spain—American colonies

Colorado, State Historical Society, 60

430

# F

FMP. *See* Federal Music Project
FSA. *See* Farm Security Administration
FTP. *See* Federal Theatre Project
FWP. *See* Federal Writers' Project
Fabyan, George, gift, 73
Faden, William, maps used by, 74; *illus.*, p. 104
Fair, Ethel M., gift, 75
Fairchild family, correspondence, 26
Fairmont, W. Va., map, *illus.*, p. 126
Fairy tales, by H. C. Andersen, 114
Far Eastern Law Division, p. 403
Farm and rural life
    photos, 23, 76, 133, 190
    *see also* Agriculture—photos
Farm Security Administration
    migrant camps, recordings in, 242
    photos by, 76, 177; *illus.*, p. 108
    and Resettlement Administration, 196
Farrar, Geraldine, material, 77; *illus.*, p. 110
Fashion, photos, 90, 147
Fauré, Gabriel, correspondence, 144
Federal Civil Works Administration, 117
Federal Emergency Relief Administration, 72
Federal Music Project, 78, 264
Federal Theatre Project
    folklore activities, 264
    MS. and pictorial material, 78
Federal Writers' Project, 72, 264
*The Federalist,* Jefferson's copy, *illus.*, p. 190
Feinberg, Charles E., 79, 261
Feminism, 16, 43
Fenton, Frances M., 80
Fenton, Roger, photos by, 80
Fewkes, Jesse Walter, field recordings, 181, 227
Fife, Alta, field recordings, 81
Fife, Austin E., field recordings, 81
Fillmore, Millard, maps collected by, 82
Film industry, early, MS. material, 135
Film music
    Antheil, G., 15
    Herbert, V., 113

Film music (continued)
    recordings, 15
    Rodgers, R., 203
    Romberg, S., 206
Film scripts, 93, 95, 206
Film stills, 93, 147, pp. 406-7
Films, pp. 406-7
    with Afro-American casts, 8
    American, 8, 69, 135, 180, 185, 207, 246
    cartoon, 246
    with Edison, T., 69
    French, early, 135, 180
    German, 93
    Japanese, 129
    Italian, 126, 135
    news and actuality, 8, 69, 93, 126, 129, 135, 180, 207
    with Pickford, M., 185
    with Roosevelt, T., 207
    silent, 8, 69, 93, 129, 135, 180, 185, 207, 246
    Yiddish, 8
Fine, Irving, material, 83
Fine printing. *See* Printing, fine
Finns in the U.S.
    folk music recordings, 196
    folklife study (Chicago), 45
Fire insurance maps, 215
Fitch, John, MS. material, 84
Fladoes, Mrs. Martin, gift, 162
*Flair,* photos, 147
Fleischer Studios, Inc., films by, 246
Flemish books (pre-1600), 211
Fletcher, Alice Cunningham, field recordings, 227
Florida
    architecture, photos, 39
    folk music recordings, 264
    history, early, MS. material, 139
    Lowery, W., research, 148
Flutes and flute playing, 159; *illus.*, p. 236
Fogarty, Thomas, drawings by, 37
Foley, Charles, 140
Folk drama, British, pictorial material and recordings, 41
Folk music and ethnological photos
    California, 264
    Great Britain, 41
    Morocco, 33
    Native Americans, 55, 100, 227
    Ozarks, 193
    Upper Volta, 209

France (continued)
    *see also* French Revolution *and*
        names of wars
Franck, César, autograph music MS.,
    223
*Frank Leslie's Illustrated Newspaper,*
    drawings for, 47
Franklin, Benjamin, early editions and
    MS. material, 87
Franklin, William Temple, MS. ma-
    terial, 87
Frederick the Great, prints, 124
Freemantle, W. T., 262
Fremstad, Olive, correspondence, 77
French, Herbert E., photos by, 170
French and Indian War, maps, 74,
    84
French-Canadians in Wisconsin, folk
        music recordings, 250
French literature, 243
    Caribbean, recordings, 18
    Verne, J., 253
French Political Cartoon Collection,
    88
French Revolution, 238
    autographs, 238
    pictorial material, 24, 88
Freud, Sigmund, MS. material and
        early editions, 89
Freud family, gift, 89
Freud (Sigmund) Archives, Inc., 89
Frissell, Toni, MS. material and
        photos by, 90
Frontier life
    photos, 100
    *see also* The West (U.S.)
Frost, Arthur B., drawings by, 37
Frothingham, Robert, correspondence,
    98
Fullam, William F., MS. material, 173

# G

Gaelic music recordings, 196
Galician drama, 230
Galli-Curci, Amelita, correspondence,
    77
Galt, Nellie, 98
Gambling, 154
Gardens
    France, drawings (copies), 156
    photos, 39, 131
Gardner, Alexander, photos by, 48

Gardner, Isabella Stewart, correspond-
        ence, 144
Gardner, James, photos by, 48
Gardner, Lester D., 10
Garfield, James A., MS. material, 189
Garland, Hamlin, correspondence, 150
Gastronomy, history, 28, 183
Gates, William, 231
Gatti-Casazza, Giulio, correspondence,
    **77**
Gaumont, early films, 135
*Gems of California Scenery,* 142
Genealogy, p. 400
    Portuguese, MS. material, 188
General book collections, p. 398
General Film Company, 135
General Foods Corporation, gift, 91
General Reading Rooms Division,
        pp. 399–400
Genthe, Arnold, photos by, 92
Geography
    Kohl, J., material, 136
    *see also* Maps and atlases
Geography and Map Division,
        pp. 400–402
Geography and Map Reading Room,
    p. 401
Geologic maps, p. 401
George Mason University, Research
        Center for the Federal
        Theatre Project, 78
Georgia
    architecture, photos, 39
    Civil War drawings, 47
    Civil War maps, 224
    folk music recordings, 98, 229
    slave narratives, 72
    wiregrass region, folklife study,
        229
German Collection, 93; *illus.,* p. 136
German Speech and Monitored Broad-
        cast Collection, 94
Germans in the U.S.
    folk music recordings, 250
    folklife study (Chicago), 45
Germany
    law, p. 403
    maps, 68, 109
Germany, Nazi
    books owned by Nazi leaders, 239
    confiscated material transferred
        to LC, 93, 94, 97, 102,
        **237, 239**

436

437

Gutenberg Bible, 255
Guthrie, Woody
    MS. material, 104; *illus.*, p. 152
    recordings, 104

# H

HABS. *See* Historic American Buildings Survey
HAER. *See* Historic American Engineering Record
Haas and Peale, photos by, 48
Hadley, Henry K., autograph music MSS., 218
Halberstadt, Ernst, 54
Hale, Philip, correspondence, 144
Hall, Joseph S., field recordings, 105
Halpert, Herbert, 264
Halsey, William F., MS. material, 173
Hamilton, Thomas, MS. material, 84
Hammerstein, Dorothy, gift, 106, 203
Hammerstein, Oscar, II, 203
    material, 106; *illus.*, p. 154
Hampton Institute, photos, 131
Handicrafts
    Appalachian, photos, 23
    of Chicago ethnic groups, 45
Handy, Levin C., photos by, 34
Handy (L. C.) Studio, 34
Hanford, J. H., 98
Hanson, Howard
    autograph music MS., 52
    correspondence, 138
Harding, Warren, photos, 170
Harkness, Edward Stephen, gift, 107
Harlem Renaissance, MS. material, 168
Harper, Ida Husted, correspondence, 43
Harper's Ferry, W. Va., Civil War map, *illus.*, p. 178
*Harper's Weekly,* drawings for, 47
Harrington, John Peabody, field recordings, 227
Harris, Roy
    autograph music MS., 52, p. 409
    biography by N. Slonimsky, 225
    correspondence, 52, 138, 225
Harrison, Benjamin, MS. material, 189
Harrison, William H., MS. material, 189

Harrisse, Henry, gift, 108
Hart, Anna T., gift, 15
Hart, Lorenz, 203
Hart, Stanley, correspondence, 15
Hartley, David, correspondence, 87
Harvard University, Peabody Museum, gift, 181
Hauslab, Franz Ritter von, 109
Hauslab-Liechtenstein Collection, 109; *illus.*, p. 160
Hawaii, music recordings, 200
Hawaiian Imprint Collection, 110
Haydn, Joseph, autograph music MSS., 262
Haydn, Michael, autograph music MS., 223
Hazard, Ebenezer, 84
*Heartbeat Theatre,* broadcast recordings, 151
Hebraic Section, pp. 393–94
Hebrew-language material, pp. 393–94
Heider, Wally, gift, 111
Heider (Wally) Recording, 111
Heineman, Dannie N., 112
Heineman Foundation for Research, Educational, Charitable, and Scientific Purposes, Inc., gift, 112; *illus.*, p. 164
Henry, Mellinger Edward, 98
Herbert, Victor, autograph music MSS., 113
Herford, Oliver, drawings by, 37
Hersholt, Mr. and Mrs. Jean, gift, 114
Hewson, Mary Stevenson. *See* Mary Stevenson
Hidatsa Indians, recordings, 227
Hill, Edward Burlingame, correspondence, 138, 144
Hills, John, maps by, 115
Himmler, Heinrich, books owned by, 239
Hindemith, Paul
    autograph music MS., 52
    correspondence, 138
Hine, Lewis, photos by, 12, 169; *illus.*, p. 250
Hines, John L., MS. material and maps, 116
Hispanic art and architecture, photos, 17
Hispanic Division, p. 402
Hispanic Law Division, p. 403
Hispanic literature, recordings, 18

439

Jones, John Paul, MS. material, 84, 173

Journalism. *See* News and actuality films, News and public affairs broadcasts, News photographs, *and* Newspapers

Judaism, p. 394

Jung, Carl G., correspondence, 31

# K

Kahnt, C. F., Liszt's letters to, 210

Kalem Company, 135

Kandinsky, Wassily, letter, 219

Kapp, Jack, 132

Kapp, Mrs. Jack, gift, 132; *illus.,* p. 194

Karales, James H., photo by, *illus.,* p. 218

Karl Alexander, Grand Duke of Saxe-Weimar-Eisenach, Liszt's letters to, 210

Kay, Ulysses Simpson, autograph music MS., 153

Kekchi Indians, recordings, 269

Kellen, William Vail, 71

Kennan, George, correspondence, 178

Kennerley, Mitchell, correspondence, 99

Kent, Harry Watson, 204

Kentucky, folk music recordings, 98

Kern, Jerome, 106

Kern County, Calif., photos and maps, 133

Kern County Survey Collection, 133

King, Ernst, MS. material, 173

King, Martin Luther, *illus.,* p. 218

Kiowa Indians, recordings, 198

Kipling, Rudyard, material, 134

Kirstein, Lincoln, correspondence, 163

Kitty Hawk, N.C., 1st flight, *illus.,* p. ii

Klein, Rudolf, correspondence, 197

Kleine, George, MS. material and films, 135

Kohl, Johann Georg, MS. material and maps by, 136

Kolisch, Rudolf, correspondence, 219

Koran, studies, 155

Korea
maps (pre–1900), 259
photos (1919–24), 162

Korean-language material, p. 397

Koreans in Chicago, folklife study, 45

Korson, George Gershon, field recordings, 137

Koshetz, Nina, correspondence, 192

Koussevitzky, Natalie Ushkov, MS. material, 138

Koussevitzky, Olga Naumoff, MS. material, 138

Koussevitzky, Serge
autograph music MSS., 138
MS. material, 138, 192

Koussevitzky Archives, 138

Koussevitzky Music Foundation, gift, 138

Kraus, Hans P., gift, 139

Kreisler, Fritz
material, 140
violin, 140; *illus.,* p. 208

Křenek, Ernst, correspondence, 197, 219

Krieger, Herbert W., field recordings, 227

Kristensen, Evald Tang, field recordings, 101

Krüger, Paul, 205

Krutch, Joseph Wood, correspondence, 31

Kufic calligraphy specimen, *illus.,* p. 238

Kupferman, Meyer, autograph music MS., 153

# L

Labels (19th cent.), 67, 241

Labor disputes
NAACP MS. material, 168
New York City, photos, 174

Laderman, Ezra, autograph music MS., 153

La Flesche, Francis, field recordings, 227

Lamaism, 202

Lampkin, Daisy, correspondence, 168

Landauer, Bella C., 10

Landauer Collection, 10

Lange, Dorothea, photos by, 76

Lanner, August, sheet music, 145

Lanner, Josef, sheet music, 145

Laos, p. 397

La Rosa, Julius, broadcast recordings, 21

442

# N

449

New Orleans
  jazz, 164
  photos, 92
  War of 1812 map, 127
New York City
  folk music recordings, 264
  photos, 22, 174, 199
  theater (1930s), 78
New York State
  architecture, photos, 186
  folk music recordings, 258, p. 395
  folklore studies (WPA), 264
*New York World-Telegram,* photos, 174
*New York World-Telegram and Sun,* photos, 174
*The New Yorker,* drawings for, 175
Newcomb, Mary, 98
Newman, C. A., George, scrapbooks, 154
News and actuality films, 8, 69, 93, 126, 129, 135, 180, 207
News and public affairs broadcasts, 94, 158, 167, 177, 236
  *see also* Political figures, recordings
News photographs, 22, 90, 131, 147, 170, 174, p. 411
Newspaper and Current Periodical Room, p. 417
Newspaper illustrations, American
  Civil War, 47
  1880s–1910s, 37
  *see also* Caricatures and cartoons *and* News photographs
Newspapers, p. 417
  American, early, 84
  in East and South Asian languages, p. 397
  in Near Eastern languages, pp. 393–94
  "underground" (U.S.), 4
Nez Percé Indians, recordings, 181
*Die Nibelungen,* film still, *illus.,* p. 136
Nicaragua, E. Squier material, 231
Nicholas II, emperor of Russia, books owned by, 214
Niver, Kemp R., 180
Noel, Wes, *illus.,* p. 286
Nootka Indians, recordings, 227
North America
  coastline study by J. Kohl, 136
  maps, 136, pp. 400–401
  pre-1800, 11, 108, 123

*The North American Indian,* 55
North Carolina
  architecture, photos, 39
  Civil War maps, 224
  folklife, photos, 23
  folklore and music recordings, 36, 42, 98, 105, 149, 258
Norton, Charles Eliot, correspondence, 231
Norwegians in the U.S.
  folk music recordings, 250
  folklife study (Chicago), 45
Nott, Josiah Clark, correspondence, 231
Noyes, Crosby Stuart, gift, 176; *illus.,* p. 258
Núñez Cabeza de Vaca, Alvar, 139
Nuremberg Chronicle, map from, *illus.,* p. 96

# O

OSRD. *See* Office of Scientific Research and Development
OWI. *See* Office of War Information
Occult sciences, 122, 154
Oceania, music recordings, 200
Office of Education, technical reports, 237
Office of Indian Affairs. *See* Bureau of Indian Affairs
Office of the Publication Board, reports, 237
Office of Scientific Research and Development, reports, 237
Office of Technical Services, reports, 237
Office of War Information
  MS. material and recordings, 177
  photos, 76, 177
Ohio, folk music recordings, p. 395
Oklahoma, migrants (1930s). *See* Migrant communities
Olbrechts, Frans M., field recordings, 227
"Old Songs That Men Have Sung," 98
Olivais e Penha Longa, conde de, 188
Opera, 24, p. 409
  Bloch, E., 30
  Damrosch family, 56
  Farrar, G., 77
  films by L. De Forest, 8

450

451

452

Science (continued)
  *see also* Science and Technology Division
Science and Technology Division, p. 416
Science fiction
  Jules Verne Collection, 253
  *see also* Pulp Fiction Collection
*Science* magazine, A. G. Bell MS. material, 26
Science Reading Room, p. 416
Scientific reports (1940s to present), 237
Scot, Reginald, *The Discoverie of Witchcraft, illus.,* p. 228
Scotland, folk music recordings, 41
Scottsboro Defense Committee, MS. material, 168
Scovasso, Anthony, gift, 140
Scripts, 64, 77, 78, 91, 93, 95, 106, 140, 151, 206, 236
Scudder, Horace E., correspondence, 114
Sea chanties, recordings, 41
Seaside Library, 61
Sebastianism, MS. material, 188
Secrist, Mr. and Mrs. J. B., gift, 221; *illus.,* p. 324
Secrist, John, 221
Seeger, Charles Louis, gift, 196, 222
Segreda, Luis Dobles. *See* Dobles Segreda, Luis
Segregation, racial, NAACP MS. material, 168
Selden-Goth, Gisella, gift, 223
Selfridge, Thomas, MS. material, 173
Seligmann, Herbert, correspondence, 168
Senate. *See* Congress
Serbians in the U.S.
  folk music recordings, 196
  folklife study (Chicago), 45
Seri Indians, recordings, 269
Serial and Government Publications Division, p. 417
Serials. *See* Periodicals
Session laws, 65
Sessions, Roger, autograph music MS., 138
Shahn, Ben, photos by, 76
*Shāhnāmah,* illuminations, 160
Shakespeare, William
  authorship controversy, 73
  early editions, 24

Shaliapin, Fedor. *See* Chaliapin, Feodor
Sharecroppers, photos, 76
Shapiro, S. R., gift, 204
Sheet music
  art songs, American, 251
  covers (19th cent.), 166
  for the flute, 159
  Lincoln-related, 233
  protest songs (1930s), 222
  Viennese (19th cent.), 145
Sherman, William Tecumseh, MS. material and maps, 224
Shevenell, Lucy Forbes, gift, 197
Shillady, John R., correspondence, 168
Shoshone Indians, recordings, 198
*Show Boat,* costume design, *illus.,* p. 154
Shufeldt, Robert W., MS. material, 173
Siberia, 268
  attack by Manchu forces, scroll map, *illus.,* p. 184
Siegmeister, Elie, autograph music MS., 153
Silent films, 8, 69, 93, 129, 135, 180, 185, 207, 245
Sills, Beverly, application for *Amateur Hour, illus.,* p. 8
Simms, Charles, MS. material, 84
Sims, William S., MS. material, 173
Singapore, p. 397
Singers. *See* Musicians
Sioux Indians, recordings, 198, 227
Skagit Indians, recordings, 198
Slavery, U.S., 233
  American Colonization Society, MS. material, 7
  narratives, 72
  pamphlets, 165
  *see also* Abolitionist movement
Slavic material. *See* European Division
Slonimsky, Nicolas, autograph music MSS. and MS. material, 225
Slovaks in Chicago, folklife study, 45
Slovenians in Chicago, folklife study, 45
Smedley, William T., drawings by, 37
Smith, Delos, photos by, 186
Smith, Erwin Evans, photos by, 226
Smith, Maurice G., field recordings, 227

459

Topographic maps, 109, p. 401
Tottell, Richard, works printed by, 71
Tousey, Frank, 61
Trade jargon, 264
Transportation, photos, 40, 100, 142, 174, 177
Trevisan manuscript, in Thacher Collection, 238
Tsar's Library, 214
Turkey
    maps, 109
    photos (19th cent.), 1
Turkish-language material, p. 394
Tuskegee Institute, photos, 131
Tutors, woodwind, 159
Tyler, John, MS. material, 189
Typography
    Goudy, F., material, 99
    specimens, 102
Tzeltal Indians, recordings, 269
Tzotzil Indians, recordings, 269

# U

UN. See United Nations
UPI. See United Press International
USSR. See Union of Soviet Socialist Republics
Ukrainians in Chicago, folklife study, 45
Underground newspapers, 4
    see also World War II—underground publications
Union of Soviet Socialist Republics
    law, p. 403
    see also European Division
United Artists Corporation, gift, 246;
    illus., p. 358
United Nations, recordings of proceedings, 247
United Press International, 174
United States
    almanacs, 6
    ethnic communities
        anarchism publications for, 14
        WPA studies, 264
    foreign relations, MS. material, 173
        Central America (19th cent.), 231
        France (18th cent.), 87
        Mexico, colonial, 139

United States (continued)
    government organizations. See name of body, e.g., Farm Security Administration, Supreme Court
    government publications, 237, 248
        early, 63
        history, MS. material, 84, p. 404
        law, pp. 402–3
            state and territorial, 65
        maps, 11, 82, 84, 85, 213, 215, pp. 400–401
        views by Detroit Publishing Company, 60
    see also America, Great Britain—American colonies, names of wars and states, and under specific subjects, e.g., Architecture—U.S.
United States Congressional Publications Collection, 248
Universal Pictures Corporation, 8
University of Arkansas, Folklore Archives, field recordings, 249
University of the District of Columbia, 72
University of Wisconsin, field recordings, 250
Upper Volta, folklore and music recordings, 209
Upton, William Treat, gift, 251
Urban life
    Chicago, ethnic groups, 45
    prints by J. Pennell, 183
    U.S., photos, 54, 76, 120, 169, 177, 199
Ursúa, Pedro de, 139
Utah, folklore and music recordings, 81
Utah Humanities Research Foundation, 81
Ute Indians, recordings, 198, 227

# V

VOA. See Voice of America
Vachon, John, photos by, 76
Valiant, Margaret, 196
Van Buren, Martin, MS. material, 189

461

463

World War II (continued)
  joke and rumor studies (OWI), 177
  naval operations, MS. material, 173
  news and public affairs broadcasts, 94, 167, 177, 236
  photos (OWI), 177
  racial discrimination (U.S.) during, MS. material, 168
  underground publications, Danish, 114
  *see also* Germany, Nazi *and* News photographs
Wormser, Richard S., 231
Wright, George H., drawings by, 37
Wright, Orville, MS. material and photos, 266; *illus.,* p. ii
Wright, Wilbur, MS. material and photos, 26
Wyoming, photos (19th cent.), 100

# X

Xenakis, Iannis, autograph music MS., 138

# Y

Yang, Piao-cheng, *Ch'in p'u ta ch'üan, illus.,* p. 288
Yanker, Gary, gift, 267
Yaqui Indians, recordings, 227, 269
Year Books (legal), 71
Yiddish films, 8
Yiddish-language material, pp. 393–94
Yiddish music recordings, 212, 232
Yohn, Frederick C., drawings by, 37
Yosemite, photos, 92, 142
Young, Chesley V., gift, 154; *illus.,* p. 228
Young, Morris N., gift, 154; *illus.,* p. 228
Yudin, Gennadiĭ, Vasil'evich, 268
Yuma Indians, recordings, 227
Yurchenco, Henrietta, field recordings, 269

# Z

Zapotecan literature, recordings, 18
*Zarzuelas,* 230
Zemlinsky, Alexander, correspondence, 219
Zumárraga, Juan de, 139
Zuñi Indians, recordings, 181, 198

☆ U.S. GOVERNMENT PRINTING OFFICE: 1980 O—300-080